Con Campbell's book, *Basics of Verbal Aspect in Biblical Greek* is a model for its genre and right at the top of books I recommend to students of the Greek New Testament. Written by a master teacher and scholar, it is not trying to impress anyone with unnecessarily technical vocabulary. He aims to teach and explain things clearly—things of *considerable* importance for understanding the New Testament. Hence, for many years I've used the first edition for intermediate Greek classes, and as a "taste of things to come" in introductory Greek courses. But scholarship has developed since the arrival of the first edition in 2008. Hence this second edition, which responds to feedback, updates the scholarship, and makes things, in certain sections, even more instructionally clear. This is a book to buy, use in classes, read and reread, and recommend to all.

CHRIS TILLING, head of research and senior lecturer in
New Testament studies, St. Mellitus College, London

For years, Con Campbell's *Basics of Verbal Aspect in Biblical Greek* has been the most accessible introduction to verbal aspect on the market. This book takes a complex topic with many differing voices and presents the Greek verbal system with the right balance of simplified clarity and nuance to Greek students. I have used this book for years in both beginning Greek and intermediate Greek exegesis classes. I was excited, therefore, to read the second edition of this important resource, which incorporates recent developments, debates, and monographs on verbal aspect in Koine Greek. Two excursuses, one on tense and another on space and time (further explaining Campbell's use of the terms *remoteness* and *proximity*; formerly a postscript), deepen the discussion without taking away from the book's focus on the *basics* of verbal aspect. A new chapter on non-indicative verbs and an appendix on *The Greek Verb Revisited* are welcome additions to this second edition. Finally, the "praxis" part of the book now includes Septuagintal examples, further expanding the book's scope. I look forward to incorporating this second edition of an already helpful resource that has only gotten better.

DANA M. HARRIS, professor of New Testament, Trinity Evangelical
Divinity School, and author of *An Introduction to Biblical Greek Grammar*

With this second edition, Campbell improves what was already an invaluable resource for those beginning their study of the Greek verb—updating the secondary literature and enhancing the book's accessibility for students.

MADISON N. PIERCE, associate professor of New
Testament, Western Theological Seminary

The issue of verbal aspect in New Testament Greek is one of the most confusing issues in all of New Testament scholarship. That is why I so highly recommend this book and use it as a textbook. Not only is Campbell's view the most defensible view on the topic, but he is by far the clearest communicator. He has the ability to cut through the linguistic jargon to communicate effectively to those just learning how the Greek verbal system works. I strongly commend this book to you and your students.

DAVID A. CROTEA, dean of the seminary and school of counseling, professor of New Testament and Greek, Columbia International University

Although I don't accept all of Campbell's conclusions about verbal-aspect theory for Koine Greek, you will not find a clearer or more charitable presentation of different views. Also, Campbell consistently shows the exegetical significance of a topic that can too easily become an academic abstraction.

ROBERT L. PLUMMER, professor of biblical studies, Southern Baptist Theological Seminary, founder and host, Daily Dose of Greek

The last twenty-five years of academic discussion of biblical Greek have been wild and wooly. Important conceptual shifts have occurred in several areas of Koine Greek, including pronunciation, the middle voice, and, most dramatically, how to understand the verbal system in relation to time and type of action communicated. As we have tried to understand and teach the ideas of verbal aspect to the next generation of students, we have needed guides. Con Campbell has served for decades as a faithful Sherpa for this Himalayan task. I have used his clear and accessible introduction to verbal aspect as a textbook for years. I am thrilled that he has revisited this helpful volume, with notable revisions based on practical experience in the classroom. Highly recommended.

JONATHAN T. PENNINGTON, professor of New Testament, Southern Baptist Theological Seminary

A proper understanding of how Greek verbs function is crucial to the accurate interpretation of the New Testament. Verbal-aspect theory has helped expand our awareness, but it is often difficult to understand for the nonspecialist. In this clearly written and helpful volume, Con Campbell demystifies verbal aspect, explains its importance, and gives numerous examples of where it makes a difference for biblical exegesis and translation.

CLINTON E. ARNOLD, research professor of New Testament, Talbot School of Theology, Biola University

BASICS *of*
VERBAL
ASPECT
in
BIBLICAL GREEK

SECOND EDITION

BASICS *of*
VERBAL
ASPECT

in

BIBLICAL GREEK

CONSTANTINE R. CAMPBELL

ZONDERVAN ACADEMIC

Basics of Verbal Aspect in Biblical Greek
Copyright © 2024 by Constantine R. Campbell

Published in Grand Rapids, Michigan, by Zondervan. Zondervan is a registered trademark of The Zondervan Corporation, L.L.C., a wholly owned subsidary of HarperCollins Christian Publishing, Inc.

Requests for information should be addressed to customercare@harpercollins.com.

Zondervan titles may be purchased in bulk for educational, business, fundraising, or sales promotional use. For information, please email SpecialMarkets@Zondervan.com.

Library of Congress Cataloging-in-Publication Data

Names: Campbell, Constantine R., author.
Title: Basics of verbal aspect in biblical Greek / Constantine R. Campbell.
Description: Second edition. | Grand Rapids, Michigan : Zondervan Academic, 2024. | Includes
   bibliographical references and index.
Identifiers: LCCN 2023051529 (print) | LCCN 2023051530 (ebook) | ISBN 9780310150220 (paperback)
   | ISBN 9780310150237 (ebook)
Subjects: LCSH: Greek language, Biblical—Verb. | Greek language, Biblical—Aspect. | Bible. New
   Testament—Language, style. | BISAC: RELIGION / Biblical Reference / Language Study |
   RELIGION / Biblical Reference / Handbooks
Classification: LCC PA847 .C35 2024 (print) | LCC PA847 (ebook) | DDC 487/.4—dc23/
   eng/20240116
LC record available at https://lccn.loc.gov/2023051529
LC ebook record available at https://lccn.loc.gov/2023051530

Excerpt from *Linguistics and New Testament Greek* by David Alan Black and Benjamin L. Merkle, copyright © 2020. Used by permission of Baker Academic, a division of Baker Publishing Group.

All Scripture quotations are author's unless explicitly noted.

Scripture quotations marked CSB® are taken from the Christian Standard Bible®, Copyright © 2017 by Holman Bible Publishers. Used by permission. Christian Standard Bible®, and CSB®, are federally registered trademarks of Holman Bible Publishers.

Any internet addresses (websites, blogs, etc.) and telephone numbers in this book are offered as a resource. They are not intended in any way to be or imply an endorsement by Zondervan, nor does Zondervan vouch for the content of these sites and numbers for the life of this book.

Cover photo: CC by 3.0 / University of Michigan Papyrology Collection
Interior design: Sara Colley

Printed in the United States of America

24 25 26 27 28 29 30 31 32 33 34 35 36 / TRM / 16 15 14 13 12 11 10 9 8 7 6 5 4 3 2 1

For George Athas,
my favorite biblical Greek.

Contents

Preface to the Second Edition

Since the first edition of this book was published in 2008, I have been gratified to discover how widely it has been used in universities, seminaries, and colleges throughout the world as students (and their professors) seek to grasp the significance of verbal aspect for understanding ancient Greek. While understanding of verbal aspect has certainly become more widespread in that time, it would be incorrect to assume that we don't still need a primer to introduce the topic to nonspecialists, and there is still no comparable resource to make mine obsolete. Alongside the growing general understanding of verbal aspect has been a noticeable increase in scholarship addressing the topic since 2008, and this—encouraging though it may be—has caused my first edition to become quite dated. So one of the key reasons to produce this second edition is to bring it up to date with what has been happening in scholarly discussions during the past fifteen years.

Another motivating factor was my own experience teaching from the book for more than a decade. Though the book had been carefully designed to help teachers and students as much as possible, I discovered some ways that it could do so more effectively. One major addition to this end has been to offer more discussion of answers to exercises, along with anticipating where students might have reached different conclusions. These expansions in the answer key will, I hope, go a long way to assuage potential student confusion or disillusionment. I also noticed from teaching that the treatments of nonindicative verbs tended to get lost in the middle of chapters, so I decided to pull all that material out of their original homes and to create an extra chapter just dealing with nonindicatives.

This should give them the attention that students need. Also, in a desire to keep things as simple as possible, some oversimplifications actually made things more complicated, such as leaving out voice in the chapter on verbal lexemes. This edition now includes some discussion of voice, which—while adding another element to consider—should actually help to keep things clearer. In a similar vein, this new edition includes more footnotes that add nuances here and there or reveal more of how the discussion relates to wider scholarship. Again, the original desire to keep things simple may have raised questions for curious readers and then left them hanging. Now they have a little more direction and nuance if they need it.

I have also changed some things in light of feedback from others. For example, some had suggested that the concluding postscript on space and time should not be kept at the back of the book, since reading that earlier would help students to grasp pertinent issues more quickly. I have beefed up that discussion, and it is now an excursus in the first section of the book. There is also a new excursus teasing out the discussion about tense, and an appendix addressing the 2016 volume, *The Greek Verb Revisited*. Finally, I had always felt uneasy about a book called *Basics of Verbal Aspect in Biblical Greek* that only dealt with the Greek of the New Testament. The second edition now includes examples and exercises from the Septuagint, thus alleviating my discomfort. I hope this will also give more advanced students some less familiar Greek to read and ponder. All in all, anyone familiar with the first edition will see that the heart of the book remains the same, but I think it is now much improved for teachers and students, and I hope it will serve them well for the next fifteen years.

As ever, I am grateful to Zondervan Academic for sharing in the vision for this book, and in particular I thank Chris Beetham for his enthusiasm and excellent work. I also thank Katya Covrett, who—I learned years later—was instrumental in seeing the first edition published in the first place.

This book is dedicated to my Greek partner in crime, George Athas, who has long shared with me in Greekness, travels, laughter, jazz, and friendship.

CONSTANTINE R. CAMPBELL

Verbal Aspect and Exegesis

WHY VERBAL ASPECT?

Some people who pick up this book will need no encouragement to read it in its entirety. They know that verbal aspect in biblical Greek is a matter to be dealt with. They understand that verbal aspect represents a controversial area of research with wide-ranging exegetical implications. They also know that most publications about verbal aspect are written by specialists for specialists and that there is a lot of confusion surrounding the topic for everyone else. Yet they want to understand. They want to know what all the fuss is about and why it matters. How will verbal-aspect research affect exegesis and translation? Will it change the way we read the Bible? How, and to what extent?

Such people will welcome a book like this and may even have skipped the introduction and moved straight into the business part of the book.

But what about the reader who is not convinced that reading a book like this is worth the time and investment? Perhaps you are a student for whom this book has been allocated as required reading in a Greek course but is otherwise not all that interested. Or perhaps you are a pastor who wants to keep up to speed with their Greek but wonders if tackling verbal aspect is worth it. Or perhaps you are a New Testament scholar who is not yet convinced that verbal aspect represents an improvement on the way you learned Greek and have taught it for years.

I have encountered many questions about verbal aspect. What difference does it really make to get verbal aspect right? Is this whole enterprise just something to challenge the academic mind with fine nuances that do not bear directly on exegesis and exposition? Are the results much different from those reached by earlier approaches to the verbal system? And if not, what's the point of it all? Let's be frank. Some readers have approached this subject with the most important question of all: "So what?"

This introduction explores some of the exegetical implications and applications that may be derived from verbal aspect. It may seem a little strange to attempt to do this at the beginning of the book. We haven't even addressed what verbal aspect is yet. But because it's important to try to show why verbal aspect matters, we will raise some questions about Greek verbs without trying to answer them at this stage. Raising the questions themselves will, I think, satisfy the "So what?" question. To achieve this, we will approach the implications of aspect for exegesis from both a negative and positive standpoint.

From a negative point of view, a good understanding of verbal aspect will enable us to assess and critique some of the scholarly conclusions reached about various Greek passages. New Testament commentaries frequently engage with the Greek text as a matter of course and often build the case for their conclusions using arguments arising from their understanding of Greek verbs. These conclusions then filter down to classes or sermons heard in church on Sunday. Teachers and pastors consult the commentaries and shape their content around the conclusions reached there. Lectures and sermons affect the understanding of regular people, who take their teachers' or pastors' conclusions to their Bible discussion groups, and before we know it the view that originated in the commentary has become folklore. But what if the original argument was flawed? What if the argument hinged on a misinformed understanding of the Greek verbal system? What if our understanding of biblical texts has been distorted, even just a little, by incorrect handling of Greek verbs?

Do you think such a phenomenon is rare? It's more common than you may think. Understanding Greek verbs matters. It does make a difference, as we will see.

From a positive point of view, a good understanding of verbal aspect will enable us to see how narratives are shaped by verbs and to see new possibilities for exegesis that were previously hidden from view. We will be able to describe verbal usage in a manner that is accurate, coherent, and neither too much nor too little. All these things represent a useful advance.

NEGATIVE INSIGHTS

In commentaries, classes, and sermons certain tendencies are clearly evident when it comes to the use of some Greek verbs. In this section, I suggest that such tendencies are unhelpful and at times misleading. Consider the following examples.

Romans 5:6 ἔτι γὰρ Χριστὸς ὄντων ἡμῶν ἀσθενῶν ἔτι κατὰ καιρὸν ὑπὲρ ἀσεβῶν **ἀπέθανεν.**

For while we were still weak, at the right time Christ **died** for the ungodly.

Some commentators write that because an aorist indicative is used here, Romans 5:6 proves that Christ's death was a once-for-all event, never to be repeated, and therefore Christ could not be reoffered time and time again (as in the Roman Mass). While I do not want to deny the once-for-all nature of Christ's death (cf. 1 Pet 3:18), the aorist in Romans 5:6 does not prove the point at all. Why not? Because that's not what an aorist indicative means. People who argue such things about this verse base their argument on a faulty understanding of the aorist indicative. A proper understanding of verbal aspect avoids such an error.[1]

1 Timothy 2:12 διδάσκειν δὲ γυναικὶ **οὐκ ἐπιτρέπω** οὐδὲ αὐθεντεῖν ἀνδρός, ἀλλ᾽ εἶναι ἐν ἡσυχίᾳ.

I do not permit a woman to teach or to have authority over a man; instead, she is to be silent.

Some recent attempts to explain this controversial verse have resorted to the meaning of the present indicative as key to their interpretation. The argument states that the present indicates an action in progress. As such, Paul does not permit this action at the time of his writing—he currently does not permit women to teach or to have authority over a man. But this is the current situation for Paul; it does not speak to our current situation, because that would not make sense of the present indicative.

---

1. Carson helpfully lists a catalogue of exegetical errors made by scholars with reference to the aorist indicative. See D. A. Carson, *Exegetical Fallacies*, 2nd ed. (Grand Rapids: Baker, 1996), 68–73.

Whatever one makes of this verse and the arguments surrounding it, it is clear that this particular argument is misleading insofar as it is based on an erroneous understanding of the verb.

John 17:17 ἁγίασον αὐτοὺς ἐν τῇ ἀληθείᾳ· ὁ λόγος ὁ σὸς ἀλήθειά ἐστιν.

Sanctify them by the truth; your word is truth.

The aorist imperative in this verse has been taken by some to prove that sanctification is an instantaneous event. This is especially the case within the so-called holiness movement, which asserts that Christians are made morally pure at the moment of conversion. It is argued that because aorist imperatives issue commands that are to be performed instantaneously, this verse and others like it provide evidence to support the concept of instantaneous sanctification. This is yet another error that has arisen from misunderstanding verbs.[2]

There are many similar examples of exegesis to be found throughout commentaries, classes, sermons, and the like. Some of these exegetical mistakes arise from common misapplications of traditional theories that have to do with the Greek verbal system. Others arise from correct applications of theories that have been shown to be lacking, imprecise, or just plain wrong. To do responsible exegesis and translation, we simply must understand Greek verbs better.

POSITIVE INSIGHTS

The ability to critique earlier patterns of exegesis is not the only benefit to be derived from the study of Greek verbal aspect. Many positive advances in understanding the New Testament (and the whole Greek Bible) may be ventured.

For example, verbal aspect enables us to articulate why certain verbs are used within their particular contexts. Consider the following passage.

John 7:28–32 ἔκραξεν οὖν ἐν τῷ ἱερῷ διδάσκων ὁ Ἰησοῦς καὶ λέγων, Κἀμὲ οἴδατε καὶ οἴδατε πόθεν εἰμί· καὶ ἀπ᾽ ἐμαυτοῦ οὐκ ἐλήλυθα,

---

2. See Randy L. Maddox, "The Use of the Aorist Tense in Holiness Exegesis," *Wesleyan Theological Journal* 16 (1981): 168–79.

ἀλλ' ἔστιν ἀληθινὸς ὁ πέμψας με, ὃν ὑμεῖς οὐκ οἴδατε· ἐγὼ οἶδα αὐτόν, ὅτι παρ' αὐτοῦ εἰμι κἀκεῖνός με ἀπέστειλεν. Ἐζήτουν οὖν αὐτὸν πιάσαι, καὶ οὐδεὶς ἐπέβαλεν ἐπ' αὐτὸν τὴν χεῖρα, ὅτι οὔπω ἐληλύθει ἡ ὥρα αὐτοῦ. Ἐκ τοῦ ὄχλου δὲ πολλοὶ ἐπίστευσαν εἰς αὐτὸν καὶ ἔλεγον· ὁ χριστὸς ὅταν ἔλθῃ μὴ πλείονα σημεῖα ποιήσει ὧν οὗτος ἐποίησεν; Ἤκουσαν οἱ Φαρισαῖοι τοῦ ὄχλου γογγύζοντος περὶ αὐτοῦ ταῦτα, καὶ ἀπέστειλαν οἱ ἀρχιερεῖς καὶ οἱ Φαρισαῖοι ὑπηρέτας ἵνα πιάσωσιν αὐτόν.

As he was teaching in the temple, Jesus cried out, "You know me and you know where I am from. Yet I have not come on my own, but the one who sent me is true. You don't know him; I know him because I am from him, and he sent me."

Then they tried to seize him. Yet no one laid a hand on him because his hour had not yet come. However, many from the crowd believed in him and said, "When the Messiah comes, he won't perform more signs than this man has done, will he?" The Pharisees heard the crowd murmuring these things about him, and so the chief priests and the Pharisees sent servants to arrest him. (CSB)

Why are the aorist indicatives ἔκραξεν, ἐπέβαλεν, and ἐπίστευσαν used for actions that outline the basic events of this narrative? And then, why are the imperfect indicatives ἐζήτουν and ἔλεγον, and the pluperfect ἐληλύθει, used for descriptive and explanatory parts of the narrative? Why are the perfects—οἴδατε (x2), ἐλήλυθα, and οἶδα—only found within direct speech? Prior to advances in our understanding of verbal aspect, it would have been difficult to give good explanations for these fairly typical phenomena.

Verbal aspect also opens new exegetical possibilities.

2 Timothy 4:6–7 Ἐγὼ γὰρ ἤδη σπένδομαι, καὶ ὁ καιρὸς τῆς ἀναλύσεώς μου **ἐφέστηκεν**. τὸν καλὸν ἀγῶνα **ἠγώνισμαι**, τὸν δρόμον **τετέλεκα**, τὴν πίστιν **τετήρηκα**·

For I am already being poured out as a drink offering, and the time for my departure **has come. I have fought** the good fight, **I have finished** the race, **I have kept** the faith.

These well-known verses witness Paul at the end of his apostolic ministry, speaking as though it is all over. But what if these perfect indicatives were not translated in the traditional manner? What if verbal aspect made it possible to translate these perfect indicatives more like present indicatives: the time *is coming*; *I am fighting* the good fight; *I am finishing* the race; *I am keeping* the faith? If this were a legitimate reading of the text, its meaning would be somewhat transformed.[3] Paul has not yet reached the end but is still actively engaged in his apostolic work. The study of verbal aspect opens up these kinds of exegetical possibilities that provide fresh insights into a number of texts.

CONCLUSION

Quite apart from all the exegetical possibilities it offers, the study of verbal aspect has brought some of the most significant developments in our understanding of ancient Greek over the last hundred years. In what follows, we will trace the history of research concerning verbal aspect in ancient Greek. We will look into linguistic theory and competing theoretical models. We will explore the aspectual constituency, meaning, and function of each tense-form across the moods, infinitive, and participle. We will aim to get verbal aspect right.

---

3. See Constantine R. Campbell, "Finished the Race? 2 Timothy 4:6–7 and Verbal Aspect," in *Donald Robinson: Selected Works, Appreciation*, ed. Peter G. Bolt and Mark D. Thompson (Sydney: Australian Church Record/Moore College, 2008), 169–75.

PART 1

Verbal Aspect Theory

CHAPTER 1

What Is Verbal Aspect?

In this chapter, a definition of verbal aspect is offered, and aspect is distinguished from two other important terms—tense and *Aktionsart*. Following this, the linguistic distinction between semantics and pragmatics is explained and is then applied to aspect, *Aktionsart*, and tense.

VERBAL ASPECT

While there are various ways of defining verbal aspect, the simplest and historically most established description is *viewpoint*.[1] An author or speaker views an action, event, or state either from the *outside* or from the *inside*. The view of an action, event, or state from the outside is called *perfective aspect*, while the view from the inside is called *imperfective aspect*. Buist Fanning describes aspect in this way:

> The action can be viewed from a reference-point within the action, without
> reference to the beginning or end-point of the action, but with a focus instead

---

1. Other definitions of aspect exist within the wider linguistic world, but Greek aspect studies have more or less kept in line with the original understanding of aspect, which is *viewpoint*. Another major understanding of aspect was popularized by Bernard Comrie's 1976 publication *Aspect: An Introduction to the Study of Verbal Aspect and Related Problems*, Cambridge Textbooks in Linguistics (Cambridge: Cambridge University Press, 1976). Comrie defines aspect through a set of internal temporal relationships, but this approach has been critiqued for resorting to temporal understandings of a spatial concept. Since aspect is about viewpoint, it is a spatial concept, viewing activities and actions either internally or externally.

on its internal structure or make-up. Or the action can be viewed from a vantage-point outside the action, with focus on the whole action from beginning to end, but without reference to its internal structure.[2]

An illustration that has become standard in describing verbal aspect involves a reporter who is to report on a street parade.[3] If the reporter views the street parade from a helicopter, he sees the whole parade from a distance. He can describe the parade in a general way because he sees the whole thing rather than seeing its details up close. This viewpoint, from the helicopter, represents what we call *perfective aspect*. It is the view from the outside—the external viewpoint. If, however, that same reporter views the same street parade from the level of the street rather than from a helicopter, his view of the parade is quite different. This time the reporter is up close to the parade and watches as it unfolds before him. Rather than seeing the parade from a distance and as a whole, the parade is now seen from within. This viewpoint, from the street, represents what we call *imperfective aspect*. It is the view from the inside—the internal viewpoint.[4]

Most, if not all, languages have ways of expressing these two different viewpoints. In English, we can see the two viewpoints contrasted in the following sentences:

a. *I walked down the street. A man talked to me.*
b. *I was walking down the street when a man began talking to me.*

Both A and B might be describing the exact same events, but they nevertheless portray the events differently. The difference between them is verbal aspect. The actions portrayed in A are viewed as a whole; this is the view from the helicopter—perfective aspect. The same actions are portrayed in B as though unfolding; this is the view from the street—imperfective aspect.

Verbal aspect in Greek is called a *synthetic semantic category*. This means

---

2. Buist M. Fanning, *Verbal Aspect in New Testament Greek*, Oxford Theological Monographs (Oxford: Clarendon, 1990), 27.

3. The illustration originates with Isačenko and is adopted by Stanley Porter. See A. V. Isačenko, *Grammaticheskij stroj russkogo jazyka v sopostavlenii s slovatskim: Morfologija* (Bratislava: The Slovak Academy of Sciences Press, 1960); Stanley E. Porter, *Verbal Aspect in the Greek of the New Testament with Reference to Tense and Mood*, Studies in Biblical Greek 1 (New York: Peter Lang, 1989), 91.

4. Strictly speaking, the reporter is not "within" the parade as he views it from the street. The point is that his view focuses on the inner features of the parade and does not include its beginning or end.

that aspect is realized (= semantic) in the morphological forms (= synthetic) of verbs.[5] In Greek, verbal aspect is encoded in the verb form of the verbal network. While this is not the same for all languages, most scholars agree that this is the case for Greek. This means that certain verbs encode certain aspects. For example, aorists express one aspect, while presents express another. We'll look more closely at this later.

Verbal aspect represents a subjective choice. This point is important: aspect is, within certain bounds, subjective. An author chooses which aspect to use when portraying a particular action, event, or state. So, to take the English examples mentioned above, to say *I was walking down the street when a man began talking to me* is no different in reality from *I walked down the street. A man talked to me.* In both cases, I walked down the street, and a man talked to me. Both examples describe the same events. But each portrays these events differently. When I'm telling the story, I decide which way I will tell it. Neither choice affects what really happened; the choice simply reflects my storytelling preference. This is what it means when we say that aspect represents a subjective choice.

TENSE, *AKTIONSART*, AND ASPECT

Verbal aspect is often discussed in relation to two other terms: tense and *Aktionsart*. Careful delineation must be made between the three terms.

TENSE

In Greek, the indicative verbs have traditionally been assigned tenses. The aorist indicative is a past tense, the present indicative is a present tense, the future indicative is a future tense, and so on. While there are more technical ways of defining tense, it normally refers to a verb's temporal reference. That is, referring to a particular time frame is the built-in meaning of a tense.

It doesn't take long when beginning to read the Greek New Testament, however, to discover that tense is not the whole story. We quickly discover present indicative tense-form verbs that refer to the past. There are also forms traditionally considered past tenses that refer to the present. There are even future-referring past tenses. Furthermore, what's the difference between two past

---

5. In linguistic terminology, *synthetic* indicates that meaning is signaled by inflection—that is, changes in morphological forms.

tenses in Greek? Tense cannot be the whole story with Greek verbs, since there is a difference in meaning between the aorist and imperfect—both past tenses.[6] The nineteenth-century answer to this question—the difference between two past tenses in Greek—is the type of action, or *Aktionsart*.

AKTIONSART

Aktionsart is a German word meaning "type of action." There are various types of action, such as punctiliar actions, iterative actions, ingressive actions, and so on. The category of *Aktionsart* describes what sort of action is depicted. If an action is depicted as a once-occurring, instantaneous event, it is called punctiliar. If the action is depicted as repeated over and over, it is called iterative. If the verb focuses on the beginning of an action, it is called ingressive.

The early academic discussion about such things exhibited much confusion between *Aktionsart* and aspect. These days, there is a general consensus as to the difference between the two terms, and it is vital that we properly understand the distinction. *Aktionsart* refers to *what sort of action* is depicted. Aspect refers to viewpoint—how the action is viewed. They are two different categories.

Let's take Romans 5:14 as an example. In that verse we are told that "death reigned from the time of Adam to Moses." The verb "reigned" expresses perfective aspect (the helicopter view). We are presented with a summary of what happened; we are told simply that it happened. This is the external viewpoint. But when we ask *what sort of action* is depicted, we are able to say a range of other things. For starters, this action took a long time! There were many years between Adam and Moses. Death's reign between Adam and Moses is understood as an ongoing, expansive event. This was not a once-occurring, instantaneous type of action.

This example clearly demonstrates the difference between aspect and *Aktionsart*. Aspect refers to how the action is viewed: death's reign is viewed externally as a whole. *Aktionsart* refers to what sort of action is depicted: it was an ongoing event that spanned many years.

The difference between aspect and *Aktionsart* leads us to another important distinction.

---

6. Indeed, the same is true for English—tense is not the whole story, as the above English examples demonstrate.

SEMANTICS AND PRAGMATICS

The terms *semantics* and *pragmatics* come from modern linguistics and refer to a distinction that is now applied to the discussion about Greek verbs.[7] Again, it is important that we understand what these terms mean.

SEMANTICS

When speaking of verbs, *semantics* refers to the values that are encoded in the verbal form. These values are unchanging and are always there when the particular verbal form occurs, allowing for exceptional circumstances (such as anomalous expressions and certain fixed idioms). Apart from exceptional circumstances, a semantic value is *uncancelable*—it is always there and cannot be canceled out. Semantics refers to what the verb means at its core. What does an aorist encode? What is core to an aorist that is different from an imperfect? What meaning does an aorist *always* carry with it?

By the way, it is worth noting a little issue to do with terminology. Often the term *semantics* is used in a nontechnical sense to refer to the range of meaning that a word may have. This is not the sense in which it is now used in academic discussion. The range of meaning of a particular word is better termed *lexical semantics*, and the type of semantics that we are interested in at the moment is *verbal semantics* or *grammatical semantics*, which refers to the uncancelable properties of the verb form.

PRAGMATICS

When speaking of verbs, *pragmatics* refers to the expression of semantic values in context and in combination with other factors. In other words, pragmatics refers to how it all ends up—the way language is used in context.

Semantics and pragmatics relate together a little like this: we take the semantic elements and plug them into a text that will have a range of things going on within it already, which bounce off and interact with the semantic values; the outcome is pragmatics. Pragmatic values (or *implicatures*) can

---

7. For a helpful overview of the use of these categories in Greek studies, as well as potential shortcomings of the distinction between semantics and pragmatics, see Francis G. H. Pang, *Revisiting Aspect and Aktionsart: A Corpus Approach to Koine Greek Event Typology*, Linguistic Biblical Studies 14 (Leiden: Brill, 2016), 227–34.

change from context to context; they are cancelable and not always there when particular verb forms are used.[8]

Perhaps an illustration will help to clarify further the differences between semantics and pragmatics. Semantics asks, "Who am I?" while pragmatics asks, "What do I do?" These are two different questions (though our Western culture tends to blur them together). *Who I am* is about who I am at the core of my being—what it is that makes me uniquely me. Who I am might be expressed by what I do, but what I do is not who I am. If you were to ask me, "Who are you?" and I reply that I am a lawyer, I haven't really answered the question. Who am I? I'm Constantine. What do I do? I'm a lawyer. But I might quit law and take up jazz music. If I do that, I haven't changed who I am; I've just changed what I do. (I know life's not quite as simple as that, but bear with the analogy.) Discovering the semantics of the aorist is to ask, "Who are you, aorist?" To discover the pragmatics of the aorist, we ask, "And what do you do, aorist?"

The distinction between semantics and pragmatics is useful in sharpening the difference between aspect and *Aktionsart*. Aspect is a semantic value. The aspect of a particular tense-form doesn't change. An aorist will always be perfective in aspect. This will be the case no matter which word (lexeme) is used as an aorist or in what context it is used. Aspect is uncancelable. When asked, "Who are you, aorist?" the answer is, "I am perfective in aspect."

Aktionsart, on the other hand, is a pragmatic value. The *Aktionsart* of a particular tense-form can change. Sometimes an aorist indicative will be punctiliar in *Aktionsart*. Sometimes it will be iterative, sometimes ingressive. It all depends on which lexeme is used as an aorist, on the context, and on what actually happened. *Aktionsart* is cancelable. When asked, "What do you do, aorist?" the answer is, "Well, I do many things. I have many possible *Aktionsart* outcomes."[9] Many scholars working with Greek verbs now employ this distinction between semantics and pragmatics.

---

8. Not all Greek scholars are comfortable with the terms *semantics* and *pragmatics*, but the distinction they articulate is nevertheless normally affirmed. Some prefer terms such as *grammatical* or *essential meaning* in place of *semantics*. Terms such as *procedural character* or *situational meaning* might be substituted for *pragmatics*. Regardless of the terms used, it remains important to distinguish between the essential meaning of a tense-form and the way it functions within texts.

9. In older grammars and commentaries, various claims are made about the *Aktionsarten* of verb tenses as though the forms themselves denote categories such as punctiliar, ingressive, constative, and the like. This is simply not the case. There is nothing about an aorist, for example, that is punctiliar in nature. Nevertheless, an aorist is capable of punctiliar expression when used with a punctiliar lexeme in a context that allows it. In other words, punctiliarity is a pragmatic *function*, or *implicature*, of the aorist under certain conditions; it is not what the aorist itself means at the semantic level. See Constantine R. Campbell, *Advances in the Study of Greek: New Insights for Reading the New Testament* (Grand Rapids: Zondervan Academic, 2015), 120–21.

The remaining question related to the distinction, however, is this: Is temporal reference semantic or pragmatic? If temporal reference is semantic, then Greek verbs truly are tenses. An indicative verb's temporal reference is uncancelable and is a core part of its meaning. An aorist indicative is a past tense and must always be a past tense.

But here, of course, lies a problem. We learn early on that aorist indicatives are *not* always past referring. Therefore, we are led to ask: Is past temporal reference a semantic value of the aorist indicative? Some scholars say no, the aorist indicative is not a past tense. Even though the aorist indicative often ends up expressing past temporal reference when used in Greek texts, this is a *pragmatic implicature* rather than semantic encoding.[10] After all, these scholars point out, there are plenty of other elements in the text that indicate how the time frame is to be understood.

In fact, in several languages time frame is indicated purely by such *deictic markers*—words like "yesterday," "now," "later," and so forth.[11] Even genre can set the time frame. For example, narratives naturally refer to the past (even without needing to use words like "yesterday") simply because it is understood that they are about events that have already happened. If the time frame is indicated by deictic markers and/or genre, why do we think that indicative verbs must indicate time as well? The answer to that question, for most of us I think, is that we are used to that being the case in English (or so we think, anyway).[12]

But such is not the case in at least some other languages, and now the question has been raised with reference to the Greek verbal system. We will return to this issue at several points. Regardless of one's position on this matter, however, I think the term "tense-form" is more helpful than "tense" when referring to verbs, because it reminds us that it is the morphological *form* that is being addressed, whatever the form happens to communicate.

---

10. The linguistic term *implicature* refers to the specific function of a form when in combination with certain pragmatic features. Every verbal form is capable of expressing a variety of implicatures, depending on the combination of pragmatic features at work in any given text; Campbell, *Advances in the Study of Greek*, 121.

11. Deictic markers indicate time, person, or location in a text. Temporal deixis encompasses words such as "earlier," "shortly," "now," "tomorrow," and so forth. Narrative will often express temporal deixis without explicit markers since it is usually assumed to be referring to the past.

12. In fact, English verbs are more complicated than most of us probably realize, and there is academic debate about its "tenses" too. Some scholars, for example, argue that the English present tense is not a tense at all, since it can refer to the present, past, and future.

CONCLUSION

We have seen in this chapter that aspect refers to the viewpoint that an author subjectively chooses when portraying an action, event, or state. There are two viewpoints from which to choose: the view from the outside—perfective aspect—and the view from the inside—imperfective aspect. We have seen that aspect is different from *Aktionsart* in that the latter term describes how an action is portrayed to take place (in any particular context), whereas aspect refers simply to viewpoint. Finally, we have seen that aspect is a semantic value encoded in the verb and is therefore uncancelable, whereas *Aktionsart* is a pragmatic value affected by a range of contextual factors and is therefore cancelable.

CHAPTER 2

The History of Verbal Aspect

Throughout the debate about verbal aspect in ancient Greek, there has been not a little confusion created by the merging of three quite distinct academic disciplines: general linguistics, Greek philology, and biblical research. In *general linguistics*, there are various linguistics schools, each with its own terminology and methodological principles. It is from this sphere that terms such as *semantics*, *pragmatics*, and *implicature* come. *Greek philology* is the study of ancient Greek generally. The corpus of literature written in ancient Greek is huge and ranges from Homer, through classical Greek literature, right through to the New Testament and beyond. *Biblical research* has its own idiosyncrasies, but with reference to Greek is particularly interested in understanding for the sake of theological nuance, exegetical argument, and so forth. There is, of course, a strong focus on Koine—or *postclassical*—Greek within this discipline.

Among the scholars who have engaged in debates about Greek verbal aspect, it is rare to find one who is equally comfortable on all three academic fronts. Most scholars have come from one, or at most two, of these three fields. Often scholars are critical of those who come from fields other than their own. Linguists sometimes claim that philologists are linguistically naïve; they may know the language well, but they lack the theoretical tools needed to analyze and describe it properly. Greek philologists tend to criticize biblical scholars and particularly linguists for not knowing enough Greek. In their view, biblical scholars are stuck in a narrow corpus of Koine, and linguists are just theorists interested in making generalizations without really knowing the language. Then again, biblical scholars may defiantly declare that linguistics and classics both pale in comparison to God's Word!

The study of Greek aspect has evolved through significant contributions from all three academic fields, as we will now see.

THE EARLY PERIOD

GEORG CURTIUS

Georg Curtius was a nineteenth-century comparative philologist who was interested in Indo-European languages.[1] He made the first breakthrough with reference to the Greek verbal system.[2] Curtis argued that in contrast to Latin, temporal meaning in the Greek verbal system was limited to the indicative mood. It is taken for granted now that there is no tense outside the indicative mood in Greek, but this was not formally acknowledged prior to Curtius.

A second major contribution of Curtius was to differentiate between distinct types of meaning expressed by the present and aorist verbal stems. He described this as a durative action as opposed to a "quickly passing" action. His term for this distinction was called *Zeitart*, literally meaning "type of time." Curtius's type of time was different from a mere time lapse (short vs. long); he was interested in describing time in terms of a point versus a line. This description became standard and is still sometimes used today.

Curtius's insights were largely accepted in the late nineteenth century, and his analysis of the Greek verbal system became dominant. However, his term *Zeitart* was later replaced by the term *Aktionsart*, since "type of action" was regarded as a more precise label than "type of time."

Curtius was aware of advances that had been made in the study of Slavonic languages, which predated his own discoveries and through which the term *aspect* was introduced to the discussion.

THE EARLY TWENTIETH CENTURY

Buist Fanning describes the period of 1890–1910 as witnessing a flowering of aspect studies. Curtius had sparked a period of productive investigation

---

1. Much of this section is reliant on Buist M. Fanning, *Verbal Aspect in New Testament Greek*, Oxford Theological Monographs (Oxford: Clarendon, 1990), 9–33.

2. Georg Curtius, *The Greek Verb: Its Structure and Development*, trans. Augustus S. Wilkins and Edwin B. England (London: John Murray, 1880).

into the nature of the Greek verbal system. Among the issues being investigated, an important question arose concerning the range of aspect values that occur in Greek and Indo-European languages. The result of this, however, was that a multiplicity of categories was born, complete with conflicting terminology. Confusion resulted from the interchangeable usage of the three terms *Zeitart*, *Aktionsart*, and aspect.

In the mid-1920s attempts were made to definitively delineate between *Aktionsart* and aspect (*Zeitart* was dropped). The definitions that ensued were as follows: *Aktionsart* refers to the portrayal of how an action actually occurs and is primarily lexically determined; aspect refers to a way of viewing an action (as articulated in ch. 1). This distinction is held today.

K. L. MCKAY

While there were several important contributions made through the middle of the twentieth century, such as those of J. Holt[3] and M. S. Ruipérez,[4] none had quite the same impact on the modern discussion as the work of K. L. McKay.[5] A classical Greek philologist with an interest in the Greek of the New Testament, McKay first published on Greek aspect in 1965. In his 1965 article, McKay suggested that aspect was a more important feature of the Greek verbal system than was time.[6]

McKay posited that there were three or four aspects, depending on whether the future was regarded as a proper aspect. He viewed the present and imperfect tense-forms as imperfective in aspect, while the aorist was perfective (using our terminology). The future, though not actually an aspect, was labeled by McKay as a quasi, fourth aspect anyway. The perfect and pluperfect tense-forms were described as stative in aspect, a concept to be explored more fully below.

McKay wrote about aspect for the following thirty years and became progressively stronger in his assertions. In fact, he ended up saying not just that aspect is more important than time in the Greek verb but that time is

---

3. Jens Holt, *Études d'aspect*, Acta Jutlandica Aarsskrift for Aarhus Universitet 15.2 (Copenhagen: Munksgaard, 1943).

4. Martín S. Ruipérez, *Estructura del Sistema de Aspectos y Tiempos del Verbo Griego Antiguo: Análisis Funcional Sincrónico*, Theses et Studia Philologica Salmanticensia 7 (Salamanca: Colegio Trilingüe de la Universidad, 1954).

5. K. L. McKay, *A New Syntax of the Verb in New Testament Greek: An Aspectual Approach*, Studies in Biblical Greek 5 (New York: Peter Lang, 1994).

6. K. L. McKay, "The Use of the Ancient Greek Perfect Down to the Second Century A.D.," *Bulletin of the Institute of Classical Studies* 12 (1965): 1–21.

not there at all, except by implication from the verb's relationship to its context.[7] McKay's work did not gain wide acceptance within classical philology or biblical studies for much of this period, but he had planted the seeds of the revolution.

THE MODERN PERIOD

It was the contributions of Stanley E. Porter[8] and Buist M. Fanning[9] that put verbal aspect firmly on the map within biblical studies. Both men completed doctorates in England at the same time, which were published in 1989 and 1990 respectively. They were not aware of each other's simultaneous research, and it is therefore encouraging that there is a great deal of agreement between the two authors. There are, however, several strong differences, which have set the shape of the subsequent debate.

STANLEY E. PORTER

Porter is one of the few scholars who have been trained formally in both linguistics and biblical studies. As such, he brings a robust theoretical linguistic framework to his analysis of the Greek verbal system. In particular, his analysis is conducted through the prism of the functional school of systemic linguistics.

Porter self-consciously builds on the framework established by McKay. He too concludes that Greek is aspectual and not tense based at all. But unlike McKay, Porter rigorously defends this view from a theoretical basis. Since temporal reference is not always expressed by the verb, it therefore cannot be a grammatical feature of the verb (semantics). Temporal reference must be derived from context (pragmatics).

Porter also acknowledges three aspects in the Greek verbal system: perfective, imperfective, and stative. The future is nonaspectual according to his analysis.

It is Porter's contribution that has caused the fiercest debate. The "tenseless" position is still in the minority, being rejected by many traditionalists.

---

7. McKay, *New Syntax of the Verb*, 39.
8. Stanley E. Porter, *Verbal Aspect in the Greek of the New Testament with Reference to Tense and Mood*, Studies in Biblical Greek 1 (New York: Peter Lang, 1989).
9. Fanning, *Verbal Aspect*.

BUIST M. FANNING

Fanning's analysis is more traditional than Porter's. For him, while aspect is regarded as dominant, tense remains a legitimate category. The aorist is still to be regarded as a past tense and the present as a present tense, and so on, but the dominance of aspect over tense explains those cases in which the temporal expression is not consistent. According to Fanning, there are only two aspects, not three, since stativity is properly regarded as an *Aktionsart* category rather than an aspect.

Fanning provides a detailed analysis of how aspect relates to *Aktionsart*, indicating how each aspect interacts with certain lexical types to produce predictable *Aktionsart* outcomes. His work has been more readily accepted by traditionalists, provoking considerably less controversy than Porter's work, though it is less rigorously linguistic in framework and methodology.

MARI BROMAN OLSEN

Mari Broman Olsen is the first major contributor to follow Porter and Fanning, and her work reflects the enormous debt that the modern discussion owes them.[10] Her contribution is very much on the linguistic side of things, with one chapter on English aspect, one chapter specifically on Koine Greek aspect, and the remainder providing a detailed study of theoretical issues.

Olsen defines aspect a little differently, as "internal temporal constituency," following Bernard Comrie and others.[11] This is not quite the same thing as defining aspect simply as viewpoint, and as such it yields somewhat different results. Like Fanning, Olsen advocates only two aspects, again affirming that stativity is an *Aktionsart* value rather than being aspectual.

Interestingly, Olsen utilizes the semantic/pragmatic distinction to argue that some Greek verb forms are tenses and others are not. This is simply a matter of which forms are consistent in their temporal reference and which are not. Those that are consistent encode temporal reference at the semantic level, and those that are not consistent do not encode temporal reference at the semantic level.

In terms of the reception of Olsen's work, it is not as well known within biblical-studies circles as it deserves to be, and this is probably due in part to its

---

10. Mari Broman Olsen, *A Semantic and Pragmatic Model of Lexical and Grammatical Aspect*, Outstanding Dissertations in Linguistics (New York: Garland, 1997).

11. Bernard Comrie, *Aspect: An Introduction to the Study of Verbal Aspect and Related Problems*, Cambridge Textbooks in Linguistics (Cambridge: Cambridge University Press, 1976).

highly technical nature. The work is linguistically rigorous, which means that it is somewhat inaccessible to the uninitiated.

RODNEY J. DECKER

Rodney J. Decker came from the New Testament scholarship stable. The burden of his work was to test Porter's non-tense position.[12] He admits that he began his investigations into aspect somewhat skeptical toward Porter's approach, but later accepted its validity.

A unique feature of Decker's work (at the time) is the source limitation imposed within it, focusing on Mark's Gospel. The strength of this method is that it allows for thorough testing, whereas some other studies had been too broad in their sampling. However, it also limits the comprehensiveness of the results: What does it say about the rest of the New Testament? What about Greek more widely?

Decker has made a significant contribution to the discussion by isolating one particular issue—the existence or otherwise of semantic temporal reference—and investigating that question thoroughly. As for the reception of his work, classicists tend to overlook it, probably due to its limited scope. For biblical-studies students, however, Decker explains Porter's approach in an accessible manner, and the testing of the controversial issue of temporal reference is of great value.

T. V. EVANS

T. V. Evans is a classical philologist who seeks to respect linguistic considerations and the input of biblical scholarship.[13] Because of his classicist background, he brings a broader knowledge of Greek literature to the discussion, having done extensive work on aspect in classical texts and the Septuagint (LXX).

On the temporality issue, Evans is a traditionalist, arguing that tense is indeed expressed by the verbal system. On the question of aspect, he affirms the existence of two aspects, rejecting the category of stative aspect.

In terms of reception, Evans's work is well regarded within classical scholarship and has been influential within biblical studies.

---

12. Rodney J. Decker, *Temporal Deixis of the Greek Verb in the Gospel of Mark with Reference to Verbal Aspect*, Studies in Biblical Greek 10 (New York: Peter Lang, 2001).

13. T. V. Evans, *Verbal Syntax in the Greek Pentateuch: Natural Greek Usage and Hebrew Interference* (Oxford: Oxford University Press, 2001).

CONSTANTINE R. CAMPBELL

I have approached verbal aspect through biblical studies. My first book deals with verbal aspect in the indicative mood and its role in narrative texts.[14] Wanting to gain the benefits of a limited sample (following Decker) and yet also attempting to minimize the trade-off of such an approach, I investigated a couple of New Testament narrative texts as well as a series of nonbiblical texts. My second book looks at verbal aspect in the non-indicative verbs.[15]

I follow Porter and Decker on the issue of tense: the indicative mood does not express tense at the semantic level (except for the future indicative), even though each tense-form has a characteristic temporal reference on the pragmatic level. I argue for only two aspects, rejecting the category of stative aspect. Following Evans, I argue that the perfect and pluperfect tense-forms are imperfective in aspect. I also argue that the future tense-form is perfective in aspect.

DAVID L. MATHEWSON

David L. Mathewson focuses on the function of verbal aspect in the book of Revelation.[16] Addressing the phenomenon of shifting tenses in Revelation's visionary segments, Mathewson accounts for such behavior through verbal aspect. His understanding of aspect and its attendant issues follows Porter in his helpful genre-specific study.

WALLY V. CIRAFESI

Wally V. Cirafesi offers an interesting study that applies verbal aspect to the Synoptic problem.[17] It is an example of how verbal aspect can interact with longstanding problems within New Testament studies. Whereas traditional approaches to Synoptic parallels have assumed *Zeitart* or *Aktionsart* values for the verbal system, Cirafesi demonstrates that verbal aspect has stronger explanatory power in accounting for Synoptic tense-form differences.[18] As with Mathewson, Cirafesi follows Porter on theoretical issues.

---

14. Constantine R. Campbell, *Verbal Aspect, the Indicative Mood, and Narrative: Soundings in the Greek of the New Testament*, Studies in Biblical Greek 13 (New York: Peter Lang, 2007).

15. Constantine R. Campbell, *Verbal Aspect and Non-Indicative Verbs: Further Soundings in the Greek of the New Testament*, Studies in Biblical Greek 15 (New York: Peter Lang, 2008).

16. David L. Mathewson, *Verbal Aspect in the Book of Revelation: The Function of Greek Verb Tenses in John's Apocalypse*, Linguistic Biblical Studies 4 (Leiden: Brill, 2010).

17. Wally V. Cirafesi, *Verbal Aspect in Synoptic Parallels: On the Method and Meaning of Divergent Tense-Form Usage in the Synoptic Passion Narratives*, Linguistic Biblical Studies 7 (Leiden: Brill, 2013).

18. Cirafesi, *Verbal Aspect in Synoptic Parallels*, 166.

DOUGLAS S. HUFFMAN

Douglas S. Huffman applies verbal aspect to prohibitions in the Greek New Testament.[19] He argues that verbal aspect provides better explanatory power than *Aktionsart* in understanding prohibitions. From a theoretical point of view, Huffman primarily follows Porter, though he follows my work in some key respects, including the interaction between pragmatics and semantics in the imperatival mood.[20]

ROBERT S. D. CRELLIN

Robert S. D. Crellin addresses the problem of the perfect tense-form in literary Koine Greek.[21] Affirming the existence of imperfective and perfective aspects, he does not accept a third stative aspect to describe the Greek perfect. He demonstrates that the Greek perfect sometimes behaves like an imperfective verb and sometimes like a perfective but ultimately differs from both in its relationship to the subject of the verb—"the perfect is fundamentally participant-focused."[22] While heavily influenced by the work of Wolfgang Klein, Crellin's solution bears some parallel to McKay in this respect (see chapter 5 for more on this).

THE GREEK VERB REVISITED

Following the so-called "Perfect Storm"—a debate between Porter, Fanning, and me on the aspectual nature of the Greek perfect at the 2013 Society of Biblical Literature annual meeting—a group of scholars led by Steven Runge addressed various questions regarding the Greek verbal system at a conference in Cambridge in 2015.[23] This led to the publication of *The Greek Verb Revisited*—a collection of essays addressing tense, aspect, mood, and voice in the Greek verbal system.[24] While not all contributors are completely uniform, the volume taken as a whole argues for tense within the indicative mood, and two aspects—rejecting

---

19. Douglas S. Huffman, *Verbal Aspect Theory and the Prohibitions in the Greek New Testament*, Studies in Biblical Greek 16 (New York: Peter Lang, 2014).

20. Huffman, *Verbal Aspect Theory and the Prohibitions*, 100–103, 511.

21. Robert S. D. Crellin, *The Syntax and Semantics of the Perfect Active in Literary Koine Greek*, Publications of the Philological Society 47 (West Sussex: Wiley Blackwell, 2016).

22. Crellin, *The Syntax and Semantics of the Perfect*, 252.

23. This paragraph is taken from my essay, "Aspect and Tense in New Testament Greek," in *Linguistics and New Testament Greek: Key Issues in the Current Debate*, ed. David Alan Black and Benjamin L. Merkle (Grand Rapids; Baker Academic, 2020), 42. Used with permission.

24. Steven E. Runge and Christopher J. Fresch, eds., *The Greek Verb Revisited: A Fresh Approach for Biblical Research* (Bellingham, WA: Lexham, 2016).

stative aspect but arguing for "combinative" aspect for the perfect and pluper-fect forms. These forms represent a combination of perfective and imperfective aspects that allows the perfect to retain a more or less traditional expression of perfective (past) action with an imperfective (present) resulting state.[25]

SAMUEL J. FRENEY

Freney examines the role of verbal aspect in New Testament quotations of the Septuagint in which the original tense-form has been changed by the New Testament authors.[26] He demonstrates that New Testament authors sometimes change Septuagint tense-forms for rhetorical and theological purposes, and these changes shed light on verbal aspect, especially for the future tense-form. Freney adduces evidence that confirms my view that the future indicative is perfective in aspect (see chapter 3 for more on this).[27]

THE PERFECT STORM

Though the Perfect Storm debate between Porter, Fanning, and me occurred in 2013, the resulting publication was not released until 2021.[28] *The Perfect Storm* contains essays from each scholar on the semantics of the Greek perfect tense-forms, along with essay responses to each other. Thus, this volume helpfully puts side by side the three most widely cited protagonists in the debate about the Greek perfect along with their critiques of each others' work, so that interested students and scholars can more easily evaluate their commonalities and differences.

CURRENT ISSUES

AREAS OF AGREEMENT

There are several areas of agreement within current debate about Greek verbal aspect. Perhaps the most important among these is the common assent

---

25. Since *The Greek Verb Revisited* presents itself as a major alternative to the "Perfect Storm" debate of Porter-Fanning-Campbell, I have included my review of the volume as an appendix at the back of this book.

26. Samuel J. Freney, *Aspectual Substitution: Verbal Change in New Testament Quotations of the Septuagint*, Studies in Biblical Greek 20 (New York: Peter Lang, 2020).

27. Freney, *Aspectual Substitution*, 245.

28. Constantine R. Campbell, Buist M. Fanning, and Stanley E. Porter, *The Perfect Storm: Critical Discussion of the Semantics of The Greek Perfect Tense under Aspect Theory*, ed. D. A. Carson, Studies in Biblical Greek 21 (New York: Peter Lang, 2021).

that aspect is a major category in our understanding of Greek. It is more important than tense and must be reckoned with. There are other areas of agreement
as well:

- Aspect is defined as *viewpoint*, which is a spatial rather than temporal
  concept.
- Aspect holds the key to understanding the Greek verbal system.
- There are at least two aspects in Greek: perfective and imperfective.
- Debate about aspect must come to some kind of resolution as quickly as
  possible.
- Greek grammars and biblical commentaries need to update and come to
  grips with the new playing field.
- Responsible exegesis of the biblical Greek text must incorporate
  aspectual awareness.

UNRESOLVED AREAS

Nevertheless, there are a few areas that are as yet unresolved.

Temporality and tense. The relationship between Greek verbs and tense
remains unresolved. Do Greek indicative verbs encode temporal reference at the
semantic level? It is worth pointing out a common misconception that scholars
believe in *either* aspect or tense. We are not talking about "aspect or tense" as
though students must choose to accept either aspect or tense as the correct way
to understand Greek verbs. All scholars agree about the importance of aspect,
though there is ongoing debate about some issues. Nevertheless, it is *yes* to aspect,
and *maybe* to tense—depending on whom you ask.

Number of aspects. The issue of how many aspects are encoded in the Greek
verbal system is of enormous importance and is also as yet unresolved. Are there
two aspects or three (or four)? Both perfective and imperfective aspects are
established, but what about stative aspect? Generally speaking, among those
who teach and learn ancient Greek, many accept the existence of three aspects.
But many major contributors to the modern debate clearly prefer the two-aspect
position, rejecting stative aspect. Indeed, within the wider linguistic world, two-
viewpoint aspects are standard across languages. To regard stativity as an aspect
is odd.

Related to this issue is how to understand the perfect and pluperfect
tense-forms, which many describe as stative in aspect. The advantages of this
understanding are that stative aspect would account for the apparent stativity of

much perfect and pluperfect usage, and that these forms share a different morphological verbal stem when compared to aorist and present stems (more on this later). On the other hand, it has been argued that stativity is an *Aktionsart* value (or a lexical element) rather than an aspect. Still others have argued for a *combinative* approach to the perfect, seeing both perfective and imperfective aspects at work.

The aspectual nature of the future tense-form is also debated, with some arguing that it is nonaspectual, others that it is perfective in aspect, and yet others that it expresses a combination of perfective and imperfective aspects.

THE WAY FORWARD

In order to reach some kind of consensus on these issues, a range of approaches will aid the discussion.

1. Methodological issues need to be sharpened and clarified. The impact of various linguistic approaches needs to be understood and appreciated.
2. The three academic disciplines involved in the debate (general linguistics, Greek philology, and biblical studies) must display greater sensitivity to one another. All three spheres should listen to one another with respect and without assuming that one is naturally more authoritative than the others.
3. The power of explanation should be appreciated as a key methodological principle. We must seek the model with the greatest power of explanation. Is a particular model of the verbal system able to account for all uses of Greek verbs?
4. We must further uncover the relationship of aspect to discourse analysis, but more on this later.
5. It would help to take the heat out of debates about Greek verbs. It's weird that tense-forms of an ancient language should generate so much passion and, at times, acrimony. Greek scholars are all trying to achieve more or less the same thing: to arrive at a more accurate understanding of how Greek verbs contribute meaning to ancient texts (including the Bible). Other disciplines within biblical studies manage to work through their differences without denouncing, mocking, or discrediting their opponents. Why can't Greek scholars?[29]

---

29. I confess my own complicity in this sorry state of affairs.

More Tense Discussion

WHAT IS TENSE?

When we discuss *tense*, we are not referring to verbal morphology.[1] This can be confusing because we are often used to referring to verbs as "tenses"—the present tense, the past tense, the future tense, and so forth. With those labels, "tense" really refers to the morphological forms we call present, past, and future. In this excursus, however, we are not addressing verbal morphology but one facet of verbal function.

Additionally, when we discuss tense, we are not referring simply to temporal reference. Temporal reference can occur in a number of ways. Words such as "now," "later," "today," and "tomorrow" can all help to establish temporal reference. These are *deictic markers* that indicate the time frame. *Tense*, however, is a very specific way of referring to time. It concerns the ways in which verbs indicate time—specifically, the time at which verbal actions take place. So, the present tense indicates that an action is to be understood as occurring at the time of speaking (or writing). The past tense indicates that an action is to be understood as occurring before the time of speaking (or writing).

Finally, tense always indicates time in relation to something else—usually the time of speaking or writing. So if an action is conveyed with a present tense,

---

1. This excursus is adapted from my essay, "Aspect and Tense in New Testament Greek," 44–48. Used with permission.

it does not mean that it is happening "now"—perhaps two thousand years after it was written about. The action is "present" only in its temporal reference with respect to the author's or speaker's portrayal of the event, not in relation to actual reality. Talking about time can be confusing in that way: there really is no such thing as absolute time in language, only relative time. For example, a speaker may use the future tense to say that they will travel tomorrow, but if that tomorrow was two thousand years ago, in what sense is the travel in the future? It was only in the future in the past. Now, it is all actually in the past. The future tense still points to a future event—but only from the perspective of the speaker at the time.

So, the question here is: Does the Greek verbal system express tense? In other words, when we encounter a Greek present tense-form, does it indicate present temporal reference, or is its temporal reference flexible? When we encounter an aorist indicative, will it necessarily refer to the past?

DEBATE CONCERNING TENSE

While Curtius laid the groundwork for Greek aspect studies in the nineteenth century, he also made significant advances in understanding tense in the Greek verbal system. The most significant advance was to demonstrate that tense does not exist outside the indicative mood.[2] Prior to Curtius, the common assumption had been that all the Greek moods conveyed tense—the subjunctive, imperative, and optative, as well as participles and infinitives. This assumption was derived from Latin, which conveys tense across all its moods, and Latin was the lens through which Greek (among other languages) was studied after the Renaissance period. Curtius's claim that tense existed only within the indicative mood was a radical suggestion at the time but is now the standard understanding. No one today considers tense to be a factor within non-indicative Greek moods.

But what about the indicative mood? For some scholars, Curtius did not go far enough. For them, tense does not play a role within any mood, whether indicative or non-indicative. The first scholar to move in this direction was McKay,

2. Georg Curtius, *Die Bildung der Tempora und Modi im Griechischen und Lateinischen sprachvergleichend dargestellt* (Berlin: Wilhelm Besser, 1846), 148–52.

who as early as 1965 asserted that tense was less of a factor in the Greek verbal system than aspect.[3] His assertions about tense in the indicative mood became progressively stronger, until in 1994 he denied that tense existed in that mood.[4] But before McKay had evolved fully to this point, Porter had already argued for this position in 1989.

Porter argues that the Greek indicative mood conveys aspect only, without tense, and that any verb's temporal reference comes about through the combination of aspect and context.[5] In other words, aorist indicatives often refer to past events because of the nature of perfective aspect (which is particularly apt for conveying completed past actions) and because aorists are often used in contexts that are already past referring, such as narratives that are by nature set in the past. An explanation of indicative verbs that relies on aspect only, and not tense, would then account for the high number of exceptions to the rule—presents that refer to the past, aorists that refer to the present, perfects that do not refer to a past action, and so forth.

Fanning, on the other hand, in line with typical approaches to the Greek verb since Curtius, argues that tense remains a feature of the indicative mood alongside aspect.[6] Since aspect is the dominant category, it could overpower tense so that certain verb forms would not always indicate the temporal reference they are supposed to. Fanning is also sensitive to the features of certain lexemes, acknowledging that some verbal lexemes buck their tense's temporal reference for reasons related to their diachronic development through the evolution of the Greek language.

And so the first (in)famous clash between these two Greek aspect scholars (at the 1991 Society of Biblical Literature annual meeting) was focused on tense in the Greek indicative mood. Both agreed that aspect was primary, but Fanning maintained tense alongside aspect, while Porter rejected tense. Porter's position was certainly the controversial one, though it ought not to have been as controversial as it was. Curtius had done the same thing with all the other moods 120 years earlier, and McKay had been chipping away at tense in the indicative mood for a couple of decades already. Moreover, there are other languages that do not encode tense in their verbal system.

While some students and scholars gravitated to the robustly linguistic

---

3. McKay, "Use of the Ancient Greek Perfect," 1–21.
4. McKay, *New Syntax of the Verb*, 39–40.
5. Porter, *Verbal Aspect*, 76–83, 98–102.
6. Fanning, *Verbal Aspect*, 198–324.

approach of Porter, others found Fanning's work more in line with the trajectories of previous Greek studies. Most of the academic contributors following Porter and Fanning would position themselves, once again, in relation to these two on the question of tense. Olsen mediated between the two, accepting tense for some indicative forms and rejecting it for others.[7] Decker followed Porter.[8] Evans followed Fanning.[9] I followed Porter (with modifications).[10] Mathewson, Cirafesi, and Huffman followed Porter.[11] Runge and his collaborators followed Fanning.[12]

While tense is not the most important question to consider, in my opinion, it nevertheless remains a fraught one. There are really two issues to evaluate. First is the obvious fact that many Greek verbs do not conform to their expected temporal reference. The statistics are quite overwhelming for some tense-forms, such as the so-called present indicative, which refers to the present only about 70 percent of the time. The aorist, Greek's default "past" tense, refers to the present or the future about 15 percent of the time. The Greek perfect, which is supposed to refer to a past action with present consequences, does this less than half the time. In fact, the only Greek tense-form that consistently refers to the time it is supposed to is the future.

The second issue to evaluate, however, is why the Greek indicative tense-forms do nevertheless have default temporal expressions. In other words, before we jettison tense altogether, we must ask, Why then does the aorist refer to the past 85 percent of the time? Why does the present refer to the present 70 percent of the time? Any conception of the inner workings of Greek tense-forms must account for these patterns. So, an important question to ask is this: Can a "non-tense" understanding of Greek verbs account for the ways in which verbs are actually used?

The question about tense in the Greek indicative mood comes down to the distinction between semantics and pragmatics. If that theoretical distinction is held, we must ask if temporal expression is semantically encoded in indicative verbs, or if it is a pragmatic expression of verbs in context. For those who deny the existence of tense in the Greek indicative mood, it is chiefly because temporal

---

7. Olsen, *Semantic and Pragmatic Model*, 201–2.
8. Decker, *Temporal Deixis*, 149–55.
9. Evans, *Verbal Syntax in the Greek Pentateuch*, 40–51.
10. Campbell, *Verbal Aspect, the Indicative Mood, and Narrative*, 84–91.
11. Mathewson, *Verbal Aspect in the Book of Revelation*, 17–18; Cirafesi, *Verbal Aspect in Synoptic Parallels*, 14–15; Huffman, *Verbal Aspect Theory and the Prohibitions*, 69–74.
12. Runge and Fresch, *Greek Verb Revisited*, chs. 4 (122–60), 11 (353–78), and 12 (379–415).

reference is not a semantic value of the morphological form. This is why so many verbs behave in ways that are contrary to their supposed tense—temporal reference is not semantic, and it is therefore flexible to some degree. Temporal reference, rather, is regarded as a pragmatic feature of verbs in context.[13]

For others, however, temporal reference is regarded as semantic despite the many exceptions to the rule. They are therefore comfortable with the claim that tense exists alongside aspect in the indicative mood because both are regarded as semantic features of verbal morphology. But how, then, do they account for the many exceptions to the rule? In Fanning's case, for example, he does not regard the distinction between semantics and pragmatics to be a tight one. There is some blurring at the edges between semantics and pragmatics, or, at least, semantic values can be rubbed out in certain contexts. This means, for Fanning, that while tense is a semantic value of Greek indicative verbs, in certain instances a verb's semantic temporal reference may be overpowered by other factors, such as aspect.[14]

Thus, in the end, one's position on tense in the Greek indicative mood largely depends on the methodological presuppositions one holds. If a clear distinction between semantics and pragmatics is held, it is almost inevitable that temporal reference will not be accepted as semantic. If the distinction is less tightly held, there is room to accept temporal reference as semantic without exceptions to the rule carrying much weight. The debate about tense, therefore, is actually a debate about linguistic methodology.

---

13. McKay, *New Syntax of the Verb*, 39–40; Constantine R. Campbell, *Advances in the Study of Greek: New Insights for Reading the New Testament* (Grand Rapids: Zondervan Academic, 2015), 114–17.

14. Fanning, *Verbal Aspect*, 323–24; Christopher J. Fresch, "Typology, Polysemy, and Prototypes: Situating Nonpast Aorist Indicatives," in Runge and Fresch, *Greek Verb Revisited*, 379–415.

CHAPTER 3

Perfective Aspect

Perfective aspect is the external viewpoint, with which an author portrays an action, event, or state from the outside. Perfective aspect is like a reporter who describes a street parade from a helicopter. It provides an all-encompassing, or summary, view of an action. From the view in the helicopter, the street parade is seen at a distance, and the details of the parade are not appreciated. Exactly how the parade is unfolding is not in view.

THE AORIST INDICATIVE TENSE-FORM

The aorist indicative tense-form is universally regarded as being perfective in aspect.[1] This means that the aorist provides an external view of an action. It presents events in summary, from a distance, and does not view the details of how the action took place. An example from Matthew 4 demonstrates this well.

Matthew 4:21–22 καὶ προβὰς ἐκεῖθεν **εἶδεν** ἄλλους δύο ἀδελφούς, Ἰάκωβον τὸν τοῦ Ζεβεδαίου καὶ Ἰωάννην τὸν ἀδελφὸν αὐτοῦ, ἐν τῷ πλοίῳ μετὰ Ζεβεδαίου τοῦ πατρὸς αὐτῶν καταρτίζοντας τὰ δίκτυα αὐτῶν, καὶ **ἐκάλεσεν** αὐτούς. οἱ δὲ εὐθέως ἀφέντες τὸ πλοῖον καὶ τὸν πατέρα αὐτῶν **ἠκολούθησαν** αὐτῷ.

---

1. The perfective aspect of non-indicative aorists will be explored in chapters 10 and 11.

And going on from there **he saw** two other brothers, James the son of
Zebedee and John his brother, in the boat with Zebedee their father,
mending their nets, and **he called** them. Immediately they left the boat
and their father and **followed** him.

We see here that the main actions in this little extract are communicated
through the use of aorist indicatives: "he saw . . . he called . . . they followed."
These aorists are not used for presenting the details of what happened. The content of what Jesus saw is provided through a participial clause. We are not told
what Jesus said when he called them. We are not told about James's and John's
thoughts in response to Jesus. We are not told whether they spoke to their father
as they left him in the boat. We are told, quite simply, that they followed Jesus,
and that's that.

It is worth mentioning that just because an action is presented in summary
does not necessarily mean that the action is unimportant. To think this way
would be to make a category error. No, some actions that are presented in summary, and indeed as aorists, are tremendously important.

Furthermore, aorists may portray actions that in reality took a long time to
take place or occur. Just because the action is presented in summary does not
mean that it happened quickly. Take Romans 5:14, for example:

Romans 5:14 ἀλλ᾽ ἐβασίλευσεν ὁ θάνατος ἀπὸ Ἀδὰμ μέχρι Μωϋσέως.

But death **reigned** from the time of Adam to Moses.

The period of time set by the phrase "from the time of Adam to Moses"
indicates that death's reign occurred over a long interval. There are many years
during which this event took place. This example demonstrates that the use of
the aorist does not indicate that an action occurred in an instant. Rather, the
event is simply viewed from a distance in summary.

Thus, it is important to dispel an old myth about the aorist. The term
punctiliar aorist is a common one and refers to a legitimate use of the aorist.
Unfortunately, some scholars have mistakenly concluded that the term *punctiliar* describes the aorist tense-form in general. They think that the aorist always
depicts a punctiliar, once-occurring, instantaneous action. The aorist in Romans
5:6 is sometimes treated this way.

Romans 5:6 Ἔτι γὰρ Χριστὸς ὄντων ἡμῶν ἀσθενῶν ἔτι κατὰ καιρὸν ὑπὲρ ἀσεβῶν **ἀπέθανεν.**

For while we were still weak, at the right time Christ **died** for the ungodly.

Some commentators write that because an aorist is used here, Romans 5:6 proves that Christ's death was a once-occurring event, never to be repeated, and therefore Christ could not be reoffered time and time again as in the Roman Mass. While I do not want to deny the once-for-all nature of Christ's death (cf. 1 Pet 3:18), the aorist in Romans 5:6 does not prove the point at all. If we look ahead a few verses, we come to 5:14 (see above), where we see an aorist that plainly depicts death reigning from the time of Adam to Moses. To reiterate, this is not a once-for-all action just because the aorist is used. Though the aorist can sometimes convey a punctiliar action in certain contexts (as discussed later), its use does not in and of itself guarantee a puntiliar action.

Confusion about the so-called punctiliar aorist has no doubt arisen from the fact that the aorist presents an action in summary. A street parade may look like a dot when you're looking at it from a helicopter high in the sky, but that does not mean that the parade actually is a dot. Just because an action is viewed in summary through use of an aorist does not mean that it occurred like a dot. The use of the aorist does not mean that an action is once occurring just because it is conveyed with perfective aspect. It must be remembered that aspect is viewpoint. Perfective aspect refers to the viewpoint from which the action is viewed; it says nothing about how the action actually occurred.

TENSE?

An important issue to consider is whether the aorist indicative tense-form expresses past tense. The traditional answer to this question is, of course, yes. There are, however, many problematic instances. Mark 1:11 provides us with a famous example.

Mark 1:11 καὶ φωνὴ ἐγένετο ἐκ τῶν οὐρανῶν, Σὺ εἶ ὁ υἱός μου ὁ ἀγαπητός, ἐν σοὶ **εὐδόκησα.**

And a voice came from heaven, "You are my beloved Son; in you **I am well pleased.**"

Suffice to say that no one translates the last clause of this verse as "*in you I was well pleased.*" It simply doesn't fit the theological or literary context to read the aorist that way. There are many such instances within the usage of the aorist where it is obviously not past referring.

To recall the discussion in the first chapter (and the excursus above), if we take seriously the distinction between semantics and pragmatics, we are forced to ask how past temporal reference can be a semantic value of the aorist. In fact, only about 85 percent of aorist indicatives refer to the past in New Testament usage.[2] Theoretically, if past temporal reference were a semantic value, we would expect the aorist to refer to the past in every instance (or something close to that, allowing for the humanity of language use). Because of the importance of the semantic/pragmatic distinction, past temporal reference is not here regarded a semantic value of the aorist. If, however, the aorist is not a past tense, then what is it?

REMOTENESS

Traditionally, the aorist indicative tense-form has been regarded as perfective in aspect and past in tense. If we do not accept the tense part of that equation, the aorist tense-form is perfective in aspect and . . . *what*? Some scholars have argued that *remoteness* is a better description of the semantics of the aorist indicative tense-form, alongside perfective aspect.[3]

Remoteness refers to the metaphorical value of distance. This fits nicely with perfective aspect, since we have already described perfective aspect as the view "from afar." It goes hand in hand with viewing the parade from the helicopter; the view is a summary view precisely because the parade is viewed from a distance.

Remoteness is regarded as a semantic value—it is always there when the aorist tense-form is used. But it has a range of pragmatic functions. It may not be a surprise to learn that the major pragmatic function that remoteness effects is past temporal reference. In fact, the semantic value of remoteness will be pragmatically expressed as past temporal reference approximately 85 percent of the

2. D. A. Carson, "An Introduction to the Porter/Fanning Debate," in *Biblical Greek Language and Linguistics: Open Questions in Current Research*, ed. Stanley E. Porter and D. A. Carson, Journal for the Study of the New Testament Supplement Series 80 (Sheffield: Sheffield Academic Press, 1993), 25.

3. Along with this, it has been suggested that the augment is a morphological marker of remoteness rather than a marker of past temporal reference, as traditional analyses describe it. For an overview, see Constantine R. Campbell, *Verbal Aspect, the Indicative Mood, and Narrative: Soundings in the Greek of the New Testament*, Studies in Biblical Greek 13 (New York: Peter Lang, 2007), 88–91.

time. An event that is in the past is naturally remote—temporally remote. Thus, past temporal reference is still regarded as one of the major uses of the aorist tense-form, but it is understood as a pragmatic expression of the aorist rather than as part of its semantic meaning.

Remoteness also offers an explanation for the 15 percent of aorist indicatives that do not refer to the past. Such aorists may refer to the present or even to the future, but they would still be regarded as remote. The difference with these cases is that the remoteness is not temporal remoteness. There are other kinds of remoteness besides temporal remoteness, such as logical remoteness.

To return to the example above from Mark 1:11, remoteness offers the key to understanding the aorist indicative εὐδόκησα. The semantic value of remoteness that is encoded in the aorist indicative does not in this instance function to provide past temporal reference. Instead, remoteness functions together with perfective aspect to provide a bird's-eye view of the scene. As the Father speaks from heaven, he gives his assessment of his Son—he is well pleased. Certain things in the context indicate that this assessment comes from heaven itself and breaks into the earthly scene. We are told that the heavens were *torn open* and that the Spirit *descended* like a dove (v. 10). The effect of these elements is that the "verdict" of heaven upon Jesus is being delivered *from heaven to earth*, as it were.

This verdict is not given with reference to any particular action but refers to Jesus—his person and works—as a whole. As such, there could not be a more appropriate choice of tense-form here. The aorist offers a summary view because of perfective aspect and because Jesus's life is viewed from afar. This does not imply that the Father is relationally *distant* from the Son, or some such viewpoint, but that on this occasion he views his Son from afar in order to view the whole. God may not be in a helicopter (!), but this scene is depicted from a vantage point somewhat similar to a helicopter—namely, from heaven itself.

NARRATIVE FUNCTION

As a remote perfective tense-form, the aorist indicative plays an important role in narrative texts. Because the aorist indicative provides a bird's-eye view of an action (or a helicopter view) and portrays actions in summary, it is often used to outline the skeletal structure of a narrative. The basic outline of events in the story is presented by the aorist in quick succession: Jesus went . . . this happened . . . Jesus said . . . and so on. This basic outline, or skeletal structure, is called the mainline of a narrative. Consider the following passage.

Matthew 8:32–34 καὶ εἶπεν αὐτοῖς . . . οἱ δὲ . . . ἀπῆλθον . . .
ὥρμησεν πᾶσα ἡ ἀγέλη . . . ἀπέθανον . . . οἱ δὲ βόσκοντες ἔφυγον . . .
ἀπήγγειλαν . . . πᾶσα ἡ πόλις ἐξῆλθεν . . . παρεκάλεσαν . . .

He [Jesus] **said** to them . . . and they [the evil spirits] **departed** . . .
the whole herd **rushed** . . . they **died** . . . the herdsmen **fled** . . . they
announced . . . the whole town **came out** . . . they **begged** . . .

In just three short verses, a huge amount of action is portrayed. The story
moves from Jesus casting out the evil spirits right through to the town casting
out Jesus. The passage is fast, compressed, and covers a lot of ground. Such is the
effect of the narrative aorist.

Narratives usually provide more information besides the skeletal outline of
events, but such details are typically conveyed by other tense-forms. The basic
actions are normally aorists, and this fact helps us to recognize the elemental
structure of narratives. It is important to note, however, that this narrative
function is pragmatic; it is a function that the aorist has within narrative, arising from its semantic nature. Aorists are often found performing different roles
within narrative texts, and other tense-forms may be found outlining the narrative mainline, but this is of no concern, since we are talking about pragmatics,
which are variable and cancelable.

THE FUTURE INDICATIVE
TENSE-FORM

Verbal aspect in the future indicative tense-form is an unresolved issue within
academic discussion. Some scholars have suggested that the future indicative is
nonaspectual (e.g., Porter),[4] while others say it is perfective in aspect, and yet
others say that it is a combination of perfective and imperfective (e.g., de Witt
Burton).[5] Assessing the aspectual nature of the future indicative tense-form is
complicated by not being able to analyze future events (since they have not yet
occurred at the time of speaking/writing), but we cannot address that issue in

---

4. Stanley E. Porter, *Verbal Aspect in the Greek of the New Testament with Reference to Tense and Mood*,
Studies in Biblical Greek 1 (New York: Peter Lang, 1989), 410.
5. Ernest de Witt Burton, *Syntax of the Moods and Tenses in New Testament Greek*, 3rd ed. (Chicago:
University of Chicago Press, 1900; repr., Grand Rapids: Kregel, 1976), 31–33.

detail here. I have argued elsewhere that the future indicative tense-form is perfective in aspect, and that position is adopted here.[6]

Furthermore, the future indicative tense-form is a real tense. That is, future temporal reference is a semantic feature of the form. This is easily derived from the fact that all futures refer to the future. There are no past-referring futures; there are no present-referring futures. The future always refers to the future.

Thus, the semantic values of the future indicative tense-form are perfective aspect and future temporal reference. Remoteness is not a separate semantic feature of the future tense-form. Future temporal reference is naturally remote, but this is simply an outcome of future temporal reference rather than the other way around.

In this way, the aorist and future tense-forms are closely related and yet distinct. They both share perfective aspect, but they differ in their other semantic values: the former also semantically encodes the spatial value of remoteness, while the latter also semantically encodes future temporal reference.

---

6. See Campbell, *Indicative Mood*, 127–60; Samuel J. Freney, *Aspectual Substitution: Verbal Change in New Testament Quotations of the Septuagint*, Studies in Biblical Greek 20 (New York: Peter Lang, 2020), 245.

CHAPTER 4

Imperfective Aspect

Imperfective aspect provides the view from the inside—an action is presented as though unfolding before the eyes. This is the view of the parade from the street, as the parade goes by, rather than the view from the helicopter. The effect of the street view is that we watch the action unfold. While we may not see the beginning or end of the parade because they're out of view, we are able to appreciate the details of how the parade unfolds.

THE PRESENT INDICATIVE
TENSE-FORM

The present indicative tense-form is universally regarded as being imperfective in aspect.[1] This means that the present portrays actions with a view from the inside; we watch as the action unfolds before our eyes. This is easy to appreciate in English: "he is walking down the street" is clearly cast before us as though we are watching it happen. The following passage provides a good example in Greek.

> **Mark 4:14–20** ὁ σπείρων τὸν λόγον **σπείρει.** οὗτοι δέ **εἰσιν** οἱ παρὰ τὴν ὁδόν· ὅπου **σπείρεται** ὁ λόγος καὶ ὅταν ἀκούσωσιν, εὐθὺς **ἔρχεται** ὁ σατανᾶς καὶ **αἴρει** τὸν λόγον τὸν ἐσπαρμένον εἰς αὐτούς. καὶ οὗτοί

---

1. The imperfective aspect of non-indicative presents will be explored in chapters 10 and 11.

εἰσὶν οἱ ἐπὶ τὰ πετρώδη σπειρόμενοι, οἳ ὅταν ἀκούσωσιν τὸν λόγον εὐθὺς μετὰ χαρᾶς **λαμβάνουσιν** αὐτόν, καὶ οὐκ **ἔχουσιν** ῥίζαν ἐν ἑαυτοῖς ἀλλὰ πρόσκαιροί **εἰσιν**, εἶτα γενομένης θλίψεως ἢ διωγμοῦ διὰ τὸν λόγον εὐθὺς **σκανδαλίζονται**. καὶ ἄλλοι **εἰσὶν** οἱ εἰς τὰς ἀκάνθας σπειρόμενοι· **οὗτοί εἰσιν** οἱ τὸν λόγον ἀκούσαντες, καὶ αἱ μέριμναι τοῦ αἰῶνος καὶ ἡ ἀπάτη τοῦ πλούτου καὶ αἱ περὶ τὰ λοιπὰ ἐπιθυμίαι εἰσπορευόμεναι **συμπνίγουσιν** τὸν λόγον καὶ ἄκαρπος **γίνεται**. καὶ ἐκεῖνοί **εἰσιν** οἱ ἐπὶ τὴν γῆν τὴν καλὴν σπαρέντες, οἵτινες **ἀκούουσιν** τὸν λόγον καὶ **παραδέχονται** καὶ **καρποφοροῦσιν** ἓν τριάκοντα καὶ ἓν ἑξήκοντα καὶ ἓν ἑκατόν.

The sower **sows** the word. And these **are** the ones along the path, where the word **is sown**: when they hear, Satan immediately **comes** and **takes** away the word that is sown in them. And these **are** the ones sown on rocky ground: the ones who, when they hear the word, immediately **receive** it with joy. And **they have** no root in themselves, but **are** only temporary. Then, when tribulation or persecution arises on account of the word, immediately **they fall away**. And others **are** the ones sown among thorns. They **are** those who hear the word, but the cares of the world and the deceitfulness of riches and the desires for other things enter in and **choke** the word, and it **becomes** unfruitful. And those **are** the ones that **were** sown on the good soil, who **hear** the word and **accept** it and **bear fruit**, one thirtyfold and one sixtyfold and one a hundredfold.

In this passage, Jesus explains the parable of the sower by laying out its meaning before the disciples' eyes. It is interesting to note that the actual parable, told in 4:3–8, is conveyed with aorist indicatives rather than presents. This is not surprising, since a parable is a little embedded narrative, which is a natural setting for aorists. But here, as Jesus explains what the story means, it is as though he is opening the story up. By explaining what the story means, Jesus turns his original story into general teaching: this is what happens when the word is sown.

PROXIMITY

The present indicative is not the only tense-form that is regarded as being imperfective in aspect. The imperfect indicative tense-form is also universally regarded as imperfective. The question must be raised, therefore, as to how these two imperfective indicative tense-forms are to be distinguished from each other. Traditionally, the distinguishing factor between the present and imperfect indicative tense-forms was understood to be tense. The imperfect indicative is a past tense, and the present indicative is a present tense.

Consistent with the spatial approach adopted so far, however, we note that Porter has suggested that the distinguishing factor is remoteness.[2] The imperfect indicative is imperfective and remote, while the present indicative is imperfective and nonremote. I have argued elsewhere that nonremoteness, which is the absence of remoteness, should be replaced by *proximity*.[3] Proximity is not simply the absence of remoteness but is a positive value of its own, which is opposite to remoteness. As such, I regard the imperfect indicative tense-form to be imperfective in aspect, with the spatial value of remoteness, while the present indicative tense-form is imperfective in aspect, with the spatial value of proximity. This may be illustrated by the following diagrams.

Remote imperfectivity (imperfect tense-form) *Proximate imperfectivity (present tense-form)*

The unfolding event or state

The viewpoint

The unfolding event or state

The viewpoint

Imagine that these diagrams represent the imperfective view of the reporter on the street. The second diagram—imperfective aspect and proximity—depicts the view of the street parade directly in front of the reporter. He not only views the parade unfolding before his eyes but is viewing that part of the parade that

---

2. Stanley E. Porter, *Verbal Aspect in the Greek of the New Testament with Reference to Tense and Mood*, Studies in Biblical Greek 1 (New York: Peter Lang, 1989), 95. See also Rodney J. Decker, *Temporal Deixis of the Greek Verb in the Gospel of Mark with Reference to Verbal Aspect*, Studies in Biblical Greek 10 (New York: Peter Lang, 2001), 41.

3. Campbell, *Verbal Aspect, the Indicative Mood, and Narrative*, 48–57.

is directly in front of him, to which he is closest. On the other hand, the first diagram—imperfective aspect and remoteness—depicts the view of the street parade as he looks down the street a little. As he views the parade unfolding before his eyes, he is not viewing the part of the parade directly in front of him but is looking further down the parade. This part of the parade is not so close, even though he still sees it unfolding.

NARRATIVE FUNCTION

In narrative texts, the present indicative tense-form is most often found in discourse—direct, indirect, or authorial discourse. This fact fits with the semantic analysis of the present indicative given above, since discourse creates an imperfective proximate context. This means that whenever discourse is portrayed in narrative, it has the effect of drawing the readers into the story, as the discourse is presented before their eyes. It is as though we are seeing the events unfold before us. As such, discourse inherently forms an imperfective context (we see it unfold) and a proximate context (it is as though we are right there).

This is why the present indicative tense-form is so well suited to discourse: it is an imperfective proximate tense-form that fits naturally within an imperfective proximate context. This is not the only function of the present indicative tense-form, but it is one of the major pragmatic functions within narrative literature. One notable nondiscourse use of the present indicative tense-form is the so-called historical present, to which we now turn.

THE HISTORICAL PRESENT

The term "historical present" refers to the common phenomenon of present indicative tense-forms that refer to the past. In the New Testament, historical presents are particularly common in Mark and John. There are two types of historical presents, stemming from two distinct groups of lexemes used with the present. The first group of lexemes that are used as historical presents are *verbs of propulsion*. These are verbs of coming and going, giving and taking, raising up and putting down, and so forth. Basically, these are verbs where there is some kind of propulsion from one point to another.

The second group of lexemes consists of verbs that introduce discourse. There are verbs of speaking, thinking, writing, and so on, which typically segue into speech, thought, and other types of discourse. While historical presents will be explored again in chapter 7, we see both types of historical present in the following passage.

John 8:3–4 ἄγουσιν δὲ οἱ γραμματεῖς καὶ οἱ Φαρισαῖοι γυναῖκα ἐπὶ μοιχείᾳ κατειλημμένην καὶ στήσαντες αὐτὴν ἐν μέσῳ **λέγουσιν** αὐτῷ, Διδάσκαλε, αὕτη ἡ γυνὴ κατείληπται ἐπ᾽ αὐτοφώρῳ μοιχευομένη.

The scribes and the Pharisees **brought** a woman who had been caught in adultery, and placing her in the midst **they said** to him, "Teacher, this woman has been caught in the act of adultery."

The verb ἄγουσιν is a verb of propulsion, while λέγουσιν introduces the direct discourse that follows. While this will be unpacked later, the semantic description of the present tense-form as imperfective in aspect with the spatial value of proximity provides the best explanation as to why these lexemes are used with the historical present.

THE IMPERFECT INDICATIVE TENSE-FORM

As mentioned above, the imperfect indicative tense-form is imperfective in aspect with the spatial value of remoteness. In this way, the imperfect indicative shares semantic values with both the present and aorist tense-forms. It shares imperfective aspect with the present indicative tense-form, and it shares remoteness with the aorist indicative tense-form.

The sharing of remoteness with the aorist indicative means that the imperfect is also found in narrative proper rather than in discourse. While aorists provide the skeletal structure of narrative proper, imperfect indicatives tend to provide supplemental information. This supplemental information contributes to narrative by giving information beyond the narrative mainline; it describes, explains, and provides background, putting flesh on the skeleton. This key function of the imperfect indicative tense-form is a pragmatic feature and is therefore cancelable.

This supplemental function of the imperfect indicative fits with its semantic meaning. Background and supplemental information naturally create a remote context, since they supplement the remote narrative mainline. While mainline is naturally remote, it is also naturally perfective; events are presented in summary outline. In contrast, supplemental information is off the mainline—and is properly called *offline*—and presents information from the inside because it describes details, provides reasons and explanations, and elucidates motivations, all of which would not be seen through the summary external view. We may observe the complementary narrative functions of aorist and imperfect indicatives in the following example, in which the aorist indicatives are bold and the imperfects are bold and underlined.

Luke 9:42–45 ἔτι δὲ προσερχομένου αὐτοῦ **ἔρρηξεν** αὐτὸν τὸ δαιμόνιον καὶ **συνεσπάραξεν· ἐπετίμησεν** δὲ ὁ Ἰησοῦς τῷ πνεύματι τῷ ἀκαθάρτῳ καὶ **ἰάσατο** τὸν παῖδα καὶ **ἀπέδωκεν** αὐτὸν τῷ πατρὶ αὐτοῦ. **ἐξεπλήσσοντο** δὲ πάντες ἐπὶ τῇ μεγαλειότητι τοῦ θεοῦ. Πάντων δὲ θαυμαζόντων ἐπὶ πᾶσιν οἷς **ἐποίει εἶπεν** πρὸς τοὺς μαθητὰς αὐτοῦ, Θέσθε ὑμεῖς εἰς τὰ ὦτα ὑμῶν τοὺς λόγους τούτους· ὁ γὰρ υἱὸς τοῦ ἀνθρώπου μέλλει παραδίδοσθαι εἰς χεῖρας ἀνθρώπων. οἱ δὲ **ἠγνόουν** τὸ ῥῆμα τοῦτο καὶ ἦν παρακεκαλυμμένον ἀπ᾽ αὐτῶν ἵνα μὴ αἴσθωνται αὐτό, καὶ **ἐφοβοῦντο** ἐρωτῆσαι αὐτὸν περὶ τοῦ ῥήματος τούτου.

While he was coming, the demon **threw** him to the ground and **convulsed** him. But Jesus **rebuked** the unclean spirit and **healed** the boy and **gave** him back to his father. And all **were astonished** at the majesty of God. But while they were all marveling at everything he **was doing**, Jesus **said** to his disciples, "Let these words sink into your ears: the Son of Man is about to be delivered into the hands of men." But they **did not understand** this saying, and it was concealed from them, so that they might not perceive it. And they **were afraid** to ask him about this saying.

Notice here that the mainline is carried by the aorists *threw, convulsed, rebuked, healed, gave*, and *said*; these verbs convey the sequence of events in the narrative. However, the imperfects *were astonished, was doing, did not understand*, and *were afraid* do not convey mainline action but rather provide supplementary material. We are told of various reactions to the actions that have taken place and to Jesus's words, and that his disciples were afraid to ask him about his saying. This information does not contribute to the mainline of the narrative but rather gives the reader an inside view into the thought world of the disciples.

CHAPTER 5

The Problem of the Perfect

The semantic nature of the perfect and pluperfect indicative tense-forms is one of the great puzzles in Greek linguistics. There are several suggested options, ranging from the traditional analysis, to perfective aspect, stative aspect, imperfective aspect, or combinative (both perfective and imperfective). In this chapter we will briefly canvas most of these options before concluding that the perfect indicative is imperfective in aspect.

THE PERFECT INDICATIVE TENSE-FORM

Traditionally the perfect indicative tense-form was understood as indicating a past action with ongoing consequences. To use the *Aktionsart* descriptions of an earlier period, the perfect was understood to be like a dot and a line. In this way, the perfect indicative was almost a combination of aorist and present tenses—an aoristic action followed by a present state. The great problem with this analysis is that it doesn't work. It yields far too many exceptions, reflected in the multiplicity of categories of perfects listed by grammars. The following examples illustrate the problem.

Many perfect indicatives don't express a past action but only envisage the ongoing consequences:

John 1:26 ἀπεκρίθη αὐτοῖς ὁ Ἰωάννης λέγων, Ἐγὼ βαπτίζω ἐν ὕδατι· μέσος ὑμῶν **ἕστηκεν** ὃν ὑμεῖς οὐκ **οἴδατε**.

John answered them, "I baptize with water, but among you **stands** one you do not **know**."

Other examples include perfect indicatives that don't express any ongoing consequences, but only the past action:

Revelation 8:5 καὶ **εἴληφεν** ὁ ἄγγελος τὸν λιβανωτὸν καὶ ἐγέμισεν αὐτόν.

Then the angel **took** the censer and filled it.

These examples provide just two categories that indicate the problems faced by the traditional explanation of the perfect indicative. See the grammars for variations on this theme.

Unfortunately, verbal aspect has not so quickly resolved the matter. We will now briefly survey the main attempts to analyze the perfect indicative in terms of aspect.

STATIVE ASPECT

An aspect we have not explored before this point is called stative aspect. According to K. L. McKay, stative aspect views the state, or state of being, of the subject of a verb.[1]

Luke 20:21 καὶ ἐπηρώτησαν αὐτὸν λέγοντες, Διδάσκαλε, **οἴδαμεν** ὅτι ὀρθῶς λέγεις καὶ διδάσκεις καὶ οὐ λαμβάνεις πρόσωπον, ἀλλ᾽ ἐπ᾽ ἀληθείας τὴν ὁδὸν τοῦ θεοῦ διδάσκεις.

So they asked him, "Teacher, we **know** that you speak and teach rightly, and show no partiality, but truly teach the way of God."

---

1. K. L. McKay, *A New Syntax of the Verb in New Testament Greek: An Aspectual Approach*, Studies in Biblical Greek 5 (New York: Peter Lang, 1994), 31.

By McKay's approach, this perfect indicative is indicating that the spies ("we") are in a state of knowing that Jesus speaks and teaches rightly. The force of the perfect is to communicate that they are in this state of knowing. So far, so good.

Problems start to arise for McKay's conception of the perfect indicative, however, with cases where it seems difficult to attribute the state to the subject rather than the object of the verb. This problem has plagued traditional analyses of the perfect indicative also, but whereas Jakob Wackernagel suggested that the stativity should be understood as applying to the object of the verb (i.e., the resultative perfect),[2] McKay suggests something else. He is right to insist that we cannot just transfer the meaning of the perfect onto the object of the verb, and the apparent need to do so flags a problem with our understanding of the perfect indicative. In such cases, McKay argues that the subject is to be seen as *the one responsible for the action.*[3] This appears to work in many cases, but there are some significantly problematic cases also, such as we see in the example below.

John 7:22 διὰ τοῦτο Μωϋσῆς **δέδωκεν** ὑμῖν τὴν περιτομήν – οὐχ ὅτι ἐκ τοῦ Μωϋσέως ἐστὶν ἀλλ᾽ ἐκ τῶν πατέρων – καὶ ἐν σαββάτῳ περιτέμνετε ἄνθρωπον.

Moses **gave** you circumcision (not that it is from Moses, but from the fathers), and you circumcise a man upon the Sabbath.

This is a good example demonstrating that it is not the responsibility of the subject in view here. According to McKay's approach, Moses as the subject must be viewed as responsible for the giving of circumcision, yet the verse itself explicitly tells us that it was *not* Moses who gave it but "the fathers." Thus, to conclude that the emphasis of the perfect indicative is to stress the responsibility of the subject, when in the same breath we are told that that is not the point, is surely an illegitimate outcome. There are other such problems with which McKay's version of stative aspect suffers.[4]

---

2. Jakob Wackernagel, "Studien zum griechischen Perfektum," in *Studien zum griechischen Perfektum: Programm zur akademischen Preisverteilung 1904* (Göttingen: Dieterich, 1904), 3–24; repr., idem, *Kleine Schriften*, vol. 1, Akademie der Wissenschaften (Göttingen: Vandenhoeck & Ruprecht, 1953), 1000–1021.

3. McKay, *New Syntax of the Verb*, 32.

4. See Constantine R. Campbell, *Verbal Aspect, the Indicative Mood, and Narrative: Soundings in the Greek of the New Testament*, Studies in Biblical Greek 13 (New York: Peter Lang, 2007), 166–69.

A different version of stative aspect is offered by Stanley E. Porter. Stative aspect, according to him, refers to a general state of affairs.[5] This conception's strength is that it removes focus from the subject of the verb, which is problematic with stative conceptions of the perfect indicative, and creates a general state.

John 12:23 Ὁ δὲ Ἰησοῦς ἀποκρίνεται αὐτοῖς λέγων, **Ἐλήλυθεν** ἡ ὥρα ἵνα δοξασθῇ ὁ υἱὸς τοῦ ἀνθρώπου.

And Jesus answered them, "The hour **has come** for the Son of Man to be glorified."

According to Porter, the perfect indicative in this verse indicates a new state of affairs: the hour has come, and now things are different. Porter's stative aspect seems to work well here, as indeed it does with many other examples.

There are, nevertheless, significant problems with this version of stative aspect too. To begin with, Porter's stative aspect is difficult to define and does not parallel any kind of aspect in other languages. Furthermore, it is difficult to apply and sometimes results in quite forced exegesis, as the following example illustrates.

John 5:33 ὑμεῖς **ἀπεστάλκατε** πρὸς Ἰωάννην, καὶ **μεμαρτύρηκεν** τῇ ἀληθείᾳ.

You **sent** to John, and he **has borne witness** to the truth.

How do these two perfect indicatives indicate a new state of affairs? Are we to understand by the first perfect that there is a state of having-sent-to-John-ness? Does the second perfect refer to a state of John having-witnessed-to-Jesus-ness? Again, there are several such difficulties with this version of stative aspect.[6]

Perhaps most serious of all, however, is the fact that stativity is not normally regarded as an aspectual value. Across all languages and in linguistic theory, stativity is an *Aktionsart* value, not an aspectual one.

---

5. Stanley E. Porter, *Idioms of the Greek New Testament*, 2nd ed., Biblical Languages: Greek 2 (Sheffield: Sheffield Academic Press, 1994), 21–22.

6. See Campbell, *Indicative Mood*, 169–75.

PERFECTIVE ASPECT

Buist M. Fanning concludes as much about stativity—it is an *Aktionsart*, not an aspect.[7] His, and Mari Broman Olsen's, solution is to label the perfect tense-form as perfective in aspect, which at least works on the level of nomenclature. One of the reasons for regarding the perfect indicative as perfective in aspect is because it is believed in academia that over the history of the Greek language the perfect indicative eventually merged with the aorist indicative in meaning.

Olsen regards the perfect indicative as perfective in aspect and present in tense.[8] A fairly significant problem here is that there are many perfects that are not present referring, such as the ones in John 5:33 above. If present temporal reference is regarded as a semantic value of the perfect, many instances of usage of the perfect must go unaccounted.

Fanning, however, suggests a more sophisticated schema. He regards the perfect indicative tense-form as perfective in aspect, present in temporal reference, and stative in *Aktionsart*.[9] In other words, Fanning posits three distinct semantic values: perfective aspect, present tense, and stative *Aktionsart*. Aside from the question of whether an *Aktionsart* value can be semantic, this conception raises other questions: What about perfect indicatives that are not stative? What about perfect indicatives that are not present in temporal reference?

A further problem with these models is that perfective aspect itself does not work well in explaining usage of the perfect indicative tense-form. For example, perfective aspect does not accommodate stative lexemes well since the combination of perfective aspect and stative lexeme normally creates an ingressive *Aktionsart*, which is rarely intended with perfect indicatives. Lexemes such as οἶδα are not accounted for under this model, and Fanning calls lexemes like this exceptions. It is worth noting that this means that approximately two-thirds of perfect usage in the New Testament is exceptional. This means that perfective

---

7. Buist M. Fanning, "Approaches to Verbal Aspect in New Testament Greek: Issues in Definition and Method," in *Biblical Greek Language and Linguistics: Open Questions in Current Research*, ed. Stanley E. Porter and D. A. Carson, Journal for the Study of the New Testament Supplement Series 80 (Sheffield: Sheffield Academic Press, 1993), 49–50.

8. Mari Broman Olsen, *A Semantic and Pragmatic Model of Lexical and Grammatical Aspect*, Outstanding Dissertations in Linguistics (New York: Garland, 1997), 202, 232.

9. Buist M. Fanning, *Verbal Aspect in New Testament Greek*, Oxford Theological Monographs (Oxford: Clarendon, 1990), 112–20.

aspect does not demonstrate enough power of explanation when it comes to the perfect tense-form.[10]

"COMBINATIVE" ASPECT

Some proponents of *The Greek Verb Revisited* advocate the so-called "combinative" aspect as an explanation for the Greek perfect indicative. This imagines two aspects combined into one form, as endorsed by several contributors, especially Randall Buth and Nicholas Ellis. But how plausible is it that *one* form conveys *two* aspects at once? On the viewpoint understanding of aspect, this seems impossible. How is it possible to view an event from the outside as a whole *and* from within the event as it unfolds *at the same time*? On Bernard Comrie's internal temporal constituency definition of aspect, it is also impossible. Thus, the two major definitions of aspect appear to be incompatible with combinative aspect. The approach is only possible if we conceive of aspect in different ways regarding the same event—with respect to the event, plus the *effects* of that event. Ellis defines the combinative aspect as "reflecting the perfective nature of the verbal event and the imperfective nature of its ongoing relevance."[11]

In effect, each perfect indicative form conveys *two* verbal activities, each with their own aspect. But this is neither standard nor a trivial departure from the norm. Moreover, we come to the problem of usage. Some perfect indicatives clearly fit at a pragmatic level—they indicate a past action with present consequences. But many do not—they either convey a past action with no present state implied (so-called aoristic perfects—though I prefer the term *historical perfects*), or they convey a state with no past action implied. For the semantics to be *both* perfective and imperfective, we should expect to see more perfect indicatives displaying these characteristics at once, but that is not what we see.

IMPERFECTIVE ASPECT

An overlooked fact in this debate is that the perfect indicative parallels the present indicative in its usage far more than it seems to do with the aorist. In fact, the patterns of perfect indicative usage in narrative texts are virtually identical to those of the present. Nearly all perfect indicatives in narrative texts occur within

---

10. See Campbell, *Indicative Mood*, 189–93.

11. Nicholas J. Ellis, "Aspect-Prominence, Morpho-Syntax, and a Cognitive-Linguistic Framework for the Greek Verb," in *The Greek Verb Revisited: A Fresh Approach for Biblical Research*, ed. Steven E. Runge and Christopher J. Fresch (Bellingham, WA: Lexham, 2016), 122–60 (143).

discourse, just like present indicatives. More than this, when the perfect indicative does *not* occur within discourse, it demonstrates the same patterns as does the present when it is not within discourse. Just as the present indicative creates historical presents with verbs of propulsion and introducers of discourse, so too does the perfect indicative. Such evidence must provoke the question: Does the perfect indicative share the aspect of the present? Does the sharing of the same aspect account for these parallel patterns of usage?

I have argued extensively that the answer is yes. Along with T. V. Evans, I argue that the perfect indicative tense-form is imperfective in aspect, which is why it and the present indicative tense-form behave so similarly.[12]

Not only does imperfective aspect explain the parallel usage of the perfect and present indicative tense-forms, but it nicely accommodates the many stative lexemes that are found in perfect indicative usage. In most languages, imperfective aspect is the natural home of stativity.[13] As such, this model of the perfect fits with what has always been observed—that the perfect indicative often communicates stativity.

But imperfective aspect also is able to explain those perfects that are *not* stative; imperfective aspect can accommodate other types of lexemes too. It also explains past-referring perfect indicatives that might seem to behave like aorists. Just as the present indicative tense-form can be used to refer to the past (the historical present), so too can the perfect indicative (the historical perfect). Consequently, I argue that imperfective aspect demonstrates the greatest power of explanation when it comes to the semantic meaning of the perfect indicative tense-form.[14]

HEIGHTENED PROXIMITY

If, then, the perfect indicative tense-form is imperfective in aspect, we must ask what distinguishes it from the present and imperfect indicative tense-forms. I argue that the perfect indicative semantically encodes imperfective aspect and the spatial value of *heightened proximity*. In this way, the perfect indicative is proximate like the present, but more so. This may be represented through the diagrams below.

---

12. See Campbell, *Indicative Mood*, 184–89; T. V. Evans, "Future Directions for Aspect Studies in Ancient Greek," in *Biblical Greek Language and Lexicography: Essays in Honor of Frederick W. Danker*, ed. Bernard A. Taylor et al. (Grand Rapids: Eerdmans, 2004), 206.

13. As Carl Bache observes, in "most languages imperfective forms are typically used to refer to [stative] sitatuations" (Carl Bache, "Aspect and Aktionsart: Towards a Semantic Distinction," *Journal of Linguistics* 18 [1982]: 69).

14. The imperfective aspect of non-indicative perfects will be explored in chapters 10 and 11.

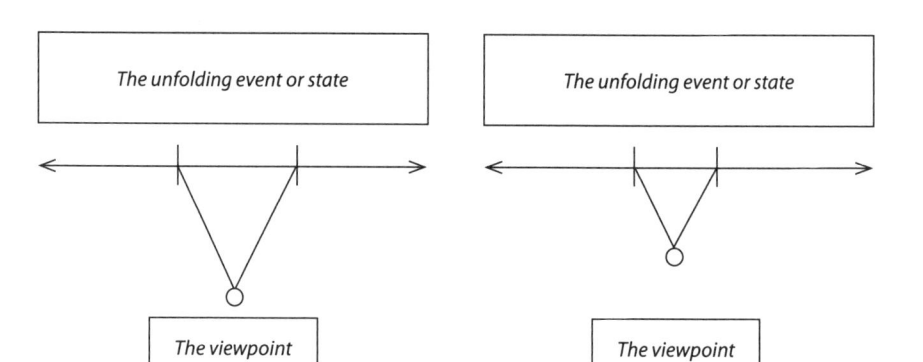

Using again the illustration of the reporter and the street parade, the second diagram represents his taking a step closer to the parade. The parade is unfolding immediately before his eyes, as before, but now is even more proximate; he is viewing the action close up. The effect of this close-up view is that it concentrates on the action by zooming in on it.

Heightened proximity, like proximity, is regarded as a semantic value alongside imperfective aspect. The perfect indicative, therefore, semantically encodes imperfective aspect and the spatial value of heightened proximity. As such, it might be appropriate to think of the perfect indicative as a *superpresent*.

THE PLUPERFECT INDICATIVE TENSE-FORM

All agree that whatever aspect the perfect indicative tense-form encodes, the pluperfect shares it. Typically the pluperfect indicative is treated this way—as piggybacking on the perfect—and therefore does not often receive due consideration on its own merit. By taking a close look at pluperfect indicative usage, we discover that it is even harder to justify stative or perfective aspect than it is with the perfect. But it seems all the more clear that imperfective aspect has great power of explanation.

Just as the perfect indicative parallels the usage of the present, so the pluperfect indicative parallels the usage of the imperfect. It demonstrates the same functions within narrative, providing supplemental information that describes, explains, and gives background. This all fits well with imperfective aspect. It also fits well with the spatial value of remoteness. But if the pluperfect indicative is distinct from the imperfect in its usage, it can function as providing information that is even more backgrounded compared to that provided by the imperfect. In other words, the pluperfect indicative sometimes provides information that supplements information that is already supplemental, as the following example illustrates.

Mark 1:34 καὶ ἐθεράπευσεν πολλοὺς κακῶς ἔχοντας ποικίλαις νόσοις καὶ δαιμόνια πολλὰ ἐξέβαλεν καὶ οὐκ **ἤφιεν** λαλεῖν τὰ δαιμόνια, ὅτι **ᾔδεισαν** αὐτόν.

And he healed many who were sick with various diseases and cast out many demons. And **he would not permit** the demons to speak, because **they knew** him.

Here we see that the imperfect indicative tense-form (ἤφιεν) provides supplementary material; further description of the scene is given as we are told that Jesus did not permit the demons to speak. However, the pluperfect indicative (ᾔδεισαν) provides information that is supplemental to that supplemental information; we are told *why* Jesus did not allow the demons to speak—because they knew him.

Accordingly, the pluperfect indicative is regarded as more remote than the imperfect. Just as the perfect indicative encodes heightened proximity in parallel to the proximity of the present, so the pluperfect indicative encodes heightened remoteness in parallel to the remoteness of the imperfect. Thus, the pluperfect indicative semantically encodes imperfective aspect and the spatial value of heightened remoteness.

Space and Time

Some readers may find the connection between spatial and temporal concepts confusing, and this excursus is intended to further clarify this relationship without making the main body of the book more complicated than it need be.[1]

In the literature addressing Greek verbal aspect, the concept of remoteness was first suggested by K. L. McKay and was later developed further by Stanley E. Porter.[2] This was posited as an alternative understanding of the meaning of the Greek augment and as a way to distinguish tense-forms that share the same aspect, such as the present and imperfect. The Greek augment has long been regarded as an indicator of past temporal reference, adorning the Greek aorist, imperfect, and pluperfect indicative tense-forms. Though there are several examples of aorists dropping their augment while still referring to the past in Homeric poetry, this was most likely for purposes of style and meter. But the augment could indicate the spatial metaphor of remoteness rather than past temporal reference.

I have developed the concept of spatial metaphors beyond Porter and McKay

---

1. Some of this excursus is adapted from my essay, "Aspect and Tense in New Testament Greek," in *Linguistics and New Testament Greek: Key Issues in the Current Debate*, ed. David Alan Black and Benjamin L. Merkle (Grand Rapids; Baker Academic, 2020), 48–50. Used with permission.

2. K. L. McKay, "The Use of the Ancient Greek Perfect Down to the Second Century A.D.," *Bulletin of the Institute of Classical Studies* 12 (1965): 19n22; Stanley E. Porter, *Verbal Aspect in the Greek of the New Testament with Reference to Tense and Mood*, Studies in Biblical Greek 1 (New York: Peter Lang, 1989), 95.

to include the opposite of remoteness—namely, proximity.[3] While the aorist and imperfect indicatives convey remoteness, the present tense-form conveys proximity. This explains why the majority of present indicatives express present temporal reference, which is a natural expression of the spatial value of proximity. And proximity is also able to explain the uses of the present indicative that do not convey present temporal reference, since there are other pragmatic expressions of proximity besides temporal reference.

It is claimed in this book that indicative Greek verbs semantically encode aspect along with the spatial value of remoteness or proximity (with the exception of the future tense-form, which encodes aspect and future temporal reference). The difference between this description of the semantics of verbs and that of traditional analyses is that semantic temporal reference ("tense") has been replaced by semantic spatial categories. In other words, while traditional analyses might regard indicative verbs as encoding aspect and tense, here indicative verbs are regarded as encoding aspect and remoteness or aspect and proximity.

It is also claimed that these spatial values of remoteness and proximity, which are semantic, normally express temporal reference on the pragmatic level. This means that remoteness, for example, will most often be pragmatically expressed as temporal remoteness—the action is past referring. The spatial value of proximity will most often express temporal proximity—present time. The question that might be asked is: How does a spatial value transmute into a temporal one?

SPATIAL TERMS ARE METAPHORICAL

First, the terms *remoteness* and *proximity* are here best regarded as metaphors. When an aorist indicative is used, it does not mean that the action occurred far away in a geographical sense just because it encodes the spatial value of remoteness. For example, if I were to describe an action that occurred on my street, I am not forced to employ a proximate tense-form simply because it happened close to me physically. By the same token, if the action occurred in Cuba, I would not be forced to use a remote tense-form simply because Cuba is on the other side of the planet from Australia. To conclude that an action must have occurred at a physical distance because remoteness is encoded by the verb is to take remoteness literally—or concretely—rather than metaphorically.

---

3. Campbell, *Verbal Aspect, the Indicative Mood, and Narrative*, 48–57.

It should be remembered that aspect itself is a subjective depiction of an action, event, or state. Remoteness and proximity are also employed as part of such a depiction. An action may be portrayed as remote without physically being distant. An action may be portrayed as proximate without physically being near.

SPATIAL AND
TEMPORAL REMOTENESS

Second, remoteness and proximity are, by definition, spatial terms. The primary meaning of remoteness has to do with being *far away*, *distant*, and *removed*. It is by extension of this spatial meaning that remoteness can be applied to temporal expressions in English. For example, to speak of *the remote past* is to speak of time that is far away, distant, or removed. The spatial idea of remoteness has been applied to time. The "time" is remote. This can only really be a metaphorical expression, since time does not actually have a spatial dimension; it cannot actually be distant or near, because time is temporal, not spatial.

But therein lies the point. In English, we use spatial terms to describe time, and often we do it without even noticing. *The remote past* is just one example. *The near future* is another. *Near* is no more a temporal term than *remote*, and yet we use the term to express temporal ideas. Again, the use is metaphorical. The future cannot spatially be near or far; the future cannot be on my street, or in Cuba. Time just doesn't occupy space, but this doesn't stop us from speaking of it as though it does.

In truth, our conceptions of time are overlaid on spatial realities. A day is measured by the rotation of the earth on its axis, a month by the orbit of the moon around the earth, and a year by the orbit of the earth around the sun. These are spatial realities that determine our major divisions of time. But how we break a day up into twenty-four hours is arbitrary. Breaking up an hour into sixty minutes is arbitrary. Having a seven-day week is arbitrary (well, the seven-day week has a biblical precedent). And there is nothing special about ten years constituting a decade, or one hundred years constituting a century. The point is that our major measurements of time are determined by physical, spatial realities. And our minor measurements of time are arbitrary divisions within those larger measurements.

Several words in English are actually spatial descriptors but are regularly employed for statements about time. Consider the word *next*. Is it temporal or spatial? You might answer, "Actually *next* has to do with order, which is neither temporal nor spatial." If that's what you're thinking, I'd say you're right and wrong. You're right that *next* has to do with order, but you're wrong that it's neither temporal nor spatial. It is, in fact, spatial. Order itself is primarily a spatial concept. It has to do with one thing after another—like children standing in line. If they stand in alphabetical order, they arrange themselves spatially. Each child takes a position in relation to each other child's position. The phrase *in order* denotes things in a particular spatial arrangement in relation to one another. The word *next*, then, is actually a spatial term: the next street, the next house, the next room. It is only by extension that this spatial word is applied to temporal situations. When we say *next week*, we are, of course, speaking about time—*week* tells us that. The contribution of *next* is to indicate that the week in question is following the current week. We think of it as *next* in the same way that we think of the *next house* as next. It is adjacent. And so we see that this spatial word is used to describe time, and that is normal in modern English usage.

There are several other examples of this phenomenon. The following words are, I would argue, primarily spatial in meaning yet may be applied to time in normal English usage: *following* (as in *the following day*), *short* (as in *a short time*), *long* (as in *a long time*), *away* (as in *three weeks away*), *close* (as in *the day is getting close*), *distant* (as in *the distant past*), *far* (as in *far off into the future*). Thus, there is a natural relationship between space and time, and space is actually the more natural of the two. The concept of remoteness fits into this broader sense in which people may regard their world more spatially than we do today. And the beauty of remoteness is that it does not nullify the possibility of past temporal reference. Indeed, past time is simply one expression of remoteness.

The point of all this is simply to say that time and space are more closely connected, even within our own language, than we may realize. We frequently use spatial descriptions in our communication of time, and we are capable of conceiving time through spatial metaphors.

SPACE AND TIME IN HISTORY

The connection between space and time is arguably part of any language. As cognitive linguists have demonstrated, it is naturally human to think first in spatial categories before developing more abstract notions such as time.[4] This is easily observed in the development of infants. Long before they understand what time is, they are already navigating their worlds through spatial reasoning. Similarly, languages that encode time through their verbal system (i.e., languages that have tenses) did not necessarily always do this. All languages change over time, and one of the major changes that can be observed in the history of a number of languages is that the verbal system tends to begin as a spatial system and later develops into a temporal one. In other words, the idea that verbs should primarily convey actions in a spatial, rather than temporal, way is not unusual in the history of language, and several languages began in such a way.

The development from spatial to temporal systems within languages matches observations that anthropologists have made about cultures in general. They observe that many cultures develop from a spatial way of thinking to a temporal way of thinking. Tony Swain, of the University of Sydney, has observed this in relation to certain tribes of Aboriginal Australians. These tribes apparently did not conceive of time at all in the way they thought; they thought about the world in a primarily spatial manner. It was not until they encountered Europeans that these tribes began to think in temporal categories.[5] Such is the case with Greek. Most scholars would agree that the verbal system of Greek was originally spatial, back in its earliest stages of development. And, of course, the Greek verbal system is now temporal—Modern Greek has tenses. The question, however, is this: When did the verbal system cease to be primarily spatial and develop its temporal characteristics? While most scholars see the verbal system as consisting of tenses as early as Homeric Greek, and certainly by the time of Attic Greek, I have argued that the verbal system is still primarily spatial at this time and indeed continues to be so through the Koine period.

There is, nevertheless, evidence that the development from spatial to temporal meaning is taking place by this time. For example, the future indicative tense-form is the first tense-form that has a consistent temporal reference. It is a genuine tense, with its core meaning concerned with the expression of time.

---

4. E.g., H. H. Clark, "Space, Time, Semantics, and the Child," in *Cognitive Development and the Acquisitions of Language*, ed. T. E. Moore (New York: Academic Press, 1973), 61; H. Grimm, "On the Child's Acquisition of Semantic Structure Underlying the Wordfield of Prepositions," *Language and Speech* 18 (1975): 110; Martin Haspelmath, *From Space to Time—Temporal Adverbials in the World's Languages* (Munich: LINCOM Europa, 1997), 140.

5. Tony Swain, *A Place for Strangers: Towards a History of Australian Aboriginal Being* (Cambridge: Cambridge University Press, 1993), 14–44.

The existence of a real tense alongside other indicative verb forms that are not regarded as tenses at the semantic level does not constitute a problem for my analysis, nor is it inconsistent. It is no accident that the only real tense within the indicative mood is also the last of the ancient tense-forms to develop. It is thus evidence that the shift from spatial to temporal encoding is taking place in the diachronic development of the language. Eventually, the entire indicative system will consist of tenses, and the future tense is the first exponent of this new situation.

CONCLUSION

Most students grappling with the relationship between space and time in language will want to know how to think about Greek indicative verbs if they are to think of them spatially rather than temporally. The way forward, I think, is to realize that space and time often go together in English, and Greek is no different, though perhaps the ordering of the relationship is reversed. In English, an event that occurred a long time ago will often be interpreted temporally first (it was a long time ago), but it will also have spatial implications for the way we think about the event. It might feel distant. Thus, in English usage the verb primarily conveys time, and yet it has spatial implications for our thinking. Greek is like this, but in reverse. An event that is distant will be interpreted first spatially (it's the remote past), but it will also have temporal implications for the way the language user thinks about the event (it happened a long time ago). In Greek, the indicative verb primarily conveys remoteness or proximity and yet has temporal implications for our thinking.

This means that if, say, the Greek aorist indicative is regarded as perfective in aspect and spatially remote at the semantic level, this will account for the 85 percent of aorist indicatives that refer to the past—since past time is a temporal expression of remoteness. But it will also account for the 15 percent of aorist indicatives that do not express past temporal reference, since there are other ways in which remoteness may function. In other words, the spatial value of remoteness is more easily regarded as a semantic feature of the aorist indicative than as past temporal reference since it does not yield exceptions.

PART 2

Verbal Aspect and Biblical Greek Text

CHAPTER 6

Verbal Lexeme Basics

I n order to examine the function of verbal aspect within biblical texts, we must first know something about verbal lexemes. Why? Because verbal aspect operates in cooperation with various lexemes to produce *Aktionsart* expression (also known as *implicature*).

There are many different ways to analyze verbal lexemes. We will restrict our interest to the most important categorizations, which are directly relevant to our analysis of verbal pragmatics. Furthermore, our analysis would be strengthened by considering the range of usage of each lexeme by consulting a lexicon such as BDAG.[1] Even more useful for this task is *The Brill Dictionary of Ancient Greek*.[2] We will at this stage, however, restrict our analysis to consideration of the gloss definition of each lexeme. With most lexemes, categorization is relatively straightforward and unambiguous. While categorization for some lexemes is a little ambiguous, this should not give cause for concern.

The first decision we need to make when looking at a verbal lexeme is whether the lexeme is transitive or intransitive.[3]

---

1. Frederick W. Danker, Walter Bauer, William F. Arndt, and F. Wilbur Gingrich, *Greek-English Lexicon of the New Testament*, 3rd ed. (Chicago: University of Chicago Press, 2000).

2. Franco Montanari, *The Brill Dictionary of Ancient Greek*, ed. Madeleine Goh and Chad Schroeder (Leiden: Brill, 2015).

3. *The Brill Dictionary of Ancient Greek* labels certain uses of verbal lexemes as transitive or intransitive, which is enormously useful for this stage of the process, though it is understood that many readers may not have access to this resource at this stage.

TRANSITIVE LEXEMES

A lexeme is transitive if the action is *performed upon an object*. The action is performed by a subject and done *to* someone or something (the object). Whether or not a lexeme is transitive is decided simply by what the type of action is. In English, lexemes such as *hit*, *give*, *kick*, *throw*, *arrange*, and so on are all transitive. A person may hit *a target*, give *a gift*, kick *a ball*, throw *a javelin*, or arrange *a meeting*. We must note that, according to the definitions offered here, not all lexemes that take a grammatical object are necessarily transitive. The object must be *affected* or *impacted* somehow. So, for example, *to hear music* is not regarded here as transitive because the music is not affected by the action, even though it is the object of the action. To reiterate, for a lexeme to be transitive, there must be some kind of "exchange" from the subject to the object.[4]

Key question:
Is the action performed upon an object?
If yes, the lexeme is transitive.

1. Transitive	2. Intransitive
performed upon an object	*not performed upon an object*

INTRANSITIVE LEXEMES

An intransitive lexeme is one that does not require an object or does not perform an action upon its object. The action is performed by a subject, but it is not done to anyone or anything (though it may be done *with reference* to someone or something). In other words, an intransitive lexeme may take an object, but this must be *unaffected* by the action performed by the subject. For example, in the phrase *to hear music*, the hearer does not act on the music, even though it is the object of the verb. Whether or not a lexeme is intransitive is decided simply by what the type of action is. In English, lexemes such as sleep, know, live, die, and so on are all intransitive.

---

4. Linguists define transitivity in various ways, and this nuance is not always acknowledged. Lexemes are often labeled as transitive if they take an object at all. But we will adopt the more nuanced definition of transitivity, which requires the object to be affected by the verbal action.

Key question:

Is the action performed upon an object?

If no, the lexeme is intransitive.

AMBITRANSITIVE LEXEMES

Some lexemes are difficult to categorize as either transitive or intransitive. The fact is that in most languages, certain lexemes can be either transitive or intransitive, depending on the context. They may act upon an object in some situations (and so are transitive), or they may not act upon an object in other situations (and so are intransitive).[5] These lexemes are best labeled *ambitransitive* because they can go either way. In English, lexemes such as eat, read, breathe, and so on are all ambitransitive. For example, *It's time to eat* is intransitive, but *I ate my lunch* is transitive. *He's breathing* is intransitive, but *We need to breathe oxygen* is transitive.

SUBCATEGORIES

It is possible to subcategorize transitive and intransitive verbs into several other types of lexemes, but we will explore only two subcategories: punctiliar lexemes and stative lexemes.

TRANSITIVE: PUNCTILIAR

If a lexeme is transitive, it may also be punctiliar. A punctiliar action is performed upon an object and is instantaneous in nature. It is a once-occurring, immediate type of action. Whether or not a lexeme is punctiliar is decided simply by what the type of action is. While a punctiliar action can be repeated, it cannot be drawn out for any length of time. In English, lexemes such as *punch, kick, throw,* and the like are all punctiliar. A person may punch a bag for two minutes, but this must be a series of punches; one punch cannot last for two minutes.

Key questions:

Is the action performed upon an object?

If yes, the lexeme is transitive.

---

5. Again, *The Brill Dictionary of Ancient Greek* can help with this issue for certain lexemes.

Is the action instantaneous?
If yes, the lexeme is punctiliar.

If a transitive lexeme is *not* punctiliar, we will simply call it transitive without specifying further. Examples of lexemes that are transitive but not punctiliar are *give*, *arrange*, *defeat*, and so on.

INTRANSITIVE: STATIVE

If a lexeme is intransitive, it may also be stative. A stative verb is not performed upon an object and describes a state of being. It is not time bound or progressive; it simply *is*. In fact, we may even consider a stative lexeme as a verb that does not really convey an action—it simply conveys a state. Whether or not a lexeme is stative is decided simply by the type of action it conveys. In English, lexemes such as *know*, *trust*, *live*, and so on are all stative.

Key questions:
Is the action performed upon an object?
If no, the lexeme is intransitive.

Does the action describe a state of being?
If yes, the lexeme is stative.

If an intransitive lexeme is not stative, we will simply call it intransitive without specifying further. Examples of lexemes that are intransitive but not stative are *sleep*, *die*, *decide*, and the like.

Transitive	Intransitive
performed upon an object	*not performed upon an object*
Punctiliar	**Stative**
instantaneous action	*state of being*

SOME GREEK LEXEMES

Here are some common Greek verbs categorized into one of our four lexical categories. Note that some of these are not entirely clear but are affected by their lexical range of meaning and context. If a lexeme acts upon an object in some situations but does not act upon an object in others, it is categorized as ambitransitive. For the sake of specific analysis in the following chapters, these lexemes will be described as either transitive or intransitive depending on whether they act upon an object in specific contexts (even though they are technically ambitransitive).

Lexeme	Gloss	Category
εἰμί	to be	intransitive: stative
ποιέω	to do, make	transitive
τίθημι	to place, put	transitive
βάλλω	to throw	transitive: punctiliar
εὑρίσκω	to find	transitive: punctiliar
ζητέω	to seek	transitive
φέρω	to carry, bear	transitive
ἔρχομαι	to come, go	intransitive
πορεύομαι	to go	intransitive
ἐγγίζω	to draw near	intransitive
λύω	to loose, destroy	transitive
ἀκολουθέω	to follow	intransitive
ἐγείρω	to raise up	transitive
κάθημαι	to be seated	intransitive: stative
καθίζω	to sit	intransitive
λαμβάνω	to take, receive	transitive
τύπτω	to strike	transitive: punctiliar
ἅπτομαι	to touch	transitive: punctiliar
ἐσθίω	to eat	transitive
καθεύδω	to sleep	intransitive
ζάω	to live	intransitive: stative

ὁράω	to see	intransitive
βλέπω	to look at	transitive/intransitive?
ἀκούω	to hear	transitive/intransitive?
θέλω	to wish, desire	intransitive: stative
βούλομαι	to want	intransitive
ἀγαπάω	to love	transitive/intransitive?
οἶδα	to know	intransitive: stative
γινώσκω	to know	intransitive: stative

VOICE

A final factor to consider is how voice interacts with lexemes. For example, if an indicative verb is found in the passive voice, it may seem that the lexeme is stative, when really that is not the case. The passive voice creates this effect rather than the lexeme itself. For example, the present passive ἀποκαλύπτεται in Romans 1:18—ἀποκαλύπτεται γὰρ ὀργὴ θεοῦ—is often translated *For God's wrath **is revealed***. This sounds stative: God's wrath is in the state of having been revealed. But it could also be understood to mean *God's wrath **is being revealed***, which is a progressive, rather than stative, concept. This is possible because the lexeme ἀποκαλύπτω (*I reveal*) is transitive, not stative. If the lexeme were stative, this fact alone would almost guarantee a stative *Aktionsart* reading of the verb. Since it is *not* a stative lexeme, there may be other options besides stative *Aktionsart*. A stative reading is *possible*, but it is not the only possibility.

This is why it is important to take special note of indicative verbs in the passive voice—the lexeme might *seem* stative when in fact it is the voice that contributes that element rather than the lexeme. It is best to temporarily "un-passify" the lexeme to its active or middle meaning (for middle-only lexemes)[6]—as you would find it in a lexicon—to figure out if it is transitive, intransitive, or ambitransitive. A temporary suspension of the passive voice enables us to think more clearly about the lexeme in question. Once the passive voice is reintroduced and factored in, however, it is entirely possible that a stative understanding of the verb will be most appropriate.

---

6. We no longer use the term *deponent* to describe lexemes that have no active voice. They are *middle-only* or *passive-only* lexemes. See my *Advances in the Study of Greek* (Grand Rapids: Zondervan Academic, 2015), ch. 4, for more on this subject.

CHAPTER 7

Present and Imperfect Indicative Tense-Forms

SEMANTICS

VERBAL ASPECT

The present and imperfect indicative tense-forms encode imperfective aspect at the semantic level. Imperfective aspect views an action or state from the inside; it is the internal viewpoint. Using the illustration of the reporter and the street parade, the internal viewpoint is the view from the street, with the parade unfolding close-up. Unlike the view from afar (in the helicopter = perfective aspect), the reporter on the street does not view the beginning or end of the parade but has a view of the details.

SPATIAL QUALITIES

Traditional approaches described the present and imperfect indicative tense-forms as imperfective in aspect, with present and past tense respectively. Tense, however, is not here regarded as a semantic value; rather, temporal reference is a pragmatic feature, determined in part by context. Instead, the present and imperfect indicative tense-forms are regarded here as semantically encoding the spatial values of proximity and remoteness, respectively.

Thus, the present indicative tense-form is imperfective in aspect, with the spatial value of proximity. The imperfect indicative tense-form is imperfective in aspect, with the spatial value of remoteness. These are semantic values that are not cancelable but are expressed pragmatically in a variety of ways in context, which will be explored below.

Remote imperfectivity (imperfect tense-form)　　Proximate imperfectivity (present tense-form)

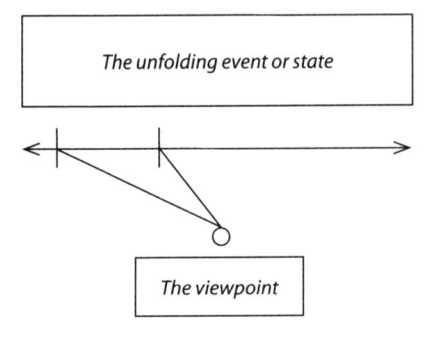
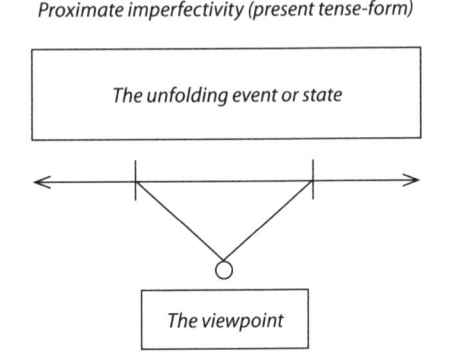

PRAGMATICS

NARRATIVE FUNCTIONS

Present Tense-Form

In narrative texts, the present indicative is most often found in discourse—direct discourse, indirect discourse, and authorial discourse, as illustrated by these examples.

> **John 5:20** ὁ γὰρ πατὴρ **φιλεῖ** τὸν υἱὸν καὶ πάντα **δείκνυσιν** αὐτῷ ἃ αὐτὸς **ποιεῖ**, καὶ μείζονα τούτων δείξει αὐτῷ ἔργα, ἵνα ὑμεῖς θαυμάζητε.

> For the Father **loves** the Son and **shows** him everything he **is doing**, and he will show him greater works than these so that you will be amazed.

> **John 16:15** πάντα ὅσα **ἔχει** ὁ πατὴρ ἐμά ἐστιν· διὰ τοῦτο εἶπον ὅτι ἐκ τοῦ ἐμοῦ **λαμβάνει** καὶ ἀναγγελεῖ ὑμῖν.

> Everything the Father **has** is mine. This is why I told you that **he takes** from what is mine and will declare it to you.

Discourse creates a proximate-imperfective context, as the speech or thought is presented immediately before the reader's eyes, as though unfolding. As such, the present indicative is attracted to discourse, being a proximate-imperfective tense-form. It is to be remembered, however, that the discourse function of the present indicative tense-form is a pragmatic feature and is therefore cancelable.

Imperfect Tense-Form

The imperfect indicative, however, is most often found in narrative proper rather than discourse. Its normal function within narrative proper is to provide offline material. While aorist indicatives typically provide the skeletal structure of the narrative mainline, imperfects most often provide supplementary information that describes, characterizes, or explains, as illustrated by these examples.

John 5:18 διὰ τοῦτο οὖν μᾶλλον **ἐζήτουν** αὐτὸν οἱ Ἰουδαῖοι ἀποκτεῖναι, ὅτι οὐ μόνον **ἔλυεν** τὸ σάββατον, ἀλλὰ καὶ πατέρα ἴδιον **ἔλεγεν** τὸν θεὸν ἴσον ἑαυτὸν ποιῶν τῷ θεῷ.

This is why the Jews **were seeking** all the more to kill him: not only **was he breaking** the Sabbath, but **he was** even **calling** God his own father, making himself equal with God.

Luke 15:16 καὶ **ἐπεθύμει** χορτασθῆναι ἐκ τῶν κερατίων ὧν ἤσθιον οἱ χοῖροι, καὶ οὐδεὶς **ἐδίδου** αὐτῷ.

He **was longing** to eat his fill from the carob pods the pigs **were eating**, but no one **would give** him any.

Offline material is inherently remote-imperfective in nature, as the supplementary information provides an internal view (imperfective), but this is not presented as being immediately before the reader's eyes. It supplements the remote mainline and thus is remote in nature. As such, the imperfect indicative is attracted to offline material, since it is a remote-imperfective tense-form. It is to be remembered, however, that the offline function of the imperfect indicative tense-form is a pragmatic feature and is therefore cancelable.

AKTIONSART INTERACTIONS—PRESENT TENSE-FORM

Aktionsart refers to the way an indicative verb behaves in the text when all features of the language and text bear upon it. There are three main elements that determine a particular verb's *Aktionsart*: semantics, lexeme, and context.

There are, therefore, three steps required to ascertain what an indicative verb is doing in the text:

1. Identify the semantic value of the indicative verb.
2. Consider the lexeme and its interaction with the semantics.
3. Consider the context.

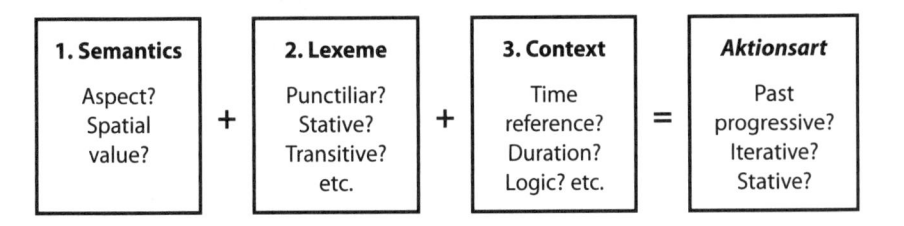

There are several ways in which the present indicative tense-form functions pragmatically. Below are the most common and important *Aktionsart* descriptions of present indicative usage and explanations of how the *Aktionsart* values are arrived at.[1]

Progressive

Present indicative tense-forms often end up depicting a process or action *in progress*. This is a common usage of the present indicative tense-form and is a natural implicature of imperfective aspect. Imperfective aspect combines with any lexeme that is not punctiliar or stative to create a progressive sense. As long as this progressive sense is not overruled by context, the *Aktionsart* is progressive.

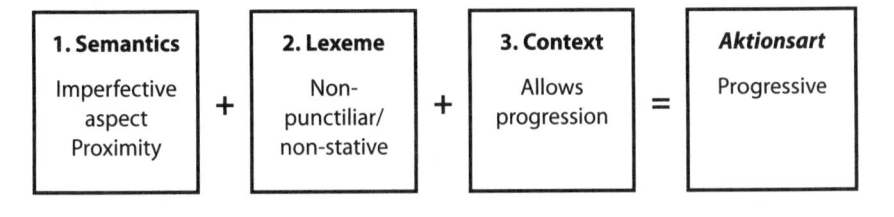

---

1. The following discussion is necessarily simplified for the sake of clarity. In his work on aspect and *Aktionsart*, Francis Pang rightly points out that the relevant elements involved (especially within context) are extremely numerous and interrelated. Pang does not doubt that it is possible to discern predictable patterns of meaning between aspect and *Aktionsart*, but he questions whether such patterns can be recognized in a systematic manner. The approach of this book is to assume that there is more complexity than we are presently able to address, but the method outlined below is nevertheless useful for students and others who seek to understand the basics of verbal aspect and *Aktionsart*. Francis G. H. Pang, *Revisiting Aspect and Aktionsart: A Corpus Approach to Koine Greek Event Typology*, Linguistic Biblical Studies 14 (Leiden: Brill, 2016), 234–40.

Luke 8:45 καὶ εἶπεν ὁ Ἰησοῦς, Τίς ὁ ἁψάμενός μου; ἀρνουμένων δὲ πάντων εἶπεν ὁ Πέτρος, Ἐπιστάτα, οἱ ὄχλοι **συνέχουσίν** σε καὶ **ἀποθλίβουσιν.**

"Who touched me?" Jesus asked. When they all denied it, Peter said, "Master, the crowds **are hemming** you in and **pressing against** you."

John 4:22 ὑμεῖς **προσκυνεῖτε** ὃ οὐκ οἴδατε· ἡμεῖς **προσκυνοῦμεν** ὃ οἴδαμεν, ὅτι ἡ σωτηρία ἐκ τῶν Ἰουδαίων ἐστίν.

You [Samaritans] **worship** what you do not know. We **worship** what we do know, because salvation is from the Jews.

Romans 8:17 εἰ δὲ τέκνα, καὶ κληρονόμοι· κληρονόμοι μὲν θεοῦ, συγκληρονόμοι δὲ Χριστοῦ, εἴπερ **συμπάσχομεν** ἵνα καὶ συνδοξασθῶμεν.

. . . and if children, also heirs—heirs of God and coheirs with Christ— seeing that we **suffer** with him so that we may also be glorified with him.

Deuteronomy 6:6 καὶ ἔσται τὰ ῥήματα ταῦτα, ὅσα ἐγὼ **ἐντέλλομαί** σοι σήμερον, ἐν τῇ καρδίᾳ σου.

These words that I **am commanding** you today are to be in your heart.

Stative

Present indicative tense-forms often end up depicting a state. This is also a natural implicature of imperfective aspect. Imperfective aspect combines with a stative lexeme to create a stative *Aktionsart* if this is not overturned by context. A stative lexeme is a word that describes a state of being rather than a process or transitive action. Sometimes the context (or passive voice) can create a stative *Aktionsart* even if the lexeme is not in itself stative.

1. Semantics		2. Lexeme		3. Context		*Aktionsart*
Imperfective aspect Proximity	**+**	Stative	**+**	Allows stativity (sometimes creates it)	**=**	Stative

John 10:14–15 Ἐγώ εἰμι ὁ ποιμὴν ὁ καλὸς καὶ **γινώσκω** τὰ ἐμὰ καὶ **γινώσκουσί** με τὰ ἐμά, καθὼς **γινώσκει** με ὁ πατὴρ κἀγὼ **γινώσκω** τὸν πατέρα, καὶ τὴν ψυχήν μου τίθημι ὑπὲρ τῶν προβάτων.

I am the good shepherd. I **know** my own sheep, and they **know** me, as the Father **knows** me, and I **know** the Father. I lay down my life for the sheep.

Matthew 9:13 πορευθέντες δὲ μάθετε τί ἐστιν, Ἔλεος **θέλω** καὶ οὐ θυσίαν· οὐ γὰρ ἦλθον καλέσαι δικαίους ἀλλ᾽ ἁμαρτωλούς.

Go and learn what this means: **I desire** mercy and not sacrifice. For I didn't come to call the righteous, but sinners.

Romans 6:8 εἰ δὲ ἀπεθάνομεν σὺν Χριστῷ, **πιστεύομεν** ὅτι καὶ συζήσομεν αὐτῷ.

Now if we died with Christ, **we believe** that we will also live with him.

Genesis 4:9 καὶ εἶπεν ὁ θεὸς πρὸς Καιν Ποῦ **ἐστιν** Αβελ ὁ ἀδελφός σου; ὁ δὲ εἶπεν Οὐ γινώσκω· μὴ φύλαξ τοῦ ἀδελφοῦ μού εἰμι ἐγώ;

And God said to Cain, "Where **is** your brother Abel?" And he said, "I do not know; surely I am not my brother's keeper?"

<u>Iterative</u>

Present indicative tense-forms can depict iterative actions, which are events that repeatedly occur. There are two key ways in which an iterative *Aktionsart* may be created. First, imperfective aspect combines with a punctiliar lexeme, which creates the sense of a repeating punctiliar action. Second, imperfective aspect combines with any nonstative lexeme in a context that requires the action to be repeating.

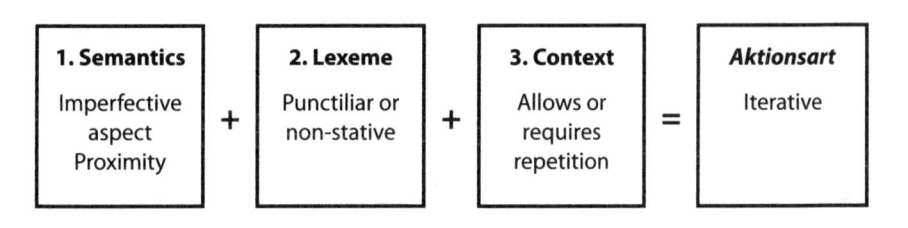

Matthew 17:15 καὶ λέγων, Κύριε, ἐλέησόν μου τὸν υἱόν, ὅτι σεληνιάζεται καὶ κακῶς πάσχει· πολλάκις γὰρ **πίπτει** εἰς τὸ πῦρ καὶ πολλάκις εἰς τὸ ὕδωρ.

"Lord," he said, "have mercy on my son, because he has seizures and suffers severely. He often **falls** into the fire and often into the water."

Luke 9:39 καὶ ἰδοὺ πνεῦμα **λαμβάνει** αὐτὸν καὶ ἐξαίφνης **κράζει** καὶ **σπαράσσει** αὐτὸν μετὰ ἀφροῦ καὶ μόγις **ἀποχωρεῖ** ἀπ᾽ αὐτοῦ συντρῖβον αὐτόν.

A spirit often **seizes** him; suddenly **he shrieks**, and it **throws** him **into convulsions** until he foams at the mouth; wounding him, it hardly ever **leaves** him.

Luke 18:12 νηστεύω δὶς τοῦ σαββάτου, **ἀποδεκατῶ** πάντα ὅσα κτῶμαι.

I fast twice a week; **I give a tenth** of everything I get.

Isaiah 58:4 εἰ εἰς κρίσεις καὶ μάχας νηστεύετε καὶ **τύπτετε** πυγμαῖς ταπεινόν, ἵνα τί μοι νηστεύετε ὡς σήμερον ἀκουσθῆναι ἐν κραυγῇ τὴν φωνὴν ὑμῶν;

If you fast for quarrels and fights and **you strike** a humble person with your fists, why do you fast for me as you do today so that your voice may be heard by its clamor?

Gnomic

Present indicative tense-forms can depict gnomic actions, which are universal and timeless. A gnomic *Aktionsart* is created through the combination of imperfective aspect and a context in which generic statements are made. These may involve any type of lexeme.

1. Semantics		2. Lexeme		3. Context		*Aktionsart*
Imperfective aspect Proximity	+	Punctiliar or non-stative	+	Allows or requires repetition	=	Iterative

Matthew 5:32 ἐγὼ δὲ λέγω ὑμῖν ὅτι πᾶς ὁ ἀπολύων τὴν γυναῖκα αὐτοῦ παρεκτὸς λόγου πορνείας **ποιεῖ** αὐτὴν μοιχευθῆναι, καὶ ὃς ἐὰν ἀπολελυμένην γαμήσῃ, **μοιχᾶται.**

But I tell you, everyone who divorces his wife, except in a case of sexual immorality, **causes** her to commit adultery. And whoever marries a divorced woman **commits adultery.**

John 3:8 τὸ πνεῦμα ὅπου **θέλει πνεῖ** καὶ τὴν φωνὴν αὐτοῦ **ἀκούεις,** ἀλλ᾽ οὐκ οἶδας πόθεν **ἔρχεται** καὶ ποῦ **ὑπάγει·** οὕτως **ἐστὶν** πᾶς ὁ γεγεννημένος ἐκ τοῦ πνεύματος.

The wind **blows** where **it pleases,** and **you hear** its sound, but you don't know where **it comes** from or where **it is going.** So **it is** with everyone born of the Spirit.

John 5:24 Ἀμὴν ἀμὴν λέγω ὑμῖν ὅτι ὁ τὸν λόγον μου ἀκούων καὶ πιστεύων τῷ πέμψαντί με **ἔχει** ζωὴν αἰώνιον καὶ εἰς κρίσιν οὐκ **ἔρχεται,** ἀλλὰ μεταβέβηκεν ἐκ τοῦ θανάτου εἰς τὴν ζωήν.

I assure you: Anyone who hears my word and believes him who sent me **has** eternal life and **will** not **come** under judgment but has passed from death to life.

Proverbs 3:34 κύριος ὑπερηφάνοις **ἀντιτάσσεται,** ταπεινοῖς δὲ **δίδωσιν** χάριν.

The Lord **resists** the arrogant, but he **gives** grace to the humble.

Historical Present

The present indicative tense-form is often used in nonpresent contexts, most often past referring. These are best translated like aorist indicatives, though they are not the same as aorists in meaning. There are two basic types of historical presents: those that introduce discourse and those that employ lexemes of propulsion.

First, historical presents that introduce discourse utilize the present tense-form because they are leading into a proximate-imperfective context (discourse).

In such cases, the proximate-imperfective nature of discourse "spills over" to the verb that introduces it.

Second, lexemes of propulsion are verbs that convey transition—movement from one point to another. These include verbs of coming and going, lifting, taking, giving, and so on. The proximate-imperfective nature of the present indicative tense-form combines with these lexemes in order to highlight the transition that is conveyed. There is no obvious way to convey this in translation.

Proximate imperfectivity and heightened transition

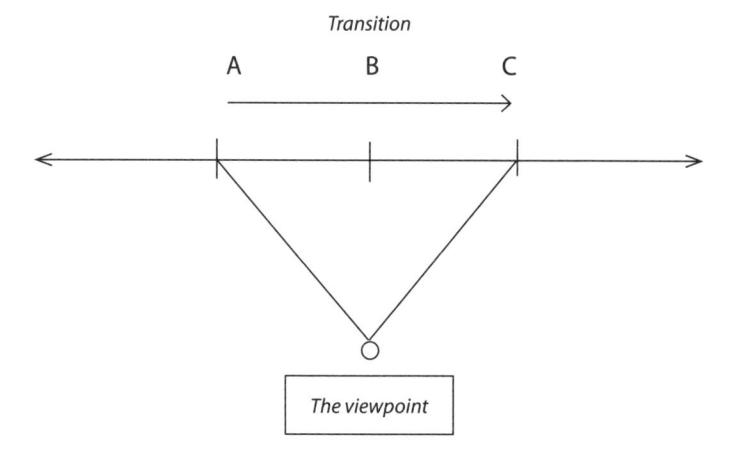

This diagram demonstrates that a proximate-imperfective depiction of an action may heighten the sense of transition as the action moves from point A to C. The transition is heightened because, in moving from A to C, point B is crossed, which is the author/speaker's center of reference in his or her imperfective viewpoint. The author/speaker, in a sense, views the action as passing in front of him or her and moving from one side of point B to the other side of point B. This movement from A, past B, to C is the element that heightens the transition in verbs of propulsion.

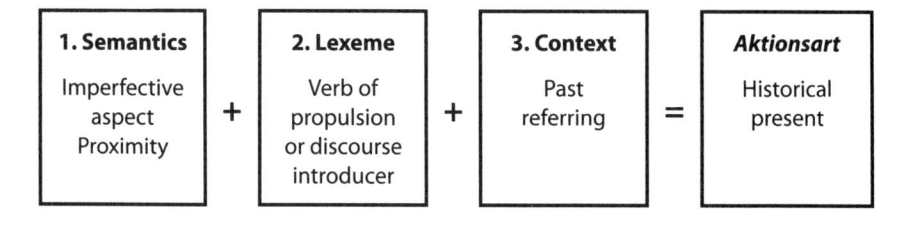

Mark 3:20 Καὶ ἔρχεται εἰς οἶκον· καὶ συνέρχεται πάλιν ὁ ὄχλος, ὥστε μὴ δύνασθαι αὐτοὺς μηδὲ ἄρτον φαγεῖν.

Then **he went** home, and the crowd **gathered** again so that they were not even able to eat.

Mark 5:22 καὶ ἔρχεται εἷς τῶν ἀρχισυναγώγων, ὀνόματι Ἰάϊρος, καὶ ἰδὼν αὐτὸν **πίπτει** πρὸς τοὺς πόδας αὐτοῦ.

One of the synagogue leaders, named Jairus, **came**, and when he saw Jesus, **he fell** at his feet.

John 19:28 Μετὰ τοῦτο εἰδὼς ὁ Ἰησοῦς ὅτι ἤδη πάντα τετέλεσται, ἵνα τελειωθῇ ἡ γραφή, **λέγει**, Διψῶ.

After this, when Jesus knew that everything was now accomplished that the Scripture might be fulfilled, **he said**, "I'm thirsty!"

1 Kings 12:1 Καὶ **πορεύεται** βασιλεὺς Ροβοαμ εἰς Σικιμα, ὅτι εἰς Σικιμα ἤρχοντο πᾶς Ισραηλ βασιλεῦσαι αὐτόν.

Then Rehoboam **went** to Shechem, for all Israel was going to Shechem to make him king.

AKTIONSART INTERACTIONS—IMPERFECT INDICATIVE TENSE-FORM

There are several ways in which the imperfect indicative tense-form functions pragmatically. Below are the most common and important *Aktionsart* descriptions of imperfect indicative usage and explanations of how the *Aktionsart* values are arrived at.

Progressive

Imperfect indicative tense-forms often end up depicting a process or action *in progress*. This is a common usage of the imperfect indicative tense-form and is a natural implicature of imperfective aspect. Imperfective aspect combines with any lexeme that is not punctiliar or stative to create a progressive sense.

As long as this progressive sense is not overruled by context, the *Aktionsart* is progressive.

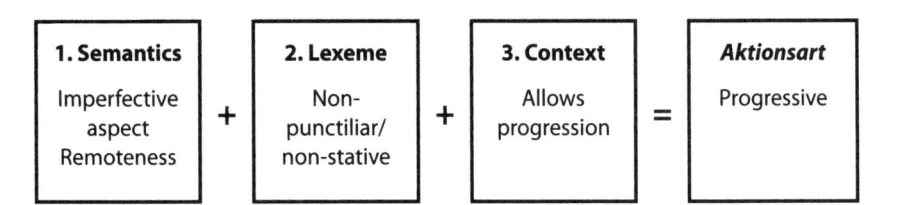

1. Semantics		2. Lexeme		3. Context		Aktionsart
Imperfective aspect Remoteness	+	Non-punctiliar/ non-stative	+	Allows progression	=	Progressive

Matthew 14:36 καὶ **παρεκάλουν** αὐτὸν ἵνα μόνον ἅψωνται τοῦ κρασπέδου τοῦ ἱματίου αὐτοῦ· καὶ ὅσοι ἥψαντο διεσώθησαν.

They were begging him that they might only touch the tassel on his robe. And as many as touched it were made perfectly well.

Mark 5:24 καὶ ἀπῆλθεν μετ᾽ αὐτοῦ. καὶ **ἠκολούθει** αὐτῷ ὄχλος πολὺς καὶ **συνέθλιβον** αὐτόν.

So Jesus went with him, and a large crowd **was following** and **pressing against** him.

John 7:25 Ἔλεγον οὖν τινες ἐκ τῶν Ἱεροσολυμιτῶν, Οὐχ οὗτός ἐστιν ὃν ζητοῦσιν ἀποκτεῖναι;

Some of the people of Jerusalem **were saying**, "Isn't this the man they want to kill?"

1 Samuel 1:13 καὶ αὐτὴ **ἐλάλει** ἐν τῇ καρδίᾳ αὐτῆς, καὶ τὰ χείλη αὐτῆς **ἐκινεῖτο**, καὶ φωνὴ αὐτῆς οὐκ ἠκούετο· καὶ ἐλογίσατο αὐτὴν Ηλι εἰς μεθύουσαν.

And **she was speaking** in her heart, and her lips **were moving**, and her voice was not heard, so Eli thought she was drunk.

Stative

Imperfect indicative tense-forms often end up depicting a state. This is also a natural implicature of imperfective aspect. Imperfective aspect combines with a stative lexeme to create a stative *Aktionsart*, if this is not overturned by context. A stative lexeme is a word that describes a state of being rather than a process or transitive action. Sometimes the context (or passive voice) can create a stative *Aktionsart* even if the lexeme is not in itself stative.

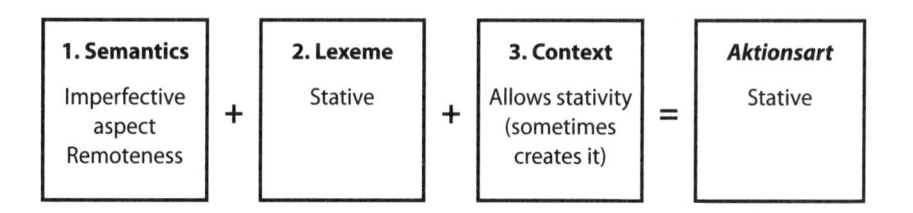

Mark 1:16 Καὶ παράγων παρὰ τὴν θάλασσαν τῆς Γαλιλαίας εἶδεν Σίμωνα καὶ Ἀνδρέαν τὸν ἀδελφὸν Σίμωνος ἀμφιβάλλοντας ἐν τῇ θαλάσσῃ· **ἦσαν** γὰρ ἁλιεῖς.

As he was passing along by the Sea of Galilee, he saw Simon and Andrew, Simon's brother. They were casting a net into the sea, since **they were** fishermen.

John 2:25 . . . καὶ ὅτι οὐ χρείαν **εἶχεν** ἵνα τις μαρτυρήσῃ περὶ τοῦ ἀνθρώπου· αὐτὸς γὰρ **ἐγίνωσκεν** τί ἦν ἐν τῷ ἀνθρώπῳ.

. . . and because he did not **need** anyone to testify about man; for he himself knew what was in man.

John 6:21 **ἤθελον** οὖν λαβεῖν αὐτὸν εἰς τὸ πλοῖον, καὶ εὐθέως ἐγένετο τὸ πλοῖον ἐπὶ τῆς γῆς εἰς ἣν ὑπῆγον.

Then **they were willing** to take him on board, and at once the boat was at the shore where they were heading.

Jeremiah 43:22 καὶ ὁ βασιλεὺς **ἐκάθητο** ἐν οἴκῳ χειμερινῷ, καὶ ἐσχάρα πυρὸς κατὰ πρόσωπον αὐτοῦ.

And the king **was sitting** in his winter house, and there was a hearth of fire in front of him.

Ingressive

The imperfect indicative tense-form is able to depict the beginning, and subsequent progression, of an action. This is similar to the progressive *Aktionsart* but differs in that the beginning of the action is in view. Most often the beginning of an action is flagged by the context, in which there is some kind of shift or new direction in the narrative.

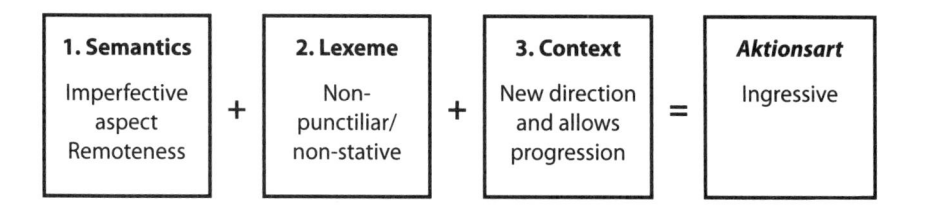

Matthew 5:2 καὶ ἀνοίξας τὸ στόμα αὐτοῦ **ἐδίδασκεν** αὐτοὺς λέγων . . .

Then he opened his mouth and **began to teach** them, saying . . .

Luke 4:39 καὶ ἐπιστὰς ἐπάνω αὐτῆς ἐπετίμησεν τῷ πυρετῷ καὶ ἀφῆκεν αὐτήν· παραχρῆμα δὲ ἀναστᾶσα **διηκόνει** αὐτοῖς.

So he stood over her and rebuked the fever, and it left her. She got up immediately and **began to serve** them.

John 5:16 καὶ διὰ τοῦτο **ἐδίωκον** οἱ Ἰουδαῖοι τὸν Ἰησοῦν, ὅτι ταῦτα ἐποίει ἐν σαββάτῳ.

Therefore, the Jews **began persecuting** Jesus because he was doing these things on the Sabbath.

Judges 12:4 καὶ συνήθροισεν Ιεφθαε πάντας τοὺς ἄνδρας Γαλααδ καὶ **ἐπολέμει** τὸν Εφραιμ, καὶ ἐπάταξαν ἄνδρες Γαλααδ τὸν Εφραιμ.

And Jephthah gathered all the men of Gilead and **began to fight** Ephraim, and the men of Gilead struck down Ephraim.

Iterative

Imperfect indicative tense-forms can depict iterative actions, which are events that repeatedly occur. There are two key ways an iterative *Aktionsart* may be created. First, imperfective aspect combines with a punctiliar lexeme, which creates the sense of a repeating punctiliar action. Second, imperfective aspect combines with any nonstative lexeme in a context that requires the action to be repetition.

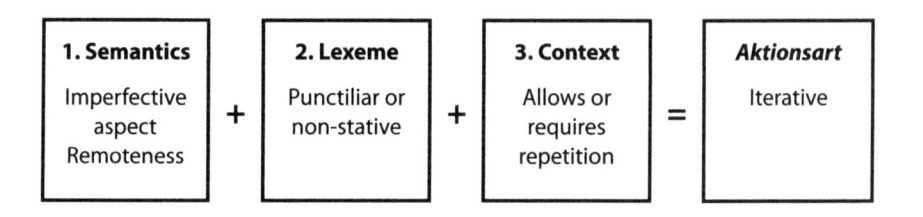

Matthew 26:55 Ἐν ἐκείνῃ τῇ ὥρᾳ εἶπεν ὁ Ἰησοῦς τοῖς ὄχλοις, Ὡς ἐπὶ λῃστὴν ἐξήλθατε μετὰ μαχαιρῶν καὶ ξύλων συλλαβεῖν με; καθ᾽ ἡμέραν ἐν τῷ ἱερῷ **ἐκαθεζόμην** διδάσκων καὶ οὐκ ἐκρατήσατέ με.

At that time Jesus said to the crowds, "Have you come out with swords and clubs, as if I were a criminal, to capture me? Every day **I used to sit**, teaching in the temple complex, and you didn't arrest me."

Matthew 27:30 καὶ ἐμπτύσαντες εἰς αὐτὸν ἔλαβον τὸν κάλαμον καὶ **ἔτυπτον** εἰς τὴν κεφαλὴν αὐτοῦ.

Then they spit at him, took the reed, and **kept hitting** him on the head.

John 3:22 Μετὰ ταῦτα ἦλθεν ὁ Ἰησοῦς καὶ οἱ μαθηταὶ αὐτοῦ εἰς τὴν Ἰουδαίαν γῆν καὶ ἐκεῖ διέτριβεν μετ᾽ αὐτῶν καὶ **ἐβάπτιζεν**.

After this, Jesus and his disciples went to the Judean countryside, where he spent time with them and **was baptizing**.

Numbers 22:27 καὶ ἰδοῦσα ἡ ὄνος τὸν ἄγγελον τοῦ θεοῦ συνεκάθισεν ὑποκάτω Βαλααμ· καὶ ἐθυμώθη Βαλααμ καὶ **ἔτυπτεν** τὴν ὄνον τῇ ῥάβδῳ.

And when the donkey saw the angel of God, it settled down under Balaam, and Balaam was angered and **kept beating** the donkey with the rod.

Conative

The imperfect indicative tense-form is sometimes used to portray an action that is attempted but not accomplished. In such cases, the imperfective aspect combines with any nonstative lexeme to present an action as being undertaken but not completed. It will always be the context that demands a conative *Aktionsart*. When the context makes it clear that the action was attempted but not achieved, a conative reading ensues.

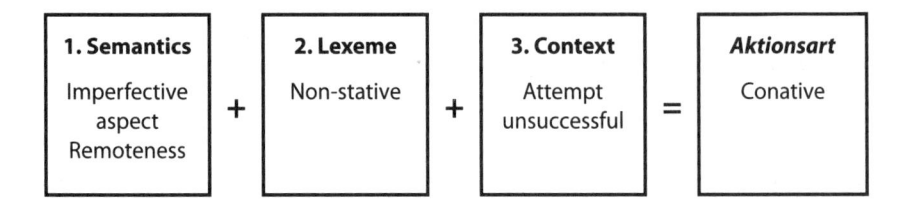

Mark 15:23 καὶ **ἐδίδουν** αὐτῷ ἐσμυρνισμένον οἶνον· ὃς δὲ οὐκ ἔλαβεν.

They **tried to give** him wine mixed with myrrh, but he did not take it.

Luke 1:59 Καὶ ἐγένετο ἐν τῇ ἡμέρᾳ τῇ ὀγδόῃ ἦλθον περιτεμεῖν τὸ παιδίον καὶ **ἐκάλουν** αὐτὸ ἐπὶ τῷ ὀνόματι τοῦ πατρὸς αὐτοῦ Ζαχαρίαν.

When they came to circumcise the child on the eighth day, **they were going to call him** by the name Zechariah, after his father.

Acts 7:26 τῇ τε ἐπιούσῃ ἡμέρᾳ ὤφθη αὐτοῖς μαχομένοις καὶ **συνήλλασσεν** αὐτοὺς εἰς εἰρήνην εἰπών, Ἄνδρες, ἀδελφοί ἐστε· ἱνατί ἀδικεῖτε ἀλλήλους;

The next day he showed up while they were fighting and **tried to reconcile** them peacefully, saying, "Men, you are brothers. Why are you mistreating each other?"

Ezra 4:4 καὶ ἦν ὁ λαὸς τῆς γῆς ἐκλύων τὰς χεῖρας τοῦ λαοῦ Ιουδα καὶ ἐνεπόδιζον αὐτοὺς τοῦ οἰκοδομεῖν.

And the people of the land were weakening the hands of the people of Judah, and **they were trying to hinder** them from building.

EXERCISES FOR PRESENT AND IMPERFECT INDICATIVE TENSE-FORMS

For each passage, (1) write about the semantic meaning of the indicative verb, (2) state the contribution of the lexeme, and (3) discuss the function of the indicative verb in context. Once you have written your answers, summarize your findings in the boxes below each passage.

When considering the context, keep an eye out for any elements that may influence the way the indicative verb is understood. This might be something obvious like a temporal word or phrase (e.g., "yesterday," "all day long," "after," etc.). Or it might be something less obvious, like a hint that an action should be understood as repeating or is part of a generalized reality. Context is an open-ended category, and it takes some practice to feel competent with it.

Example:
Luke 8:45 (x2) καὶ εἶπεν ὁ Ἰησοῦς, Τίς ὁ ἁψάμενός μου; ἀρνουμένων δὲ πάντων εἶπεν ὁ Πέτρος, Ἐπιστάτα, οἱ ὄχλοι **συνέχουσίν** σε καὶ **ἀποθλίβουσιν**.

"Who touched me?" Jesus asked. When they all denied it, Peter said, "Master, the crowds **are hemming** you in and **pressing against** you."

1. Semantic meaning of the indicative verb. The present indicative semantically encodes imperfective aspect and the spatial value of proximity.
2. Contribution of the lexeme. The lexemes are transitive (perform an action upon an object). They are not punctiliar or stative.
3. Function in context. The context makes it clear that these actions are taking place continuously at the time of speech. Thus, these indicative verbs are conveying progressive action.

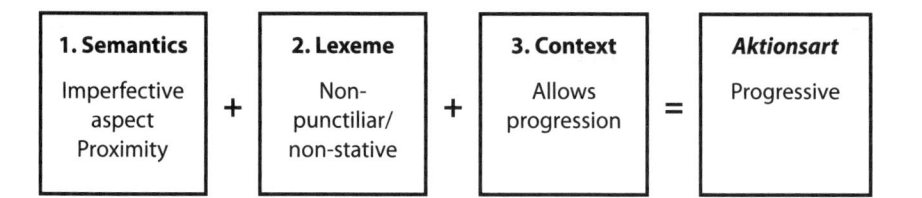

1. Semantics		2. Lexeme		3. Context		Aktionsart
Imperfective aspect Proximity	+	Non-punctiliar/ non-stative	+	Allows progression	=	Progressive

John 7:42 οὐχ ἡ γραφὴ εἶπεν ὅτι ἐκ τοῦ σπέρματος Δαυὶδ καὶ ἀπὸ Βηθλέεμ τῆς κώμης ὅπου ἦν Δαυὶδ **ἔρχεται** ὁ Χριστός;

"Doesn't the Scripture say that the Christ **comes** from David's offspring and from the town of Bethlehem, where David once lived?"

1. Semantics		2. Lexeme		3. Context		Aktionsart
	+		+		=	

John 5:16 καὶ διὰ τοῦτο **ἐδίωκον** οἱ Ἰουδαῖοι τὸν Ἰησοῦν, ὅτι ταῦτα ἐποίει ἐν σαββάτῳ.

Therefore, the Jews **began persecuting** Jesus because he was doing these things on the Sabbath.

1. Semantics		2. Lexeme		3. Context		Aktionsart
	+		+		=	

Romans 1:18 Ἀποκαλύπτεται γὰρ ὀργὴ θεοῦ ἀπ' οὐρανοῦ ἐπὶ πᾶσαν ἀσέβειαν καὶ ἀδικίαν ἀνθρώπων τῶν τὴν ἀλήθειαν ἐν ἀδικίᾳ κατεχόντων.

For God's wrath **is revealed** from heaven against all godlessness and unrighteousness of people who by their unrighteousness suppress the truth.

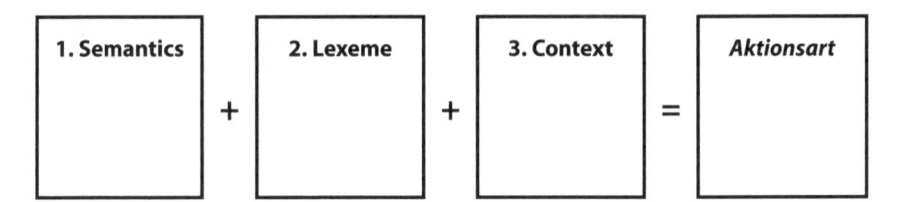

Romans 8:3 τὸ γὰρ ἀδύνατον τοῦ νόμου ἐν ᾧ **ἠσθένει** διὰ τῆς σαρκός, ὁ θεὸς τὸν ἑαυτοῦ υἱὸν πέμψας ἐν ὁμοιώματι σαρκὸς ἁμαρτίας καὶ περὶ ἁμαρτίας κατέκρινεν τὴν ἁμαρτίαν ἐν τῇ σαρκί.

What the law could not do since **it was limited** by the flesh, God did. He condemned sin in the flesh by sending his own Son in flesh like ours under sin's domain, and as a sin offering.

1. Semantics		2. Lexeme		3. Context		Aktionsart
	+		+		=	

John 15:27 (x2) καὶ ὑμεῖς δὲ **μαρτυρεῖτε**, ὅτι ἀπ᾽ ἀρχῆς μετ᾽ ἐμοῦ **ἐστε**.

You also **will testify**, because you **have been** with me from the beginning.

1. Semantics		2. Lexeme		3. Context		Aktionsart
	+		+		=	

Romans 6:8 εἰ δὲ ἀπεθάνομεν σὺν Χριστῷ, **πιστεύομεν** ὅτι καὶ συζήσομεν αὐτῷ.

Now if we died with Christ, **we believe** that we will also live with him.

1. Semantics		2. Lexeme		3. Context		Aktionsart
	+		+		=	

John 3:22 Μετὰ ταῦτα ἦλθεν ὁ Ἰησοῦς καὶ οἱ μαθηταὶ αὐτοῦ εἰς τὴν Ἰουδαίαν γῆν καὶ ἐκεῖ διέτριβεν μετ᾽ αὐτῶν καὶ **ἐβάπτιζεν**.

After this, Jesus and his disciples went to the Judean countryside, where he spent time with them and **was baptizing**.

1. Semantics		2. Lexeme		3. Context		Aktionsart
	+		+		=	

Romans 8:13 (x3) εἰ γὰρ κατὰ σάρκα **ζῆτε**, **μέλλετε** ἀποθνῄσκειν· εἰ δὲ πνεύματι τὰς πράξεις τοῦ σώματος **θανατοῦτε**, ζήσεσθε.

For if **you live** according to the flesh, **you are going** to die. But if by the Spirit **you put to death** the deeds of the body, you will live.

1. Semantics		2. Lexeme		3. Context		Aktionsart
	+		+		=	

Psalm 101:9 ὅλην τὴν ἡμέραν **ὠνείδιζόν** με οἱ ἐχθροί μου, καὶ οἱ ἐπαινοῦντές με κατ᾽ ἐμοῦ **ὤμνυον**.

All day long my enemies **reproach** me, and those who used to commend me **swear** against me.

1. Semantics		2. Lexeme		3. Context		Aktionsart
	+		+		=	

CHAPTER 8

Aorist and Future Indicative Tense-Forms

SEMANTICS

VERBAL ASPECT

The aorist indicative tense-form encodes perfective aspect at the semantic level. Perfective aspect views an action or state from the outside; it is the external viewpoint. Using the illustration of the reporter and the street parade, the external viewpoint is the view from the helicopter, with the parade seen as a whole. Unlike the close-up view (from the street = imperfective aspect), the reporter in the helicopter does not view the parade's details or how it unfolds but has an external view of the whole event.

The verbal aspect of the future indicative tense-form is a matter of debate, with options ranging from nonaspectual, perfective, imperfective, or both perfective and imperfective. In part, this confusion stems from the difficult nature of *futurity* when applied to understanding verbal meaning and function. Nevertheless, regarding the future indicative as encoding perfective aspect provides the best power of explanation, and therefore that is the position adopted here.[1]

---

1. For extensive argumentation along such lines, see Constantine R. Campbell, *Verbal Aspect, the Indicative Mood, and Narrative: Soundings in the Greek of the New Testament*, Studies in Biblical Greek 13 (New York: Peter Lang, 2007), 139–51; Samuel J. Freney, *Aspectual Substitution: Verbal Change in New Testament Quotations of the Septuagint*, Studies in Biblical Greek 20 (New York: Peter Lang, 2020), 245.

SPATIAL/TEMPORAL QUALITIES

Traditional approaches describe the aorist indicative tense-form as perfective in aspect, with past tense. Tense, however, is not here regarded as a semantic value; rather, temporal reference is a pragmatic feature, determined in part by context. Instead, the aorist indicative tense-form is regarded as semantically encoding the spatial value of remoteness. Thus, the aorist indicative tense-form is perfective in aspect, with the spatial value of remoteness. These are semantic values that are not cancelable but are expressed pragmatically in a variety of ways in context, which will be explored below.

The future indicative tense-form, however, refers to future time in its every usage and is therefore regarded as a genuine tense; that is, future temporal reference is a semantic feature of the tense-form alongside perfective aspect. Rather than being semantically aspectual-spatial (as the aorist tense-form is here regarded), the future indicative is semantically aspectual-temporal.

PRAGMATICS

NARRATIVE FUNCTIONS

Aorist Tense-Form

In narrative texts, the aorist indicative is most often found in narrative proper. While it is used in discourse and even in offline information, its main function in narrative is to provide the mainline of narrative proper, outlining the skeletal structure of the story, as these examples demonstrate.

> **Luke 1:39–41** Ἀναστᾶσα δὲ Μαριὰμ ἐν ταῖς ἡμέραις ταύταις **ἐπορεύθη** εἰς τὴν ὀρεινὴν μετὰ σπουδῆς εἰς πόλιν Ἰούδα, καὶ **εἰσῆλθεν** εἰς τὸν οἶκον Ζαχαρίου καὶ **ἠσπάσατο** τὴν Ἐλισάβετ. καὶ ἐγένετο ὡς **ἤκουσεν** τὸν ἀσπασμὸν τῆς Μαρίας ἡ Ἐλισάβετ, **ἐσκίρτησεν** τὸ βρέφος ἐν τῇ κοιλίᾳ αὐτῆς, καὶ **ἐπλήσθη** πνεύματος ἁγίου ἡ Ἐλισάβετ.

> In those days Mary set out and **went** with haste to a town in the hill country of Judah, where **she entered** Zechariah's house and **greeted**

Elizabeth. When Elizabeth **heard** Mary's greeting, the baby **leaped** inside her, and Elizabeth **was filled** with the Holy Spirit.

John 19:32–34 ἦλθον οὖν οἱ στρατιῶται καὶ τοῦ μὲν πρώτου **κατέαξαν** τὰ σκέλη καὶ τοῦ ἄλλου τοῦ συσταυρωθέντος αὐτῷ· ἐπὶ δὲ τὸν Ἰησοῦν ἐλθόντες, ὡς **εἶδον** ἤδη αὐτὸν τεθνηκότα, **οὐ κατέαξαν** αὐτοῦ τὰ σκέλη, ἀλλ᾽ εἷς τῶν στρατιωτῶν λόγχῃ αὐτοῦ τὴν πλευρὰν **ἔνυξεν**, καὶ **ἐξῆλθεν** εὐθὺς αἷμα καὶ ὕδωρ.

So the soldiers **came** and **broke** the legs of the first man and of the other one who had been crucified with him. When **they** came to Jesus, they **did not break** his legs since **they saw** that he was already dead. But one of the soldiers **pierced** his side with a spear, and at once blood and water **came out.**

Narrative mainline creates a remote-perfective context as the events of the story are presented rapidly in quick succession. As such, the aorist indicative is attracted to that mainline, being a remote-perfective tense-form. It is to be remembered, however, that the mainline function of the aorist indicative tense-form is a pragmatic feature and is therefore cancelable.

Future Tense-Form

The future indicative is most often found in discourse rather than in narrative proper. This is no doubt due to its future temporal reference: in narrative, reference to the future is performed most naturally by characters within the narrative and thus within their speech (discourse).

John 16:13–14 ὅταν δὲ ἔλθῃ ἐκεῖνος, τὸ πνεῦμα τῆς ἀληθείας, **ὁδηγήσει** ὑμᾶς ἐν τῇ ἀληθείᾳ πάσῃ· οὐ γὰρ **λαλήσει** ἀφ᾽ ἑαυτοῦ, ἀλλ᾽ ὅσα **ἀκούσει** **λαλήσει** καὶ τὰ ἐρχόμενα **ἀναγγελεῖ** ὑμῖν. ἐκεῖνος ἐμὲ **δοξάσει**, ὅτι ἐκ τοῦ ἐμοῦ **λήμψεται** καὶ **ἀναγγελεῖ** ὑμῖν.

When the Spirit of truth comes, **he will guide** you into all the truth. For **he will not speak** on his own, but **he will speak** whatever **he hears. He will** also **declare** to you what is to come. He **will glorify** me, because **he will take** from what is mine and **declare** it to you."

AKTIONSART INTERACTIONS—AORIST INDICATIVE TENSE-FORM

Aktionsart refers to the way an indicative verb behaves in the text when all features of the language and text bear upon it. There are three main elements that determine a particular verb's *Aktionsart*: semantics, lexeme, and context. Accordingly, there are three steps required to ascertain what a verb is doing in the text:

1. Identify the semantic value of the indicative verb.
2. Consider the lexeme and its interaction with the semantics.
3. Consider the context.

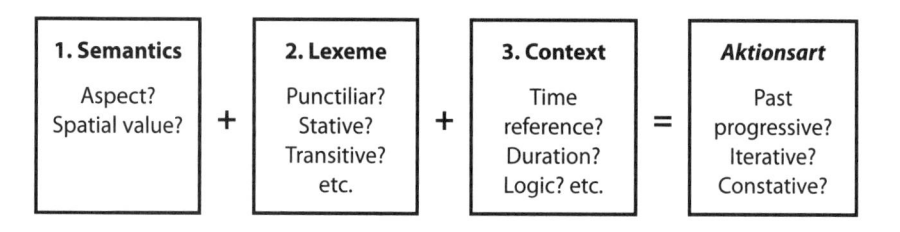

There are several ways in which the aorist indicative tense-form functions pragmatically. Below are the most common and important *Aktionsart* descriptions of aorist indicative usage and explanations of how the *Aktionsart* values are arrived at.[2]

Summary

Aorist indicative tense-forms often end up depicting a process or action *in summary*. This is the most common usage of the aorist indicative tense-form and is a natural implicature of perfective aspect. Perfective aspect combines with any lexeme that is not punctiliar or stative to create a summary sense. As long as this summary sense is not overruled by context, the *Aktionsart* is summary.

---

2. The following discussion is necessarily simplified for the sake of clarity. In his work on aspect and *Aktionsart*, Francis Pang rightly points out that the relevant elements involved (especially within context) are extremely numerous and interrelated. Pang does not doubt that it is possible to discern predictable patterns of meaning between aspect and *Aktionsart*, but he questions whether such patterns can be recognized in a systematic manner. The approach of this book is to assume that there is more complexity than we are presently able to address, but the method outlined below is nevertheless useful for students and others who seek to understand the basics of verbal aspect and *Aktionsart*. See Francis G. H. Pang, *Revisiting Aspect and Aktionsart: A Corpus Approach to Koine Greek Event Typology*, Linguistic Biblical Studies 14 (Leiden: Brill, 2016), 234–40.

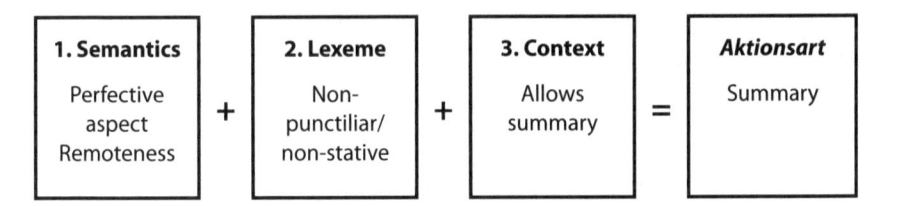

1. Semantics		2. Lexeme		3. Context		Aktionsart
Perfective aspect Remoteness	+	Non-punctiliar/ non-stative	+	Allows summary	=	Summary

John 1:17 ὅτι ὁ νόμος διὰ Μωϋσέως **ἐδόθη**, ἡ χάρις καὶ ἡ ἀλήθεια διὰ Ἰησοῦ Χριστοῦ **ἐγένετο**.

For although the law **was given** through Moses, grace and truth **came** through Jesus Christ.

John 12:41 ταῦτα **εἶπεν** Ἡσαΐας ὅτι **εἶδεν** τὴν δόξαν αὐτοῦ, καὶ **ἐλάλησεν** περὶ αὐτοῦ.

Isaiah **said** these things because **he saw** his glory and **spoke** about him.

Romans 1:21 διότι γνόντες τὸν θεὸν οὐχ ὡς θεὸν **ἐδόξασαν** ἢ **ηὐχαρίστησαν**, ἀλλ᾽ **ἐματαιώθησαν** ἐν τοῖς διαλογισμοῖς αὐτῶν καὶ **ἐσκοτίσθη** ἡ ἀσύνετος αὐτῶν καρδία.

For though they knew God, **they did** not **glorify** him as God or **give him thanks**. Instead, they **became futile** in their thinking, and their senseless minds **were darkened**.

Genesis 1:1 Ἐν ἀρχῇ **ἐποίησεν** ὁ θεὸς τὸν οὐρανὸν καὶ τὴν γῆν.

In the beginning God **made** the sky and the earth.

Punctiliar

Aorist indicative tense-forms sometimes end up depicting a punctiliar action. This is also a natural implicature of perfective aspect. Perfective aspect combines with a punctiliar lexeme to create a punctiliar *Aktionsart*, if this is not over-turned by context. A punctiliar lexeme is a word that describes an action that is, by its very nature, once occurring and instantaneous.

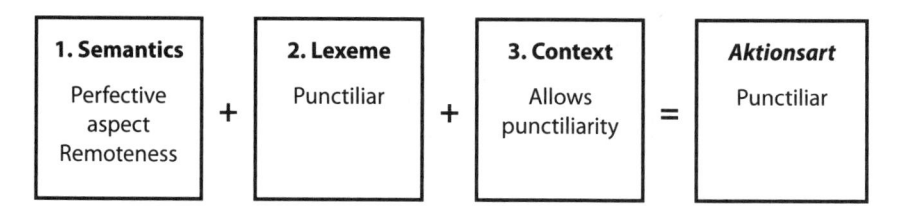

Mark 5:27 ἀκούσασα περὶ τοῦ Ἰησοῦ, ἐλθοῦσα ἐν τῷ ὄχλῳ ὄπισθεν **ἥψατο** τοῦ ἱματίου αὐτοῦ.

Having heard about Jesus, she came behind him in the crowd and **touched** his robe.

Mark 14:47 εἷς δέ τις τῶν παρεστηκότων σπασάμενος τὴν μάχαιραν **ἔπαισεν** τὸν δοῦλον τοῦ ἀρχιερέως καὶ **ἀφεῖλεν** αὐτοῦ τὸ ὠτάριον.

And one of those who stood by drew his sword, **struck** the high priest's slave, and **cut off** his ear.

John 19:34 ἀλλ᾽ εἷς τῶν στρατιωτῶν λόγχῃ αὐτοῦ τὴν πλευρὰν **ἔνυξεν**, καὶ ἐξῆλθεν εὐθὺς αἷμα καὶ ὕδωρ.

But one of the soldiers **pierced** his side with a spear, and at once blood and water came out.

Job 1:19 ἐξαίφνης πνεῦμα μέγα ἐπῆλθεν ἐκ τῆς ἐρήμου καὶ **ἥψατο** τῶν τεσσάρων γωνιῶν τῆς οἰκίας, καὶ **ἔπεσεν** ἡ οἰκία ἐπὶ τὰ παιδία σου.

Suddenly a great wind came from the wilderness and **struck** the four corners of the house, and the house **fell** on your children.

Ingressive

Aorist indicative tense-forms are able to depict the entrance into a state or the beginning of a new action. When perfective aspect combines with a stative lexeme, the entrance into the state is in view, and thus an ingressive *Aktionsart* is formed. Alternatively, non-stative lexemes can form an ingressive sense with perfective aspect due to contextual factors.

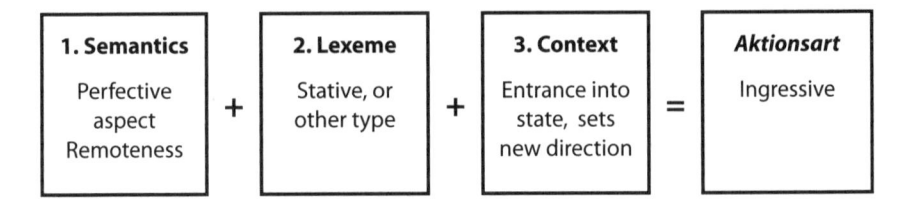

1. Semantics		2. Lexeme		3. Context		Aktionsart
Perfective aspect Remoteness	+	Stative, or other type	+	Entrance into state, sets new direction	=	Ingressive

Matthew 22:7 ὁ δὲ βασιλεὺς **ὠργίσθη** καὶ πέμψας τὰ στρατεύματα αὐτοῦ ἀπώλεσεν τοὺς φονεῖς ἐκείνους καὶ τὴν πόλιν αὐτῶν ἐνέπρησεν.

The king **became angry**, so he sent out his troops, destroyed those murderers, and burned down their city.

John 12:9 Ἔγνω οὖν ὄχλος πολὺς ἐκ τῶν Ἰουδαίων ὅτι ἐκεῖ ἐστιν καὶ ἦλθον οὐ διὰ τὸν Ἰησοῦν μόνον, ἀλλ᾽ ἵνα καὶ τὸν Λάζαρον ἴδωσιν ὃν ἤγειρεν ἐκ νεκρῶν.

Then a large crowd of the Jews **learned** he was there. They came not only because of Jesus but also to see Lazarus, the one he had raised from the dead.

Revelation 20:4 καὶ **ἔζησαν** καὶ ἐβασίλευσαν μετὰ τοῦ Χριστοῦ χίλια ἔτη.

They **came to life** and reigned with the Christ for a thousand years.

Genesis 15:6 καὶ **ἐπίστευσεν** Αβραμ τῷ θεῷ, καὶ ἐλογίσθη αὐτῷ εἰς δικαιοσύνην.

And Abram **believed** God, and it was credited to him as righteousness.

Gnomic

Aorist indicative tense-forms can depict gnomic actions, which are universal and timeless. A gnomic *Aktionsart* is created through the combination of perfective aspect and a context in which generic statements are made. These may involve any type of lexeme. Gnomic aorists are not just found in timeless contexts—they are often best translated as present in temporal reference. As such, the gnomic aorist provides a perfective aspect option for the presentation of events that are present in temporal reference in contrast to the (imperfective) present tense-form.

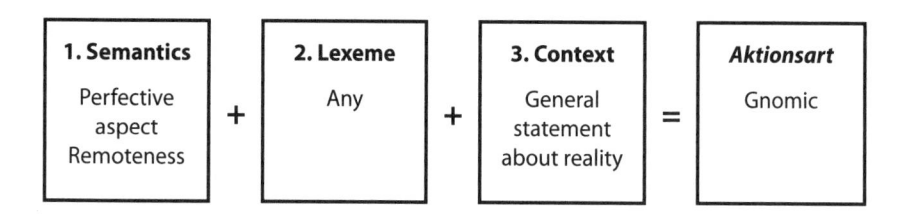

Matthew 23:2 Ἐπὶ τῆς Μωϋσέως καθέδρας **ἐκάθισαν** οἱ γραμματεῖς καὶ οἱ Φαρισαῖοι.

The scribes and the Pharisees **sit** in the chair of Moses.

Luke 7:35 καὶ **ἐδικαιώθη** ἡ σοφία ἀπὸ πάντων τῶν τέκνων αὐτῆς.

Yet wisdom **is vindicated** by all her children.

James 1:11 **ἀνέτειλεν** γὰρ ὁ ἥλιος σὺν τῷ καύσωνι καὶ **ἐξήρανεν** τὸν χόρτον καὶ τὸ ἄνθος αὐτοῦ **ἐξέπεσεν** καὶ ἡ εὐπρέπεια τοῦ προσώπου αὐτοῦ **ἀπώλετο**· οὕτως καὶ ὁ πλούσιος ἐν ταῖς πορείαις αὐτοῦ μαρανθήσεται.

For the sun **rises** with its scorching heat and **dries up** the grass; its flower **falls off**, and its beautiful appearance **is destroyed**. In the same way, the rich man will wither away while pursuing his activities.

Proverbs 14:1 σοφαὶ γυναῖκες **ᾠκοδόμησαν** οἴκους, ἡ δὲ ἄφρων **κατέσκαψεν** ταῖς χερσὶν αὐτῆς.

Wise women **build** homes, but the foolish one **tears it down** with her own hands.

Present Aorist

Though rare in the New Testament, the aorist indicative tense-form can refer to the present even outside of a gnomic usage. In such cases, the aorist indicative provides a perfective option for the depiction of actions that are present in temporal reference. These may involve any type of lexeme, while the present temporal reference is set by the context.

1. Semantics		2. Lexeme		3. Context		Aktionsart
Perfective aspect Remoteness	+	Any	+	Present referring	=	Present aorist

Mark 1:11 καὶ φωνὴ ἐγένετο ἐκ τῶν οὐρανῶν, Σὺ εἶ ὁ υἱός μου ὁ ἀγαπητός, ἐν σοὶ **εὐδόκησα**.

And a voice came from heaven, "You are my beloved Son; with you **I am well pleased**."

Luke 1:47 καὶ **ἠγαλλίασεν** τὸ πνεῦμά μου ἐπὶ τῷ θεῷ τῷ σωτῆρί μου.

And my spirit **rejoices** in God my Savior.

John 13:31 Ὅτε οὖν ἐξῆλθεν, λέγει Ἰησοῦς, Νῦν **ἐδοξάσθη** ὁ υἱὸς τοῦ ἀνθρώπου, καὶ ὁ θεὸς **ἐδοξάσθη** ἐν αὐτῷ.

When he had gone out, Jesus said, "Now the Son of Man **is glorified**, and God **is glorified** in him."

Psalm 7:2 Κύριε ὁ θεός μου, ἐπὶ σοὶ **ἤλπισα**· σῶσόν με ἐκ πάντων τῶν διωκόντων με καὶ ῥῦσαί με.

Lord my God, **I seek refuge** in you; save me from all my pursuers and rescue me.

Future Aorist

More commonly, the aorist indicative tense-form may be used in future-referring contexts. The difference between the future-referring aorist indicative and the future indicative tense-form may be seen in the fact that the aorist semantically encodes remoteness. This remoteness accounts for one of the common ways in which the aorist indicative refers to the future, which is within future conditional sentences. In such cases, remoteness functions logically and contributes to the contingency inherent to such conditions. Future aorist indicatives may involve any type of lexeme, while the future temporal reference is set by the context.

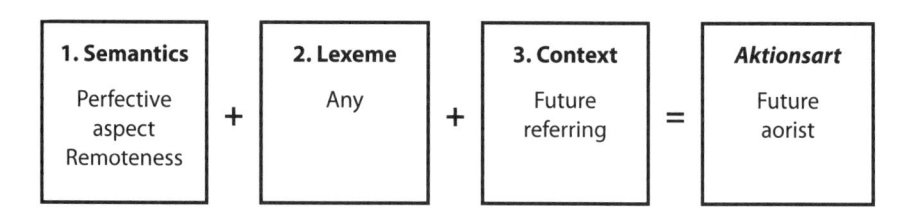

Mark 11:24 διὰ τοῦτο λέγω ὑμῖν, πάντα ὅσα προσεύχεσθε καὶ αἰτεῖσθε, πιστεύετε ὅτι **ἐλάβετε**, καὶ ἔσται ὑμῖν.

Therefore, I tell you, all the things you pray and ask for—believe that **you will receive** them, and you will have them.

Luke 17:6 εἶπεν δὲ ὁ κύριος· εἰ ἔχετε πίστιν ὡς κόκκον σινάπεως, ἐλέγετε ἂν τῇ συκαμίνῳ ταύτῃ, Ἐκριζώθητι καὶ φυτεύθητι ἐν τῇ θαλάσσῃ· καὶ **ὑπήκουσεν** ἂν ὑμῖν.

"If you have faith the size of a mustard seed" the Lord said, "you can say to this mulberry tree, 'Be uprooted and planted in the sea,' and **it will obey** you."

Revelation 10:7 ἀλλ' ἐν ταῖς ἡμέραις τῆς φωνῆς τοῦ ἑβδόμου ἀγγέλου, ὅταν μέλλῃ σαλπίζειν, καὶ **ἐτελέσθη** τὸ μυστήριον τοῦ θεοῦ, ὡς εὐηγγέλισεν τοὺς ἑαυτοῦ δούλους τοὺς προφήτας.

But in the days of the sound of the seventh angel, when he will blow his trumpet, then God's hidden plan **will be completed**, as he announced to his servants the prophets.

Zephaniah 1:11 θρηνήσατε, οἱ κατοικοῦντες τὴν κατακεκομμένην, ὅτι **ὡμοιώθη** πᾶς ὁ λαὸς Χανααν, **ἐξωλεθρεύθησαν** πάντες οἱ ἐπηρμένοι ἀργυρίῳ.

Wail, you residents of the destroyed part, for all the people **will be made like** Canaan; all those loaded with silver **will be utterly destroyed**.

AKTIONSART INTERACTIONS—FUTURE INDICATIVE TENSE-FORM

There are several ways in which the future indicative tense-form functions pragmatically. Below are the most common and important *Aktionsart* descriptions of future indicative usage and explanations of how the *Aktionsart* values are arrived at. It will be noticed that these *Aktionsarten* are parallel to those found in aorist usage. This is to be expected, given their sharing of perfective aspect.

Summary Future

Future indicative tense-forms often end up depicting a process or action *in summary*. This is the most common usage of the future tense-form and is a natural implicature of perfective aspect. Perfective aspect combines with any lexeme that is not punctiliar or stative to create a summary sense. As long as this summary sense is not overruled by context, the *Aktionsart* is summary.

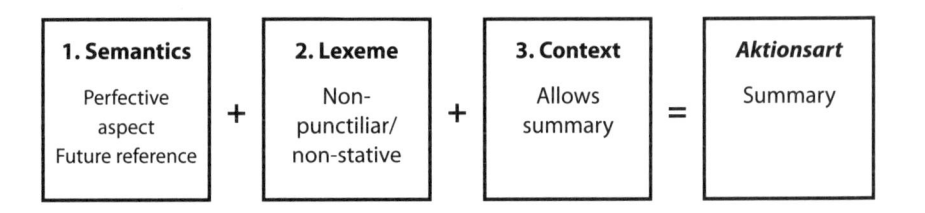

Matthew 10:21 παραδώσει δὲ ἀδελφὸς ἀδελφὸν εἰς θάνατον καὶ πατὴρ τέκνον, καὶ **ἐπαναστήσονται** τέκνα ἐπὶ γονεῖς καὶ **θανατώσουσιν** αὐτούς.

Brother **will betray** brother to death, and a father his child. Children will even **rise up** against their parents and **will put them to death**.

Luke 13:24 Ἀγωνίζεσθε εἰσελθεῖν διὰ τῆς στενῆς θύρας, ὅτι πολλοί, λέγω ὑμῖν, **ζητήσουσιν** εἰσελθεῖν καὶ **οὐκ ἰσχύσουσιν**.

Make every effort to enter through the narrow door, because I tell you, many **will try** to enter and **won't be able**.

John 16:13–14 ὅταν δὲ ἔλθῃ ἐκεῖνος, τὸ πνεῦμα τῆς ἀληθείας, **ὁδηγήσει** ὑμᾶς ἐν τῇ ἀληθείᾳ πάσῃ· **οὐ γὰρ λαλήσει** ἀφ᾽ ἑαυτοῦ, ἀλλ᾽ ὅσα ἀκούσει **λαλήσει** καὶ τὰ ἐρχόμενα **ἀναγγελεῖ** ὑμῖν. ἐκεῖνος ἐμὲ **δοξάσει**, ὅτι ἐκ τοῦ ἐμοῦ **λήμψεται** καὶ **ἀναγγελεῖ** ὑμῖν.

When the Spirit of truth comes, **he will guide** you into all the truth. For **he will not speak** on his own, but **he will speak** whatever **he hears**. He **will** also **declare** to you what is to come. He **will glorify** me, because **he will take** from what is mine and **declare** it to you.

Zechariah 14:13 καὶ **ἔσται** ἐν τῇ ἡμέρᾳ ἐκείνῃ ἔκστασις κυρίου ἐπ᾽ αὐτοὺς μεγάλη, καὶ **ἐπιλήμψονται** ἕκαστος τῆς χειρὸς τοῦ πλησίον αὐτοῦ, καὶ **συμπλακήσεται** ἡ χεὶρ αὐτοῦ πρὸς χεῖρα τοῦ πλησίον αὐτοῦ.

On that day a great panic from the Lord **will be** upon them, so that each **will seize** the hand of his neighbor, and his hand **will be joined** to the hand of his neighbor.

Punctiliar

Future indicative tense-forms sometimes end up depicting a punctiliar action. This is also a natural implicature of perfective aspect. Perfective aspect combines with a punctiliar lexeme to create a punctiliar *Aktionsart*, if this is not overturned by context. A punctiliar lexeme is a word that describes an action that is, by its very nature, once occurring and instantaneous.

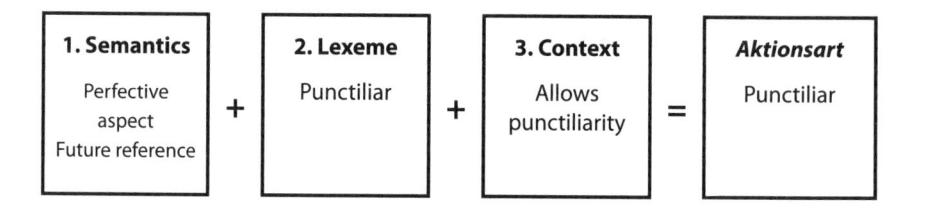

Mark 14:27 καὶ λέγει αὐτοῖς ὁ Ἰησοῦς ὅτι Πάντες σκανδαλισθήσεσθε, ὅτι γέγραπται, **Πατάξω** τὸν ποιμένα, καὶ τὰ πρόβατα διασκορπισθήσονται.

Then Jesus said to them, "All of you will run away, because it is written: '**I will strike** the shepherd, and the sheep will be scattered.'"

Luke 5:37 καὶ οὐδεὶς βάλλει οἶνον νέον εἰς ἀσκοὺς παλαιούς· εἰ δὲ μή γε, **ῥήξει** ὁ οἶνος ὁ νέος τοὺς ἀσκοὺς καὶ αὐτὸς ἐκχυθήσεται καὶ οἱ ἀσκοὶ ἀπολοῦνται.

And no one puts new wine into old wineskins. Otherwise, the new wine **will burst** the skins, it will spill, and the skins will be ruined.

Acts 1:5 ὅτι Ἰωάννης μὲν ἐβάπτισεν ὕδατι, ὑμεῖς δὲ ἐν πνεύματι **βαπτισθήσεσθε** ἁγίῳ οὐ μετὰ πολλὰς ταύτας ἡμέρας.

For John baptized with water, but you **will be baptized** with the Holy Spirit not many days from now.

Daniel 11:19 ἐπιστρέψει τὸ πρόσωπον αὐτοῦ εἰς τὸ κατισχῦσαι τὴν χώραν αὐτοῦ καὶ **προσκόψει** καὶ πεσεῖται καὶ οὐχ εὑρεθήσεται.

He will turn his face in order to strengthen his country, and **he will stumble** and will fall and will not be found.

Ingressive

As with the aorist indicative tense-form, the future indicative tense-form is able to depict ingressive actions, in which the beginning of a state or action is in view. This occurs when the perfective aspect of the future form combines with stative lexemes or when the context denotes a new situation that signals the beginning of the action.

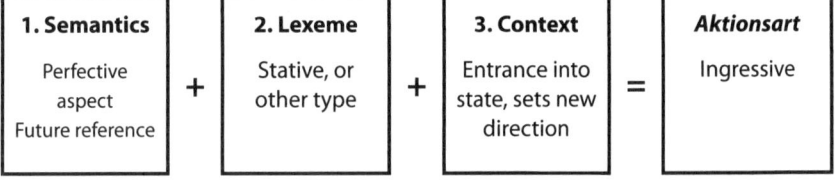

1. Semantics		2. Lexeme		3. Context		Aktionsart
Perfective aspect Future reference	+	Stative, or other type	+	Entrance into state, sets new direction	=	Ingressive

Matthew 9:18 Ταῦτα αὐτοῦ λαλοῦντος αὐτοῖς ἰδοὺ ἄρχων εἷς ἐλθὼν προσεκύνει αὐτῷ λέγων ὅτι Ἡ θυγάτηρ μου ἄρτι ἐτελεύτησεν· ἀλλὰ ἐλθὼν ἐπίθες τὴν χεῖρά σου ἐπ᾽ αὐτήν, καὶ **ζήσεται**.

While he was saying these things to them, suddenly a synagogue leader came and knelt before him, saying, "My daughter has just died; but come and lay your hand on her, and **she will live.**"

Matthew 19:21 ἔφη αὐτῷ ὁ Ἰησοῦς, Εἰ θέλεις τέλειος εἶναι, ὕπαγε πώλησόν σου τὰ ὑπάρχοντα καὶ δὸς τοῖς πτωχοῖς, καὶ **ἕξεις** θησαυρὸν ἐν οὐρανοῖς, καὶ δεῦρο ἀκολούθει μοι.

Jesus said to him, "If you want to be perfect, go, sell your possessions and give to the poor, and **you will have** treasure in heaven; then come, follow me."

Mark 4:13 Καὶ λέγει αὐτοῖς, Οὐκ οἴδατε τὴν παραβολὴν ταύτην, καὶ πῶς πάσας τὰς παραβολὰς **γνώσεσθε;**

And he said to them, "Do you not understand this parable? How then **will you understand** all the parables?"

1 Kings 1:24 καὶ εἶπεν Ναθαν Κύριέ μου βασιλεῦ, σὺ εἶπας Αδωνιας **βασιλεύσει** ὀπίσω μου καὶ αὐτὸς **καθήσεται** ἐπὶ τοῦ θρόνου μου;

And Nathan said, "My lord O king, did you say, 'Adonias **will become king** after me, and he **will sit** on my throne'?"

EXERCISES FOR AORIST AND FUTURE INDICATIVE TENSE-FORMS

For each passage, (1) write about the semantic meaning of the indicative verb, (2) state the contribution of the lexeme, and (3) discuss the function of the verb in context. Once you have written your answers, summarize your findings in the boxes below each passage.

When considering the context, keep an eye out for any elements that may influence the way the verb is understood. This might be something obvious like a temporal word or phrase (e.g., "yesterday," "all day long," "after," etc.). Or it might be something less obvious, like a hint that an action should be understood as repeating or is part of a generalized reality. Context is an open-ended category, and it takes some practice to feel competent with it.

Example:
John 19:34 ἀλλ᾽ εἷς τῶν στρατιωτῶν λόγχῃ αὐτοῦ τὴν πλευρὰν **ἔνυξεν**, καὶ ἐξῆλθεν εὐθὺς αἷμα καὶ ὕδωρ.

But one of the soldiers **pierced** his side with a spear, and at once blood and water came out.

1. Semantic meaning of the indicative verb. The aorist indicative semantically encodes perfective aspect and the spatial value of remoteness.
2. Contribution of the lexeme. The lexeme is punctiliar; it is an instantaneous action.
3. Function in context. The context allows for a punctiliar interpretation.

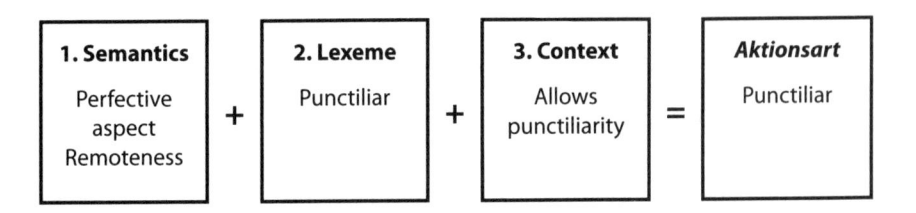

John 7:32 (x2) Ἤκουσαν οἱ Φαρισαῖοι τοῦ ὄχλου γογγύζοντος περὶ αὐτοῦ ταῦτα, καὶ **ἀπέστειλαν** οἱ ἀρχιερεῖς καὶ οἱ Φαρισαῖοι ὑπηρέτας ἵνα πιάσωσιν αὐτόν.

The Pharisees **heard** the crowd muttering these things about him, so the chief priests and the Pharisees **sent** temple police to arrest him.

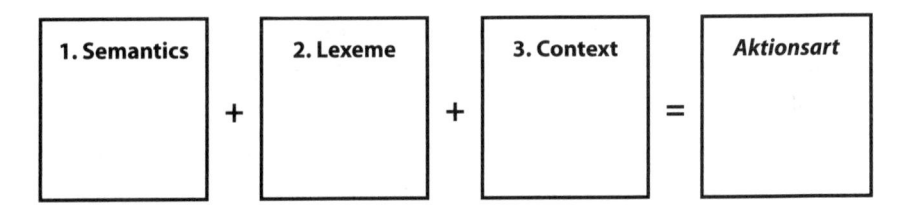

Romans 6:14 ἁμαρτία γὰρ ὑμῶν **οὐ κυριεύσει**· οὐ γάρ ἐστε ὑπὸ νόμον ἀλλὰ ὑπὸ χάριν.

For sin **will not rule** over you, because you are not under law but under grace.

1. Semantics		2. Lexeme		3. Context		Aktionsart
	+		+		=	

Romans 3:23 πάντες γὰρ **ἥμαρτον** καὶ ὑστεροῦνται τῆς δόξης τοῦ θεοῦ.

For all **have sinned** and fall short of the glory of God.

1. Semantics		2. Lexeme		3. Context		Aktionsart
	+		+		=	

John 1:10 ἐν τῷ κόσμῳ ἦν, καὶ ὁ κόσμος δι᾽ αὐτοῦ ἐγένετο, καὶ ὁ κόσμος αὐτὸν **οὐκ ἔγνω**.

He was in the world, and the world was created through him, yet the world **did not recognize** him.

1. Semantics		2. Lexeme		3. Context		Aktionsart
	+		+		=	

Mark 14:27 καὶ λέγει αὐτοῖς ὁ Ἰησοῦς ὅτι Πάντες σκανδαλισθήσεσθε, ὅτι γέγραπται, **Πατάξω** τὸν ποιμένα, καὶ τὰ πρόβατα διασκορπισθήσονται.

Then Jesus said to them, "All of you will run away, because it is written: '**I will strike** the shepherd, and the sheep will be scattered.'"

1. Semantics		2. Lexeme		3. Context		Aktionsart
	+		+		=	

John 7:26 καὶ ἴδε παρρησίᾳ λαλεῖ καὶ οὐδὲν αὐτῷ λέγουσιν. μήποτε ἀληθῶς **ἔγνωσαν** οἱ ἄρχοντες ὅτι οὗτός ἐστιν ὁ Χριστός;

Yet, look! He's speaking publicly and they're saying nothing to him. Can it be true that the authorities **know** he is the Christ?

1. Semantics		2. Lexeme		3. Context		Aktionsart
	+		+		=	

Romans 8:11 εἰ δὲ τὸ πνεῦμα τοῦ ἐγείραντος τὸν Ἰησοῦν ἐκ νεκρῶν οἰκεῖ ἐν ὑμῖν, ὁ ἐγείρας Χριστὸν ἐκ νεκρῶν **ζῳοποιήσει** καὶ τὰ θνητὰ σώματα ὑμῶν διὰ τοῦ ἐνοικοῦντος αὐτοῦ πνεύματος ἐν ὑμῖν.

And if the Spirit of him who raised Jesus from the dead lives in you, then he who raised Christ from the dead **will also bring** your mortal bodies **to life** through his Spirit who lives in you.

1. Semantics		2. Lexeme		3. Context		Aktionsart
	+		+		=	

Romans 8:30 (x6) οὓς δὲ **προώρισεν**, τούτους καὶ **ἐκάλεσεν**· καὶ οὓς **ἐκάλεσεν**, τούτους καὶ **ἐδικαίωσεν**· οὓς δὲ **ἐδικαίωσεν**, τούτους καὶ **ἐδόξασεν**.

And those **he predestines, he** also **calls**; and those **he calls, he** also **justifies**; and those **he justifies, he** also **glorifies.**

1. Semantics		2. Lexeme		3. Context		Aktionsart
	+		+		=	

Genesis 4:12 ὅτι ἐργᾷ τὴν γῆν, καὶ **οὐ προσθήσει** τὴν ἰσχὺν αὐτῆς δοῦναί σοι· στένων καὶ τρέμων **ἔσῃ** ἐπὶ τῆς γῆς.

For **you will till** the earth, and **it will not continue** to yield its strength to you; **you will be** groaning and trembling on the earth.

1. Semantics		2. Lexeme		3. Context		Aktionsart
	+		+		=	

CHAPTER 9

Perfect and Pluperfect Indicative Tense-Forms

SEMANTICS

VERBAL ASPECT

The verbal aspect of the perfect and pluperfect indicative tense-forms is a matter of debate, with options ranging from stative, perfective, imperfective, or both perfective and imperfective. In part, this confusion stems from the assumption that the perfect in Greek is similar to that in Latin. Nevertheless, regarding the perfect and pluperfect indicative tense-forms as encoding imperfective aspect provides the best power of explanation and is therefore the position adopted here.[1]

The perfect and pluperfect indicative tense-forms encode imperfective aspect at the semantic level. Imperfective aspect views an action or state from the inside; it is the internal viewpoint. Using the illustration of the reporter and the street parade, the internal viewpoint is the view from the street, with the parade unfolding close-up. Unlike the view from afar (in the helicopter = perfective aspect), the reporter on the street does not view the beginning or end of the parade but has a view of the details.

---

1. For extensive argumentation along such lines, see Constantine R. Campbell, *Verbal Aspect, the Indicative Mood, and Narrative: Soundings in the Greek of the New Testament*, Studies in Biblical Greek 13 (New York: Peter Lang, 2007), 184–89.

SPATIAL QUALITIES

Since the perfect and pluperfect indicative tense-forms are here regarded as imperfective in aspect, the question must be raised as to how they are to be distinguished from the present and imperfect indicative tense-forms. Just as the present and imperfect indicative tense-forms semantically encode the spatial values of proximity and remoteness respectively, so too the perfect and pluperfect indicatives encode these values respectively.

For these forms, however, the spatial values are heightened. Thus, the perfect indicative tense-form semantically encodes imperfective aspect with the spatial value of heightened proximity. The pluperfect indicative tense-form semantically encodes imperfective aspect with the spatial value of heightened remoteness. The diagram below demonstrates the difference between proximity (present indicative tense-form) and heightened proximity (perfect indicative tense-form).

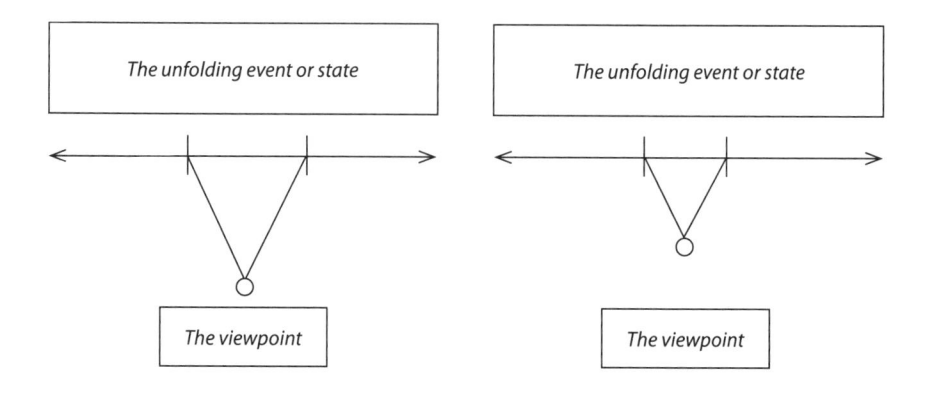

Proximate imperfectivity (present tense-form)   *Imperfectivity and heightened proximity*

The unfolding event or state   *The unfolding event or state*

The viewpoint   *The viewpoint*

PRAGMATICS

NARRATIVE FUNCTIONS
Perfect Tense-Form

In narrative texts, the perfect indicative is most often found in discourse—direct discourse, indirect discourse, and authorial discourse, as illustrated by these examples. In this way, the distribution of the perfect indicative parallels that of the present.

John 7:28 ἔκραξεν οὖν ἐν τῷ ἱερῷ διδάσκων ὁ Ἰησοῦς καὶ λέγων, Κἀμὲ **οἴδατε** καὶ **οἴδατε** πόθεν εἰμί· καὶ ἀπ' ἐμαυτοῦ **οὐκ ἐλήλυθα**, ἀλλ' ἔστιν ἀληθινὸς ὁ πέμψας με, ὃν ὑμεῖς **οὐκ οἴδατε**.

As he was teaching in the temple complex, Jesus cried out, "**You know** me and **you know** where I am from. Yet **I have not come** on my own, but the One who sent me is true. **You don't know** him."

John 15:24 εἰ τὰ ἔργα μὴ ἐποίησα ἐν αὐτοῖς ἃ οὐδεὶς ἄλλος ἐποίησεν, ἁμαρτίαν οὐκ εἴχοσαν· νῦν δὲ καὶ **ἑωράκασιν** καὶ **μεμισήκασιν** καὶ ἐμὲ καὶ τὸν πατέρα μου.

If I had not done the works among them that no one else has done, they would not have sin. Now **they see** and **hate** both me and my Father.

Discourse creates a proximate-imperfective context as the speech or thought is presented immediately before the reader's eyes, as though unfolding. As such, the perfect indicative is attracted to discourse, being a proximate-imperfective tense-form. It is to be remembered, however, that the discourse function of the perfect tense-form is a pragmatic feature and is therefore cancelable.

Pluperfect Tense-Form

The pluperfect indicative is most often found in narrative proper rather than discourse. Its normal function within narrative proper is to provide offline material. While aorists typically provide the skeletal structure of the narrative mainline, pluperfects most often provide supplementary information that describes, characterizes, or explains, as illustrated by these examples. In this way, the distribution of pluperfects parallels that of the imperfect.

Luke 4:41 ἐξήρχετο δὲ καὶ δαιμόνια ἀπὸ πολλῶν κράζοντα καὶ λέγοντα ὅτι Σὺ εἶ ὁ υἱὸς τοῦ θεοῦ. καὶ ἐπιτιμῶν οὐκ εἴα αὐτὰ λαλεῖν, ὅτι **ᾔδεισαν** τὸν Χριστὸν αὐτὸν εἶναι.

Also, demons were coming out of many, shouting and saying, "You are the Son of God!" But he rebuked them and would not allow them to speak, because **they knew** he was the Christ.

John 7:30 Ἐζήτουν οὖν αὐτὸν πιάσαι, καὶ οὐδεὶς ἐπέβαλεν ἐπ᾽ αὐτὸν τὴν χεῖρα, ὅτι **οὔπω ἐληλύθει** ἡ ὥρα αὐτοῦ.

Then they tried to seize him. Yet no one laid a hand on him because his hour **had not yet come.**

Offline material is inherently remote-imperfective in nature, as the supplementary information provides an internal view (imperfective), but this is not presented as being immediately before the reader's eyes. It supplements the remote mainline and thus is remote in nature. As such, the pluperfect indicative is attracted to offline material, since it is a remote-imperfective tense-form. It is to be remembered, however, that the offline function of the pluperfect indicative tense-form is a pragmatic feature and is therefore cancelable.

AKTIONSART INTERACTIONS—PERFECT TENSE-FORM

Aktionsart refers to the way a verb behaves in the text when all features of the language and text bear upon it. There are three main elements that determine a particular verb's *Aktionsart*: semantics, lexeme, and context. Accordingly, there are three steps required to ascertain what an indicative verb is doing in the text:

1. Identify the semantic value of the indicative verb.
2. Consider the lexeme and its interaction with the semantics.
3. Consider the context.

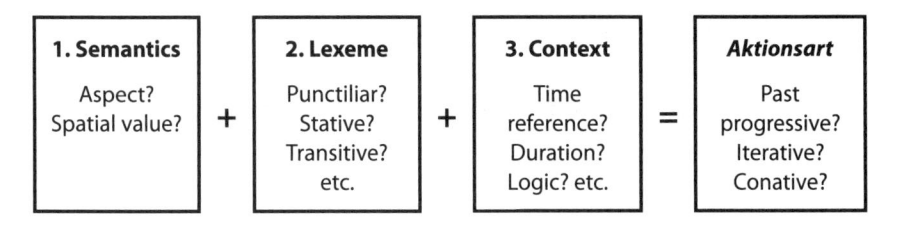

1. Semantics		2. Lexeme		3. Context		*Aktionsart*
Aspect? Spatial value?	+	Punctiliar? Stative? Transitive? etc.	+	Time reference? Duration? Logic? etc.	=	Past progressive? Iterative? Conative?

The word "have" in translation of perfect indicatives comes from the traditional understanding of the perfect, in which the verb was understood as conveying a past action with present consequences. While rendering the perfect indicative will occasionally require the word "have" in our translations, this should not be supplied by default. Context will determine whether "have" needs to be included in our translation. Perfect indicatives will normally refer either to the present (e.g., stative perfects) or to the past (e.g., historical perfects), and as such the "have" translation will only be required in certain circumstances.

There are several ways in which the perfect indicative tense-form functions pragmatically. Below are the most common and important *Aktionsart* descriptions of perfect indicative usage and explanations of how the *Aktionsart* values are arrived at.[2]

Stative

Perfect indicative tense-forms often end up depicting a state. This is also a natural implicature of imperfective aspect. Imperfective aspect combines with a stative lexeme to create a stative *Aktionsart*, if this is not overturned by context. A stative lexeme is a word that describes a state of being rather than a process or transitive action. Sometimes the context (or passive voice) can create a stative *Aktionsart* even if the lexeme is not in itself stative. Stative perfects are normally present in their temporal reference.

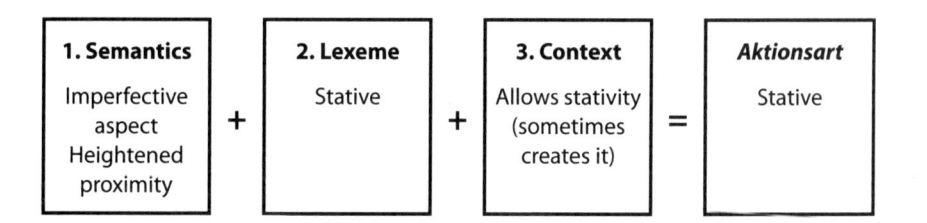

Mark 1:15 . . . καὶ λέγων ὅτι **Πεπλήρωται** ὁ καιρὸς καὶ **ἤγγικεν** ἡ βασιλεία τοῦ θεοῦ· μετανοεῖτε καὶ πιστεύετε ἐν τῷ εὐαγγελίῳ.

. . . and saying, "The time **is fulfilled**, and the kingdom of God **is near**. Repent and believe in the good news!"

---

2. The following discussion is necessarily simplified for the sake of clarity. In his work on aspect and *Aktionsart*, Francis Pang rightly points out that the relevant elements involved (especially within context) are extremely numerous and interrelated. Pang does not doubt that it is possible to discern predictable patterns of meaning between aspect and *Aktionsart*, but he questions whether such patterns can be recognized in a systematic manner. The approach of this book is to assume that there is more complexity than we are presently able to address, but the method outlined below is nevertheless useful for students and others who seek to understand the basics of verbal aspect and *Aktionsart*. See Francis G. H. Pang, *Revisiting Aspect and* Aktionsart: *A Corpus Approach to Koine Greek Event Typology*, Linguistic Biblical Studies 14 (Leiden: Brill, 2016), 234–40.

John 7:28 ἔκραξεν οὖν ἐν τῷ ἱερῷ διδάσκων ὁ Ἰησοῦς καὶ λέγων, Κἀμὲ **οἴδατε** καὶ **οἴδατε** πόθεν εἰμί· καὶ ἀπ᾽ ἐμαυτοῦ οὐκ ἐλήλυθα, ἀλλ᾽ ἔστιν ἀληθινὸς ὁ πέμψας με, ὃν ὑμεῖς **οὐκ οἴδατε**.

As he was teaching in the temple complex, Jesus cried out, "**You know** me and **you know** where I am from. Yet I have not come on my own, but the one who sent me is true. You **don't know** him."

John 11:27 λέγει αὐτῷ, Ναὶ κύριε, ἐγὼ **πεπίστευκα** ὅτι σὺ εἶ ὁ Χριστὸς ὁ υἱὸς τοῦ θεοῦ ὁ εἰς τὸν κόσμον ἐρχόμενος.

"Yes, Lord," she told him, "**I believe** you are the Christ, the Son of God, the One coming into the world."

Psalm 40:12 ἐν τούτῳ ἔγνων ὅτι **τεθέληκάς** με, ὅτι οὐ μὴ ἐπιχαρῇ ὁ ἐχθρός μου ἐπ᾽ ἐμέ.

By this I know that **you delight** in me: my enemy does not shout in triumph over me.

Historical Perfect

The perfect indicative tense-form is frequently used in nonpresent contexts, most often past-referring ones. These are best translated like aorist indicatives, though they are not the same as aorists in meaning. There are two basic types of historical perfects: those that introduce discourse and those that employ lexemes of propulsion. In this way, the historical perfect parallels the historical present almost exactly; the same functions are observed with the same group of lexemes.

First, historical perfects that introduce discourse utilize the perfect tense-form because they are leading into a proximate-imperfective context (discourse). In such cases, the proximate-imperfective nature of discourse "spills over" onto the verb that introduces it.

Second, lexemes of propulsion are verbs that convey transition—movement from one point to another. These include verbs of coming and going, lifting, taking, giving, and so on. The proximate-imperfective nature of the perfect tense-form combines with these lexemes in order to highlight the transition that is conveyed. There is no obvious way to convey this in translation.

One caveat to note is that verbs of propulsion do not necessarily form historical perfects. As with the historical present, such lexemes may also be used to refer to the present rather than the past. The point is, rather, that these lexemes may refer to the past when found in past contexts.

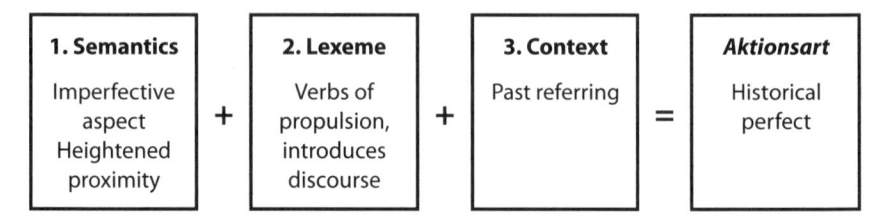

Mark 9:13 ἀλλὰ λέγω ὑμῖν ὅτι καὶ Ἠλίας **ἐλήλυθεν**, καὶ ἐποίησαν αὐτῷ ὅσα ἤθελον, καθὼς γέγραπται ἐπ᾽ αὐτόν.

But I tell you that Elijah **came**, and they did to him whatever they wanted, just as it is written about him.

Luke 4:18 Πνεῦμα κυρίου ἐπ᾽ ἐμὲ οὗ εἵνεκεν ἔχρισέν με εὐαγγελίσασθαι πτωχοῖς, **ἀπέσταλκέν** με, κηρύξαι αἰχμαλώτοις ἄφεσιν καὶ τυφλοῖς ἀνάβλεψιν, ἀποστεῖλαι τεθραυσμένους ἐν ἀφέσει.

The Spirit of the Lord is on me, because he anointed me to preach good news to the poor. **He sent** me to proclaim freedom to the captives and recovery of sight to the blind, to set free the oppressed.

John 1:15 Ἰωάννης μαρτυρεῖ περὶ αὐτοῦ καὶ **κέκραγεν** λέγων, Οὗτος ἦν ὃν εἶπον, Ὁ ὀπίσω μου ἐρχόμενος ἔμπροσθέν μου γέγονεν, ὅτι πρῶτός μου ἦν.

John testified concerning him and **exclaimed**, "This was the one of whom I said, 'The one coming after me has surpassed me, because he was before me.'"

Genesis 42:30 **Λελάληκεν** ὁ ἄνθρωπος ὁ κύριος τῆς γῆς πρὸς ἡμᾶς σκληρὰ καὶ ἔθετο ἡμᾶς ἐν φυλακῇ ὡς κατασκοπεύοντας τὴν γῆν.

The man who is the lord of the country **spoke** harshly to us and put us in custody, accusing us of spying on the country.

Progressive

Perfect indicative tense-forms sometimes end up depicting a process or action *in progress*. This usage of the perfect indicative tense-form is not widely acknowledged, though it is a natural expression of imperfective aspect. Imperfective aspect may combine with any lexeme that is not punctiliar or stative to create a progressive sense. As long as this progressive sense is not overruled by context, the *Aktionsart* may be progressive.

A word of caution: sometimes it is difficult to decide whether a perfect indicative is progressive or historical when the context would allow for either. Care must be exercised here, as the choice can significantly influence the outcome.

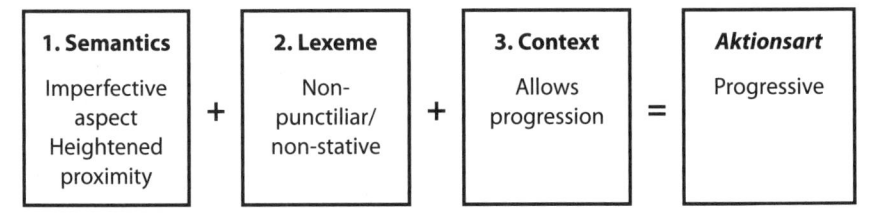

Mark 7:37 καὶ ὑπερπερισσῶς ἐξεπλήσσοντο λέγοντες, Καλῶς πάντα **πεποίηκεν**, καὶ τοὺς κωφοὺς ποιεῖ ἀκούειν καὶ τοὺς ἀλάλους λαλεῖν.

They were extremely astonished and said, "**He does** everything well! He even makes deaf people hear and people unable to speak, talk!"

John 17:6 Ἐφανέρωσά σου τὸ ὄνομα τοῖς ἀνθρώποις οὓς ἔδωκάς μοι ἐκ τοῦ κόσμου. σοὶ ἦσαν κἀμοὶ αὐτοὺς ἔδωκας καὶ τὸν λόγον σου **τετήρηκαν**.

I have revealed your name to the men you gave me from the world. They were yours, you gave them to me, and **they keep** your word.

Acts 21:28 . . . κράζοντες, Ἄνδρες Ἰσραηλῖται, βοηθεῖτε· οὗτός ἐστιν ὁ ἄνθρωπος ὁ κατὰ τοῦ λαοῦ καὶ τοῦ νόμου καὶ τοῦ τόπου τούτου πάντας πανταχῇ διδάσκων, ἔτι τε καὶ Ἕλληνας εἰσήγαγεν εἰς τὸ ἱερὸν καὶ **κεκοίνωκεν** τὸν ἅγιον τόπον τοῦτον.

. . . shouting, "Men of Israel, help! This is the man who teaches everyone everywhere against our people, our law, and this place. What's more, he also brought Greeks into the temple and **profanes** this holy place."

Acts 25:11 εἰ μὲν οὖν ἀδικῶ καὶ ἄξιον θανάτου **πέπραχά** τι, οὐ παραιτοῦμαι τὸ ἀποθανεῖν· εἰ δὲ οὐδέν ἐστιν ὧν οὗτοι κατηγοροῦσίν μου, οὐδείς με δύναται αὐτοῖς χαρίσασθαι· Καίσαρα ἐπικαλοῦμαι.

If then I am doing wrong, or **am doing** anything deserving of death, I do not refuse to die, but if there is nothing to what these men accuse me of, no one can give me up to them. I appeal to Caesar!

1 Corinthians 7:15 εἰ δὲ ὁ ἄπιστος χωρίζεται, χωριζέσθω· οὐ δεδούλωται ὁ ἀδελφὸς ἢ ἡ ἀδελφὴ ἐν τοῖς τοιούτοις· ἐν δὲ εἰρήνῃ **κέκληκεν** ἡμᾶς ὁ θεός.

But if the unbeliever leaves, let him leave. A brother or a sister is not bound in such cases. God **calls** us to peace.

2 Timothy 4:7 τὸν καλὸν ἀγῶνα **ἠγώνισμαι**, τὸν δρόμον **τετέλεκα**, τὴν πίστιν **τετήρηκα**.

I **am fighting** the good fight, I **am finishing** the race, I **am keeping** the faith.

Jeremiah 1:12 καὶ εἶπεν κύριος πρός με Καλῶς ἑώρακας, διότι **ἐγρήγορα** ἐγὼ ἐπὶ τοὺς λόγους μου τοῦ ποιῆσαι αὐτούς.

The Lord said to me, "You have seen correctly, for I **am watching** my words to accomplish them."

PRAGMATICS OF HEIGHTENED PROXIMITY

There is an extra step required in understanding perfect indicatives. The spatial value of heightened proximity adds another level to the analysis of perfect indicative tense-forms above *Aktionsart*. Once the *Aktionsart* of a particular perfect is established, the pragmatic expression of heightened proximity must be addressed. The semantic value of heightened proximity may be expressed pragmatically in one of two ways: intensification or prominence. It is not always clear which pragmatic expression is most suitable in particular instances, but a basic rule of thumb is to see if intensification is possible or likely; if not, prominence is expressed rather than intensification.

Intensification

Because heightened proximity creates a super closeup view of an action, it may cause some actions to become intensified. This means that the transitive lexeme is "sharpened" beyond its normal usage.

The following examples demonstrate the manner in which a perfect may intensify a lexeme beyond its normal meaning: ἥγημαι, "be firmly convinced" (ἡγοῦμαι, "believe, think"), τεθαύμακα, "be surprised" (θαυμάζω, "wonder, marvel"), πεφόβημαι, "be terrified" (φοβοῦμαι, "be afraid"), σεσιώπηκα, "maintain complete silence" (σιωπῶ, "be silent").[3]

Prominence

When intensification is not easily applied to a lexeme or is not deemed appropriate in the context, prominence is the pragmatic expression of heightened proximity. The concept of prominence is here taken to refer to the degree to which an element stands out from others in its environment. Thus, prominence is roughly synonymous with *stress*. Often such prominence is not easily expressed in English translation, though the use of italics should be considered as a legitimate technique for this purpose in some instances.

AKTIONSART INTERACTIONS—PLUPERFECT INDICATIVE TENSE-FORM

There are only a few ways in which the pluperfect indicative tense-form functions pragmatically. Below are the most common and important *Aktionsart* descriptions of pluperfect indicative usage along with explanations of how the *Aktionsart* values are arrived at. It will be noticed that the pluperfect indicative is similar in usage to the imperfect indicative tense-form. This is to be expected, given their sharing of imperfective aspect and remoteness.

The word "had" in translation of pluperfect indicatives comes from the traditional understanding of the pluperfect, in which the verb was understood as conveying an action antecedent to the past action of the main verb

---

3. See Albert Rijksbaron, *The Syntax and Semantics of the Verb in Classical Greek: An Introduction* (Amsterdam: Gieben, 1984), 36.

and consequences present at the time of that past action. While rendering the pluperfect indicative will often require the word "had" in our translations, this should not be supplied by default. Context will determine whether "had" needs to be included in our translation. Pluperfects will normally refer either to the past, in which they stand parallel to imperfects, or to the past-past, in which they stand "behind" imperfects and need to be rendered with "had" in translation.

Stative

Pluperfect indicative tense-forms often end up depicting a state. This is also a natural implicature of imperfective aspect. Imperfective aspect combines with a stative lexeme to create a stative *Aktionsart*, if this is not overturned by context. A stative lexeme is a word that describes a state of being rather than a process or transitive action. Sometimes the context (or passive voice) can create a stative *Aktionsart* even if the lexeme is not in itself stative.

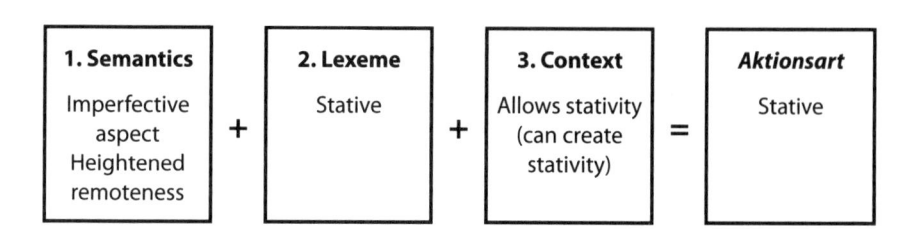

Luke 23:10 εἰστήκεισαν δὲ οἱ ἀρχιερεῖς καὶ οἱ γραμματεῖς εὐτόνως κατηγοροῦντες αὐτοῦ.

The chief priests and the scribes **were standing by**, vehemently accusing him.

John 2:9 ὡς δὲ ἐγεύσατο ὁ ἀρχιτρίκλινος τὸ ὕδωρ οἶνον γεγενημένον καὶ **οὐκ ᾔδει** πόθεν ἐστίν, οἱ δὲ διάκονοι **ᾔδεισαν** οἱ ἠντληκότες τὸ ὕδωρ, φωνεῖ τὸν νυμφίον ὁ ἀρχιτρίκλινος.

When the chief servant tasted the water (after it had become wine), **he did not know** where it came from—though the servants who had drawn the water **knew**, the chief servant called the bridegroom.

Luke 4:29 καὶ ἀναστάντες ἐξέβαλον αὐτὸν ἔξω τῆς πόλεως καὶ ἤγαγον αὐτὸν ἕως ὀφρύος τοῦ ὄρους ἐφ' οὗ ἡ πόλις **ᾠκοδόμητο** αὐτῶν ὥστε κατακρημνίσαι αὐτόν.

They got up, drove him out of town, and brought him to the edge of the hill their town **was built on**, intending to hurl him over the cliff.

Deuteronomy 32:37 καὶ εἶπεν κύριος Ποῦ εἰσιν οἱ θεοὶ αὐτῶν, ἐφ' οἷς **ἐπεποίθεισαν** ἐπ' αὐτοῖς.

And the Lord said, "Where are their gods, in whom **they trusted?**"

Past-Past ("Had")

The pluperfect indicative often depicts action that is past in the past—it refers to a time frame that stands behind an already past temporal context. This is a unique function of the pluperfect, which is suited to this because of its heightened remoteness; past-past temporal reference is doubly remote. This use of the pluperfect indicative can involve any type of lexeme and arises from contextual factors. The word "had" is appropriate in translating past-past pluperfects.

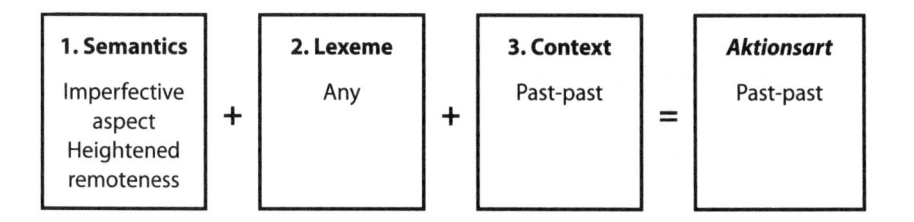

Mark 15:7 ἦν δὲ ὁ λεγόμενος Βαραββᾶς μετὰ τῶν στασιαστῶν δεδεμένος οἵτινες ἐν τῇ στάσει φόνον **πεποιήκεισαν**.

There was one named Barabbas, who was in prison with rebels who **had committed** murder during the rebellion.

Luke 22:13 ἀπελθόντες δὲ εὗρον καθὼς **εἰρήκει** αὐτοῖς καὶ ἡτοίμασαν τὸ πάσχα.

So they went and found it just as **he had told** them, and they prepared the Passover.

John 7:30 Ἐζήτουν οὖν αὐτὸν πιάσαι, καὶ οὐδεὶς ἐπέβαλεν ἐπ' αὐτὸν τὴν χεῖρα, ὅτι **οὔπω ἐληλύθει** ἡ ὥρα αὐτοῦ.

Then they tried to seize him. Yet no one laid a hand on him because his hour **had not yet come.**

Judges 19:28 καὶ εἶπεν πρὸς αὐτήν Ἀνάστηθι καὶ ἀπέλθωμεν· καὶ οὐκ ἀπεκρίθη αὐτῷ, ἀλλὰ **τεθνήκει.** καὶ ἀνέλαβεν αὐτὴν ἐπὶ τὸ ὑποζύγιον καὶ ἀνέστη ὁ ἀνὴρ καὶ ἀπῆλθεν εἰς τὸν τόπον αὐτοῦ.

"Get up," he told her. "Let's go." But there was no response; **she had died.** So the man put her on his donkey and set out for home.

EXERCISES FOR PERFECT AND PLUPERFECT INDICATIVE TENSE-FORMS

For each passage, (1) write about the semantic meaning of the indicative verb, (2) state the contribution of the lexeme, and (3) discuss the function of the verb in context. Once you have written your answers, summarize your findings in the boxes below each passage.

When considering the context, keep an eye out for any elements that may influence the way the verb is understood. This might be something obvious like a temporal word or phrase (e.g., "yesterday," "all day long," "after," etc.). Or it might be something less obvious, like a hint that an action should be understood as repeating or is part of a generalized reality. Context is an open-ended category, and it takes some practice to feel competent with it.

Example:
John 7:27 ἀλλὰ τοῦτον **οἴδαμεν** πόθεν ἐστίν· ὁ δὲ Χριστὸς ὅταν ἔρχηται οὐδεὶς γινώσκει πόθεν ἐστίν.

But **we know** where this man is from. When the Christ comes, nobody will know where he is from.

1. Semantic meaning of the indicative verb. The perfect indicative semantically encodes imperfective aspect and the spatial value of heightened proximity.

2. Contribution of the lexeme. The lexeme is stative.

3. Function in context. The context allows for a stative interpretation.

1. Semantics		2. Lexeme		3. Context		Aktionsart
Imperfective aspect Heightened proximity	+	Stative	+	Allows stativity	=	Stative

Romans 1:17 δικαιοσύνη γὰρ θεοῦ ἐν αὐτῷ ἀποκαλύπτεται ἐκ πίστεως εἰς πίστιν, καθὼς **γέγραπται**, Ὁ δὲ δίκαιος ἐκ πίστεως ζήσεται.

For in it God's righteousness is revealed from faith to faith, just as **it is written**: The righteous will live by faith.

1. Semantics		2. Lexeme		3. Context		Aktionsart
	+		+		=	

John 7:30 Ἐζήτουν οὖν αὐτὸν πιάσαι, καὶ οὐδεὶς ἐπέβαλεν ἐπ' αὐτὸν τὴν χεῖρα, ὅτι **οὔπω ἐληλύθει** ἡ ὥρα αὐτοῦ.

Then they tried to seize him. Yet no one laid a hand on him because his hour **had not yet come**.

1. Semantics		2. Lexeme		3. Context		Aktionsart
	+		+		=	

John 16:11 ... περὶ δὲ κρίσεως, ὅτι ὁ ἄρχων τοῦ κόσμου τούτου **κέκριται**.

... and about judgment, because the ruler of this world **is being judged**.

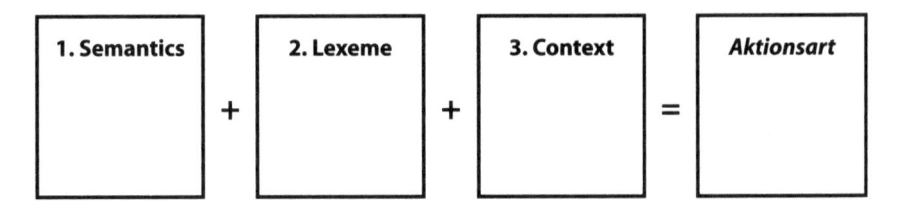

John 1:15 Ἰωάννης μαρτυρεῖ περὶ αὐτοῦ καὶ **κέκραγεν** λέγων, Οὗτος ἦν ὃν εἶπον, Ὁ ὀπίσω μου ἐρχόμενος ἔμπροσθέν μου γέγονεν, ὅτι πρῶτός μου ἦν.

John testified concerning him and **exclaimed**, "This was the one of whom I said, 'The one coming after me has surpassed me, because he was before me.'"

Romans 8:38 πέπεισμαι γὰρ ὅτι οὔτε θάνατος οὔτε ζωὴ οὔτε ἄγγελοι οὔτε ἀρχαὶ οὔτε ἐνεστῶτα οὔτε μέλλοντα οὔτε δυνάμεις...

For **I am persuaded** that neither death nor life, nor angels nor rulers, nor things present, nor things to come, nor powers...

Matthew 7:25 καὶ κατέβη ἡ βροχὴ καὶ ἦλθον οἱ ποταμοὶ καὶ ἔπνευσαν οἱ ἄνεμοι καὶ προσέπεσαν τῇ οἰκίᾳ ἐκείνῃ, καὶ οὐκ ἔπεσεν, τεθεμελίωτο γὰρ ἐπὶ τὴν πέτραν.

The rain fell, the rivers rose, and the winds blew and pounded that house. Yet it didn't collapse, because **it was founded** on the rock.

1. Semantics		2. Lexeme		3. Context		Aktionsart
	+		+		=	

John 19:30 ὅτε οὖν ἔλαβεν τὸ ὄξος ὁ Ἰησοῦς εἶπεν, **Τετέλεσται**, καὶ κλίνας τὴν κεφαλὴν παρέδωκεν τὸ πνεῦμα.

When Jesus had received the sour wine, he said, "**It is finished!**" Then after bowing his head, he gave up his spirit.

1. Semantics		2. Lexeme		3. Context		Aktionsart
	+		+		=	

John 20:11 Μαρία δὲ **εἱστήκει** πρὸς τῷ μνημείῳ ἔξω κλαίουσα. ὡς οὖν ἔκλαιεν, παρέκυψεν εἰς τὸ μνημεῖον.

But Mary **was standing** outside facing the tomb, crying. As she was crying, she stooped to look into the tomb.

1. Semantics		2. Lexeme		3. Context		Aktionsart
	+		+		=	

2 Samuel 3:22 καὶ ἰδοὺ οἱ παῖδες Δαυιδ καὶ Ιωαβ παρεγίνοντο ἐκ τῆς ἐξοδίας καὶ σκῦλα πολλὰ ἔφερον μετ᾽ αὐτῶν· καὶ Αβεννηρ οὐκ ἦν μετὰ Δαυιδ εἰς Χεβρων, ὅτι **ἀπεστάλκει** αὐτὸν καὶ **ἀπεληλύθει** ἐν εἰρήνῃ.

Just then David's soldiers and Joab returned from a raid and brought a large amount of plundered goods with them. Abner was not with

David in Hebron because David **had dismissed** him, and **he had gone** in peace.

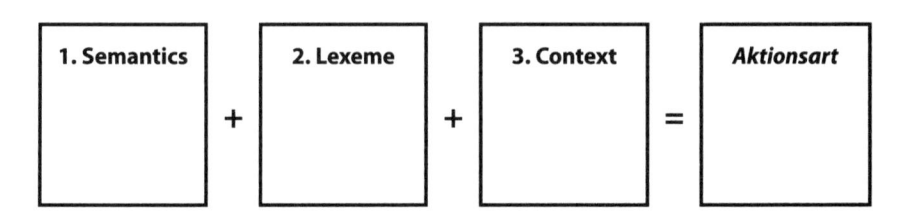

CHAPTER 10

Non-Indicative Tense-Forms

I n this chapter and the next, we turn to consider verbal aspect outside the indicative mood. On the one hand, the semantics of the non-indicative tense-forms are more straightforward than the indicative mood because we do not need to consider the issue of *tense*. Scholars have not attributed tense to non-indicative tense-forms' semantics since Georg Curtius's work in the nineteenth century (although they may convey *relative* tense; see below).

Having reinterpreted the semantics of indicative tense-forms to be *aspectual + spatial* (e.g., perfective aspect + remoteness) instead of *aspectual + temporal* (e.g., perfective aspect + past temporal reference), the absence of "tense" in the non-indicatives means that we also see an absence of spatial distinctions since they stand in for "tense" in the indicative mood but are not needed to do so in the non-indicatives (with the exception of the perfect; more on this below). In other words, we do not analyze non-indicatives as *aspectual + spatial* (e.g., perfective aspect + remoteness) but simply as *aspectual* (e.g., perfective aspect).

Without having to worry about the issue of tense or spatial distinctions in the non-indicative verbs, we can focus entirely on their aspectual meaning and function. As with the indicative mood, there are only two aspects—perfective and imperfective—and these are easily traced throughout the non-indicative verbal system. The non-indicative aspectual system is also simpler because there are no non-indicative imperfects or pluperfects, so we do not need to consider how they would differ from presents and perfects.

Another area in which non-indicatives are more straightforward than their indicative counterparts is that we do not need to examine their *Aktionsart* expressions. While some older grammars use *Aktionsart* labels for some non-indicative verbal uses, in this book *Aktionsart* categories are reserved for the indicative mood only. As we examine the various functions of the non-indicative tense-forms, we *could* describe these as *Aktionsarten*—since the word literally means "type of action"—but for the sake of simplicity and clarity we reserve the term to help us deal with the complexity of indicative verbal usage. This also means that the "four-box method" employed in previous chapters is not relevant in this chapter or the next.

Having said all that, however, understanding aspectual function in non-indicative tense-forms is in certain ways more challenging than in the indicative mood. This is because the *only* distinction between present and aorist non-indicatives is aspectual, so we are forced to reckon with a purely aspectual distinction that will sometimes be tricky to interpret, especially if we do not share parallel aspectual distinctions in English.

THE SUBJUNCTIVE MOOD

Students of Greek often have difficulty working out what meaningful difference there is between aorist and present subjunctives. This is especially the case when we are taught to translate both as *I might loose* or some variation of this gloss. If both subjunctives translate this way, why did Greek authors choose one over the other? Why does the language need more than one tense-form in the subjunctive mood?

The simplest answer is that sometimes languages make distinctions that other languages do not. Just because we might translate a present and an aorist subjunctive the same way in English does not mean that there was no distinguishable difference to the Greek speaker. It might simply mean that we have no real way of communicating the difference. But that does not mean that the student of Greek should not appreciate the original distinction.

Another reason for our difficulty in handling subjunctives may have to do with the fact that the *only* difference between them is verbal aspect. Regardless of one's position on the question of tense in the indicative mood, all agree that non-indicatives are aspectual and do not encode temporal reference at the semantic level. Some students, however, will struggle to conceive of actions that don't have any temporal reference at all, even at the pragmatic level. How may an action in the subjunctive mood be viewed internally (imperfective aspect)? How may it be viewed externally (perfective aspect)?

It may help to approach the distinction through pragmatic features. As with aspect in the indicative mood, aspect in the subjunctive mood issues a range of pragmatic implicatures, which typically arise from one aspect or the other. Just as a predictable range of pragmatic expressions arise from imperfective aspect in the indicative mood, so too a predictable range of expressions arise from imperfective aspect in the subjunctive mood. Getting a handle on these will help to grasp the differences that aspect makes in this mood.

THE PRESENT SUBJUNCTIVE

While it may be difficult to discern for English speakers, verbal aspect is fully operational within the Greek subjunctive mood. The present subjunctive encodes the semantic value of imperfective aspect. The various pragmatic functions of the present subjunctive express its imperfective aspect, viewing the action internally. Some common implicatures of imperfective aspect within present subjunctives are activities that are conceptually unfolding, temporally ongoing, stative, or personally characteristic.[1] These examples demonstrate the internal viewpoint of the imperfective aspect conveyed by the present subjunctive.

Stative Present Subjunctive

The imperfective aspect of the present subjunctive lends itself to expressing stative concepts, as the following examples demonstrate.

Luke 5:12 Καὶ ἐγένετο ἐν τῷ εἶναι αὐτὸν ἐν μιᾷ τῶν πόλεων καὶ ἰδοὺ ἀνὴρ πλήρης λέπρας· ἰδὼν δὲ τὸν Ἰησοῦν, πεσὼν ἐπὶ πρόσωπον ἐδεήθη αὐτοῦ λέγων, Κύριε, ἐὰν **θέλῃς** δύνασαί με καθαρίσαι.

When he was in one of the cities, there was a man full of leprosy. And when he saw Jesus, he fell on his face and begged him, "Lord, if **you are willing**, you can make me clean."

John 15:2 πᾶν κλῆμα ἐν ἐμοὶ μὴ φέρον καρπὸν αἴρει αὐτό, καὶ πᾶν τὸ καρπὸν φέρον καθαίρει αὐτὸ ἵνα καρπὸν πλείονα **φέρῃ**.

---

1. Constantine R. Campbell, *Verbal Aspect and Non-Indicative Verbs: Further Soundings in the Greek of the New Testament*, Studies in Biblical Greek 15 (New York: Peter Lang, 2008), 54.

Every branch in me that does not bear fruit he takes away, and every branch that does bear fruit he prunes, that **it may bear** more fruit.

In these instances, the imperfective aspect of the present subjunctives allows a stative implicature: *to be willing* and *to bear fruit* describe certain characteristics of their grammatical subjects; the tree has fruit on it. Stativity is one of the natural expressions of imperfective aspect.

General Present Subjunctive

The present subjunctive's imperfective aspect makes it especially suited to proverbial, general, and generic statements, as seen below. This is a key pragmatic function of imperfective aspect within the subjunctive mood.

John 17:3 αὕτη δέ ἐστιν ἡ αἰώνιος ζωὴ ἵνα **γινώσκωσιν** σὲ τὸν μόνον ἀληθινὸν θεὸν καὶ ὃν ἀπέστειλας Ἰησοῦν Χριστόν.

This is eternal life, **that they might know** you, the only true God, and the one you have sent—Jesus Christ.

Luke 11:33 Οὐδεὶς λύχνον ἅψας εἰς κρύπτην τίθησιν οὐδὲ ὑπὸ τὸν μόδιον ἀλλ' ἐπὶ τὴν λυχνίαν, ἵνα οἱ εἰσπορευόμενοι τὸ φῶς **βλέπωσιν**.

No one after lighting a lamp puts it in a cellar or under a basket, but on a lampstand, so that those who come in **may see** the light.

THE AORIST SUBJUNCTIVE

The aorist subjunctive encodes the semantic value of perfective aspect. The various pragmatic functions of the aorist subjunctive express its perfective aspect: activities are summarized, punctiliar, or concrete rather than abstract.[2] The aorist subjunctive is also found in certain constructions that require perfective aspect.

Summary Aorist Subjunctive

The perfective aspect of the aorist subjunctive is often used to convey summary actions, as is also normal in the indicative mood.

---

2. Campbell, *Non-Indicative Verbs*, 56.

Romans 10:14–15 Πῶς οὖν **ἐπικαλέσωνται** εἰς ὃν οὐκ ἐπίστευσαν; πῶς δὲ **πιστεύσωσιν** οὗ οὐκ ἤκουσαν; πῶς δὲ **ἀκούσωσιν** χωρὶς κηρύσσοντος; πῶς δὲ **κηρύξωσιν** ἐὰν μὴ **ἀποσταλῶσιν**;

How, then, **can they call** on one they have not believed in? And how **can they believe** without hearing about him? And how **can they hear** without a preacher? And how **can they preach** unless **they are sent**?

John 12:49 ὅτι ἐγὼ ἐξ ἐμαυτοῦ οὐκ ἐλάλησα, ἀλλ᾽ ὁ πέμψας με πατὴρ αὐτός μοι ἐντολὴν δέδωκεν τί **εἴπω** καὶ τί **λαλήσω**.

For I have not spoken on my own, but the Father himself who sent me has given me a command as to what **I should say** and what **I should speak**.

2 Corinthians 9:4 μή πως ἐὰν **ἔλθωσιν** σὺν ἐμοὶ Μακεδόνες καὶ **εὕρωσιν** ὑμᾶς ἀπαρασκευάστους καταισχυνθῶμεν ἡμεῖς, ἵνα μὴ λέγω ὑμεῖς, ἐν τῇ ὑποστάσει ταύτῃ.

For if any Macedonians **should come** with me and **find** you unprepared, we—not to mention you—**would be embarrassed** by this confidence.

Οὐ Μή + Aorist Subjunctive

The aorist subjunctive is found within certain constructions that do not normally employ the present subjunctive. The emphatic future negative construction (οὐ μή) is one that is only ever found with the aorist subjunctive or the future indicative. This is due to the fact that perfective aspect is needed when speaking of events that will *not* occur in the future.[3] We thus observe a parallel between the aorist subjunctive and the future indicative, since both verbs encode perfective aspect.

John 8:12 Πάλιν οὖν αὐτοῖς ἐλάλησεν ὁ Ἰησοῦς λέγων, Ἐγώ εἰμι τὸ φῶς τοῦ κόσμου· ὁ ἀκολουθῶν ἐμοὶ **οὐ μὴ περιπατήσῃ** ἐν τῇ σκοτίᾳ, ἀλλ᾽ ἕξει τὸ φῶς τῆς ζωῆς.

---

3. This is a complicated concept; to follow it up, see Campbell, *Non-Indicative Verbs*, 58–59.

Then Jesus spoke to them again: "I am the light of the world. Anyone who follows me **will never walk** in the darkness but will have the light of life."

Romans 4:8 μακάριος ἀνὴρ οὗ **οὐ μὴ** λογίσηται κύριος ἁμαρτίαν.

How happy is the man whom the Lord **will never charge** with sin!

Deuteronomy 1:37 καὶ ἐμοὶ ἐθυμώθη κύριος δι᾽ ὑμᾶς λέγων Οὐδὲ σὺ **οὐ μὴ εἰσέλθῃς** ἐκεῖ.

The Lord was angry with me also because of you and said, "You **will never enter** there either."

Ἕως + Aorist Subjunctive

Another construction that employs only the aorist subjunctive and never the present subjunctive is ἕως + subjunctive. Perfective aspect is suited to this construction since it often indicates a point in the future at which a new situation is inaugurated or an existing situation is brought to an end.

Luke 24:49 καὶ ἐγὼ ἀποστέλλω τὴν ἐπαγγελίαν τοῦ πατρός μου ἐφ᾽ ὑμᾶς· ὑμεῖς δὲ καθίσατε ἐν τῇ πόλει **ἕως οὗ ἐνδύσησθε** ἐξ ὕψους δύναμιν.

And I am sending you what my Father promised. As for you, stay in the city **until you are empowered** from on high.

Acts 2:35 . . . **ἕως** ἂν **θῶ** τοὺς ἐχθρούς σου ὑποπόδιον τῶν ποδῶν σου.

. . . **until I make** your enemies your footstool.

Psalm 17:38 καταδιώξω τοὺς ἐχθρούς μου καὶ καταλήμψομαι αὐτοὺς καὶ οὐκ ἀποστραφήσομαι, **ἕως** ἂν **ἐκλίπωσιν**.

I will pursue my enemies and overtake them, and I will not turn away **until they fail**.

THE IMPERATIVE MOOD

THE PRESENT IMPERATIVE

The present imperative semantically encodes imperfective aspect. Within present imperatival usage, imperfective aspect normally implicates commands that express some kind of general instruction.[4] This is due to the fact that imperfective aspect is open-ended, without the beginning or end of the action in view. Such a view is inherently suited to the portrayal of instructions that are general in intent. A general instruction is one that is issued with reference to a general situation, or perhaps more accurately, situations in general. Accordingly, it is often employed for the issuing of ethical and moral instruction that is to be characteristic of its adherents. It must be stressed, however, that this is a pragmatic function of imperfective aspect in the imperative mood and as such is cancelable.

To suggest that the present imperative conveys general instruction does not imply that the intended action is to be *continuous* in nature. Such a conclusion confuses aspect with *Aktionsart* in a similar manner to the mistake of concluding that the present indicative must always imply continuous action, which it does not. Thus, the present imperative issues a general command, but not necessarily a *continuous* command. The examples below demonstrate general instructions issued with the present imperative.

General Command Present Imperative

Luke 6:27 Ἀλλὰ ὑμῖν λέγω τοῖς ἀκούουσιν, Ἀγαπᾶτε τοὺς ἐχθροὺς ὑμῶν, καλῶς ποιεῖτε τοῖς μισοῦσιν ὑμᾶς.

But I say to you who hear, **love** your enemies, do good to those who hate you.

Luke 14:35 οὔτε εἰς γῆν οὔτε εἰς κοπρίαν εὔθετόν ἐστιν, ἔξω βάλλουσιν αὐτό. ὁ ἔχων ὦτα ἀκούειν **ἀκουέτω.**

---

4. The distinction between general commands (issued by the present imperative) and specific commands (issued by the aorist imperative) is controversial, and Fanning and Porter reach opposite conclusions about it. While Fanning affirms the distinction, Porter rejects it, and yet it is possible to mediate the two positions. In short, if the general/specific command distinction is held as semantic, it must fail, for there are numerous "exceptions." However, if the distinction is regarded as pragmatic, Porter's objections may be mollified. See Campbell, *Non-Indicative Verbs*, 81–83.

It is fit neither for the land nor for the manure pile; they throw it away.
He who has ears to hear, **let him hear.**

John 21:16 λέγει αὐτῷ πάλιν δεύτερον, Σίμων Ἰωάννου, ἀγαπᾷς με;
λέγει αὐτῷ, Ναὶ κύριε, σὺ οἶδας ὅτι φιλῶ σε. λέγει αὐτῷ, **Ποίμαινε** τὰ
πρόβατά μου.

He said to him a second time, "Simon, son of John, do you love me?"
He said to him, "Yes, Lord; you know that I love you." He said to him,
"**Shepherd** my sheep."

Proverbs 25:21 ἐὰν πεινᾷ ὁ ἐχθρός σου, **τρέφε** αὐτόν, ἐὰν διψᾷ, **πότιζε**
αὐτόν.

If your enemy is hungry, **nourish** him; if he is thirsty, **give** him **a
drink.**

Specific Command Present Imperative

Certain lexemes used with the present imperative express specific commands
instead of general commands. Interestingly, these verbs are of the same lexical
type that typically form historical presents when in the indicative mood: verbs of
propulsion and verbs of speaking. Note these examples:

John 14:31 ἀλλ' ἵνα γνῷ ὁ κόσμος ὅτι ἀγαπῶ τὸν πατέρα, καὶ καθὼς
ἐνετείλατό μοι ὁ πατήρ, οὕτως ποιῶ. Ἐγείρεσθε, ἄγωμεν ἐντεῦθεν.

But that the world may know that I love the Father, I do as the Father
has commanded me. **Rise,** let us go from here.

John 2:8 καὶ λέγει αὐτοῖς, Ἀντλήσατε νῦν καὶ **φέρετε** τῷ ἀρχιτρικλίνῳ·
οἱ δὲ ἤνεγκαν.

And he said to them, "Now draw some out and **take** it to the master of
the banquet." So they took it.

Acts 22:27 προσελθὼν δὲ ὁ χιλίαρχος εἶπεν αὐτῷ, **Λέγε** μοι, σὺ
Ῥωμαῖος εἶ; ὁ δὲ ἔφη, Ναί.

The commander came and said to him, "**Tell** me, are you a Roman citizen?" And he said, "Yes."

2 Chronicles 10:5 καὶ εἶπεν αὐτοῖς **Πορεύεσθε** ἕως τριῶν ἡμερῶν καὶ ἔρχεσθε πρός με· καὶ ἀπῆλθεν ὁ λαός.

And he said to them, "**Go** for about three days, and then **come** to me." And the people went away.

These examples demonstrate that with verbs of propulsion and speaking, the present imperative takes on a usage that would normally be associated with the aorist imperative—the actions are specific rather than general. As with the historical present in the indicative mood, the present imperative may be used with verbs of propulsion to highlight the transition inherent to such lexemes.

THE AORIST IMPERATIVE

The aorist imperative semantically encodes perfective aspect. Its main pragmatic function is to convey *specific* commands. A command is specific if it involves a specific agent acting within a specific situation. This function of the aorist imperative contrasts clearly with the present imperative, which normally conveys commands that are general in nature. Perfective aspect is ideal for the communication of specific instruction, since the external viewpoint lends itself to the expression of definiteness.

It is to be remembered that specific instruction is a pragmatic function of aorist imperatives. Sometimes specific instruction is clearly not intended, and this is to be evaluated according to context. In such cases, the aorist imperative may express general instruction, which is viewed as a whole because of its perfective aspect. When context makes it clear that this is how the aorist imperative is operating, little distinguishes it from the normal function of the present imperative.[5]

Specific Instruction Aorist Imperative

To suggest that the aorist imperative conveys specific instruction does not imply that the intended action is to be *instantaneous* or *immediate* in nature. Such a conclusion would be to confuse aspect with *Aktionsart* in similar manner to the mistake of concluding that the aorist indicative must always implicate punctiliar

---

5. For more on nonspecific aorist imperatives, see Campbell, *Non-Indicative Verbs*, 86–91.

action, which it does not. Thus, the aorist imperative issues a specific command, but not necessarily an instantaneous command. The examples below demonstrate specific instructions issued with the aorist imperative.

Luke 5:4 ὡς δὲ ἐπαύσατο λαλῶν, εἶπεν πρὸς τὸν Σίμωνα, Ἐπανάγαγε εἰς τὸ βάθος καὶ **χαλάσατε** τὰ δίκτυα ὑμῶν εἰς ἄγραν.

When he had finished speaking, he said to Simon, "**Put out** into deep water and **let down** your nets for a catch."

John 2:7-8 λέγει αὐτοῖς ὁ Ἰησοῦς, **Γεμίσατε** τὰς ὑδρίας ὕδατος. καὶ ἐγέμισαν αὐτὰς ἕως ἄνω. καὶ λέγει αὐτοῖς, **Ἀντλήσατε** νῦν καὶ φέρετε τῷ ἀρχιτρικλίνῳ· οἱ δὲ ἤνεγκαν.

"**Fill** the jars with water," Jesus told them. So they filled them to the brim. Then he said to them, "Now **draw some out** and take it to the chief servant." And they did.

John 19:6 ὅτε οὖν εἶδον αὐτὸν οἱ ἀρχιερεῖς καὶ οἱ ὑπηρέται ἐκραύγασαν λέγοντες, **Σταύρωσον σταύρωσον**. λέγει αὐτοῖς ὁ Πιλᾶτος, **Λάβετε** αὐτὸν ὑμεῖς καὶ **σταυρώσατε**· ἐγὼ γὰρ οὐχ εὑρίσκω ἐν αὐτῷ αἰτίαν.

When the chief priests and the temple police saw him, they shouted, "**Crucify! Crucify!**" Pilate responded, "**Take** him and **crucify** him yourselves, for I find no grounds for charging him."

2 Samuel 12:28 καὶ νῦν **συνάγαγε** τὸ κατάλοιπον τοῦ λαοῦ καὶ **παρέμβαλε** ἐπὶ τὴν πόλιν καὶ **προκαταλαβοῦ** αὐτήν, ἵνα μὴ προκαταλάβωμαι ἐγὼ τὴν πόλιν καὶ κληθῇ τὸ ὄνομά μου ἐπ᾽ αὐτήν.

And now **gather** the rest of the people together, **lay siege** to the city, and **capture it first**, otherwise I will capture the city, and it will be named after me.

It is sometimes difficult to ascribe this function to aorist imperatives. It is to be remembered at this point that the indication of specific commands is a pragmatic function of the aorist imperative and is therefore cancelable. In such cases, the semantic value of perfective aspect is to be understood to be pragmatically functioning in some other way.

THE PARTICIPLE

As with the subjunctive and imperative moods, verbal aspect is fully operational within the Greek participial system. Since the participle encodes a wide range of semantic information—such as aspect, voice, person, gender, number, and case—its usage is unsurprisingly complex. That is why the next chapter is dedicated to exploring participial function further. We begin here, however, with an overview of the pragmatic aspectual implicatures of relative temporal uses of the participle (also known as relative tense).

THE PRESENT PARTICIPLE

The present participle semantically encodes imperfective aspect. Its imperfective aspect produces the present participle's main pragmatic function: it nearly always expresses action that is contemporaneous with the action expressed by its leading verb (excluding substantival and periphrastic usages).

Contemporaneous Present Participle

The following examples demonstrate the very common contemporaneous temporal relationship between the present participle and its leading verb.

Matthew 20:17 Καὶ ἀναβαίνων ὁ Ἰησοῦς εἰς Ἱεροσόλυμα παρέλαβεν τοὺς δώδεκα κατ᾽ ἰδίαν καὶ ἐν τῇ ὁδῷ εἶπεν αὐτοῖς.

While going up to Jerusalem, Jesus took the Twelve aside privately and spoke to them on the way.

John 6:24 ὅτε οὖν εἶδεν ὁ ὄχλος ὅτι Ἰησοῦς οὐκ ἔστιν ἐκεῖ οὐδὲ οἱ μαθηταὶ αὐτοῦ, ἐνέβησαν αὐτοὶ εἰς τὰ πλοιάρια καὶ ἦλθον εἰς Καφαρναοὺμ **ζητοῦντες** τὸν Ἰησοῦν.

So when the crowd saw that Jesus was not there, nor his disciples, they got into the boats and went to Capernaum, **seeking** Jesus.

2 Corinthians 5:2 καὶ γὰρ ἐν τούτῳ στενάζομεν τὸ οἰκητήριον ἡμῶν τὸ ἐξ οὐρανοῦ ἐπενδύσασθαι **ἐπιποθοῦντες.**

For we groan in this tent, **desiring** to put on our heavenly dwelling.

Joshua 2:1 Καὶ ἀπέστειλεν Ἰησοῦς υἱὸς Ναυη ἐκ Σαττιν δύο νεανίσκους κατασκοπεῦσαι **λέγων** Ἀνάβητε καὶ ἴδετε τὴν γῆν καὶ τὴν Ιεριχω.

Joshua son of Nun sent two men as spies from Shittim, **saying**, "Go and scout the land, especially Jericho."

While the present participle may at times depict an action that has begun before the action of the leading verb has begun, it is not viewed as completed before the second action begins but rather remains "open-ended." In the following example, the present participle depicts a situation that, while antecedent in origin, becomes contemporaneous with the action of the leading verb. The present participle will not normally be found depicting an action that is completed before the action of the leading verb begins.

Acts 9:33 εὗρεν δὲ ἐκεῖ ἄνθρωπόν τινα ὀνόματι Αἰνέαν ἐξ ἐτῶν ὀκτὼ **κατακείμενον** ἐπὶ κραβάττου, ὃς ἦν παραλελυμένος.

There he found a man named Aeneas, who was paralyzed and had been **bedridden** for eight years.

THE AORIST PARTICIPLE

The aorist participle semantically encodes perfective aspect. Its aspect produces the aorist participle's main pragmatic function: it most often expresses action that is antecedent to the action expressed by its leading verb—though it can express a different temporal relationship to its leading verb.

Antecedent Aorist Participle

The perfective aspect of the aorist participle normally expresses antecedent action, so that the action expressed by the leading verb occurs *after* the action of the aorist participle.

Matthew 5:1 Ἰδὼν δὲ τοὺς ὄχλους ἀνέβη εἰς τὸ ὄρος, καὶ **καθίσαντος** αὐτοῦ προσῆλθαν αὐτῷ οἱ μαθηταὶ αὐτοῦ.

After he saw the crowds, he went up on the mountain, and **after he sat down**, his disciples came to him.

John 19:29–30 σκεῦος ἔκειτο ὄξους μεστόν· σπόγγον οὖν μεστὸν τοῦ ὄξους ὑσσώπῳ **περιθέντες** προσήνεγκαν αὐτοῦ τῷ στόματι. ὅτε οὖν ἔλαβεν τὸ ὄξος ὁ Ἰησοῦς εἶπεν, Τετέλεσται, καὶ **κλίνας** τὴν κεφαλὴν παρέδωκεν τὸ πνεῦμα.

A jar full of sour wine was sitting there; so **after they fixed** a sponge full of sour wine on hyssop they held it up to his mouth. When Jesus had received the sour wine, he said, "It is finished!" Then **after bowing** his head, he gave up his spirit.

Romans 5:1 Δικαιωθέντες οὖν ἐκ πίστεως εἰρήνην ἔχομεν πρὸς τὸν θεὸν διὰ τοῦ κυρίου ἡμῶν Ἰησοῦ Χριστοῦ.

Therefore, **since we have been declared righteous** by faith, we have peace with God through our Lord Jesus Christ.

Subsequent Aorist Participle

The perfective aspect of the aorist participle also enables it to express action that is temporally subsequent to its leading verb, though this is rare.

Acts 25:13 Ἡμερῶν δὲ διαγενομένων τινῶν Ἀγρίππας ὁ βασιλεὺς καὶ Βερνίκη κατήντησαν εἰς Καισάρειαν **ἀσπασάμενοι** τὸν Φῆστον.

After some days had passed, King Agrippa and Bernice arrived in Caesarea and **greeted** Festus.

Contemporaneous Aorist Participle (Attendant Circumstance)

On rare occasions the aorist participle expresses action that is contemporaneous to the action of its leading verb. This occurs only within constructions of attendant circumstance, which will be explored in the following chapter. Suffice to say, the perfective aspect of the aorist participle issues a different pragmatic usage in such constructions.

Luke 1:19 καὶ **ἀποκριθεὶς** ὁ ἄγγελος εἶπεν αὐτῷ, Ἐγώ εἰμι Γαβριὴλ ὁ παρεστηκὼς ἐνώπιον τοῦ θεοῦ καὶ ἀπεστάλην λαλῆσαι πρὸς σὲ καὶ εὐαγγελίσασθαί σοι ταῦτα.

The angel **answered** and said to him, "I am Gabriel, who stands in the presence of God, and I was sent to speak to you and tell you this good news."

THE PERFECT PARTICIPLE

The perfect participle semantically encodes imperfective aspect. Its aspect produces the perfect participle's main pragmatic function: it nearly always expresses action that is contemporaneous with the action expressed by its leading verb (including stative concepts). As with the present participle, sometimes such action begins before the action of the leading verb but becomes contemporaneous with it. The usage of the perfect participle, therefore, parallels that of the present participle.

While the spatial values of proximity and remoteness are generally not encoded in non-indicative verbs, the perfect participle encodes the spatial value of proximity, which distinguishes it from the present participle. It is not normally possible to reflect this difference in translation.

Luke 9:27 λέγω δὲ ὑμῖν ἀληθῶς, εἰσίν τινες τῶν αὐτοῦ **ἑστηκότων** οἳ οὐ μὴ γεύσωνται θανάτου ἕως ἂν ἴδωσιν τὴν βασιλείαν τοῦ θεοῦ.

I tell you the truth: there are some **standing** here who will not taste death until they see the kingdom of God.

John 1:51 καὶ λέγει αὐτῷ, Ἀμὴν ἀμὴν λέγω ὑμῖν, ὄψεσθε τὸν οὐρανὸν **ἀνεῳγότα** καὶ τοὺς ἀγγέλους τοῦ θεοῦ ἀναβαίνοντας καὶ καταβαίνοντας ἐπὶ τὸν υἱὸν τοῦ ἀνθρώπου.

Then he said, "I assure you: You will see heaven **opening** and the angels of God ascending and descending on the Son of Man."

Romans 5:3 οὐ μόνον δέ, ἀλλὰ καὶ καυχώμεθα ἐν ταῖς θλίψεσιν, εἰδότες ὅτι ἡ θλῖψις ὑπομονὴν κατεργάζεται.

And not only that, but we also rejoice in our afflictions, **knowing** that affliction produces endurance.

1 Samuel 14:16 καὶ εἶδον οἱ σκοποὶ τοῦ Σαουλ ἐν Γαβεε Βενιαμιν καὶ ἰδοὺ ἡ παρεμβολὴ **τεταραγμένη** ἔνθεν καὶ ἔνθεν.

When Saul's watchmen in Gibeah of Benjamin looked, they saw the **panicking** troops scattering in every direction.

THE INFINITIVE

Unlike the moods and participial system, the functions of verbal aspect within the Greek infinitive are primarily determined through constructions. Each aspect tends to be reserved for particular constructions that suit either imperfective aspect (present infinitive) or perfective aspect (aorist infinitive).

THE PRESENT INFINITIVE

Though difficult to appreciate at times, present infinitives semantically encode imperfective aspect. This aspect is pragmatically expressed in a variety of ways, primarily through infinitival constructions that commonly require it. For many of these constructions, the preference for the present infinitive is clearly due to its imperfective aspect.

"Begin To" / "About To" + Present Infinitive

Two key constructions are "begin to . . ." and "about to . . ." + present infinitive—as illustrated by the examples below. To portray an action as *beginning* is to choose an unfolding view of the action; an internal view gives attention to an action's unfolding and thus is able to accommodate the portrayal of the beginning of the action. Similarly, to portray an action as *about to* begin or take place is simply the latter concept displaced by one step; the beginning of the action is imminent and is almost in view.

Luke 5:21 καὶ ἤρξαντο διαλογίζεσθαι οἱ γραμματεῖς καὶ οἱ Φαρισαῖοι λέγοντες, Τίς ἐστιν οὗτος ὃς λαλεῖ βλασφημίας; τίς δύναται ἁμαρτίας ἀφεῖναι εἰ μὴ μόνος ὁ θεός;

Then the scribes and the Pharisees **began to question**, saying, "Who is this, who speaks blasphemies? Who can forgive sins but God alone?"

Luke 15:14 δαπανήσαντος δὲ αὐτοῦ πάντα ἐγένετο λιμὸς ἰσχυρὰ κατὰ τὴν χώραν ἐκείνην, καὶ αὐτὸς ἤρξατο ὑστερεῖσθαι.

After he had spent everything, a severe famine struck that country, and **he began to be in need**.

John 4:47 οὗτος ἀκούσας ὅτι Ἰησοῦς ἥκει ἐκ τῆς Ἰουδαίας εἰς τὴν Γαλιλαίαν ἀπῆλθεν πρὸς αὐτὸν καὶ ἠρώτα ἵνα καταβῇ καὶ ἰάσηται αὐτοῦ τὸν υἱόν, ἤμελλεν γὰρ ἀποθνῄσκειν.

When he heard that Jesus had come from Judea to Galilee, he went to him and asked him to come down and heal his son, for **he was about to die**.

Job 26:2 Τίνι πρόσκεισαι ἢ τίνι μέλλεις βοηθεῖν; πότερον οὐχ ᾧ πολλὴ ἰσχὺς καὶ ᾧ βραχίων κραταιός ἐστιν;

To whom are you devoted, or whom are **you about to help**? Is it not to him who has much strength and a strong arm?

Ἐν Τῷ + Present Infinitive

Another construction that is commonly used with the present infinitive is ἐν τῷ + infinitive to express contemporaneous time. This expresses an action that occurs while something else in the narrative takes place. Most often the construction expresses an open-ended action that is intersected by some other action. Since imperfective aspect portrays actions internally and as though unfolding, its suitability to both contemporaneous time and open-ended action is clear.

Mark 4:4 καὶ ἐγένετο ἐν τῷ σπείρειν ὃ μὲν ἔπεσεν παρὰ τὴν ὁδόν, καὶ ἦλθεν τὰ πετεινὰ καὶ κατέφαγεν αὐτό.

As he sowed, some seed fell along the path, and the birds came and ate it up.

Luke 9:29 καὶ ἐγένετο ἐν τῷ προσεύχεσθαι αὐτὸν τὸ εἶδος τοῦ προσώπου αὐτοῦ ἕτερον καὶ ὁ ἱματισμὸς αὐτοῦ λευκὸς ἐξαστράπτων.

And **while he was praying**, the appearance of his face changed, and his clothes became dazzling white.

Luke 17:14 καὶ ἰδὼν εἶπεν αὐτοῖς, Πορευθέντες ἐπιδείξατε ἑαυτοὺς τοῖς ἱερεῦσιν. καὶ ἐγένετο ἐν τῷ ὑπάγειν αὐτοὺς ἐκαθαρίσθησαν.

When he saw them he said to them, "Go and show yourselves to the priests." And **as they went** they were cleansed.

Genesis 38:28 ἐγένετο δὲ ἐν τῷ τίκτειν αὐτὴν ὁ εἷς προεξήνεγκεν τὴν χεῖρα· λαβοῦσα δὲ ἡ μαῖα ἔδησεν ἐπὶ τὴν χεῖρα αὐτοῦ κόκκινον λέγουσα Οὗτος ἐξελεύσεται πρότερος.

As she was giving birth, one of them put out his hand, and the midwife took it and tied a scarlet thread around it, announcing, "This one came out first."

Διὰ Τό + Present Infinitive

Yet another construction that is nearly always used with the present infinitive is the causal διὰ τό + infinitive construction. The causal infinitive explains the reasons behind various mainline actions, and thus this construction is unsurprisingly dominated by the present infinitive due to its imperfective aspect, in the same way that offline information is conveyed through imperfective aspect in the indicative mood.

Luke 8:6 καὶ ἕτερον κατέπεσεν ἐπὶ τὴν πέτραν, καὶ φυὲν ἐξηράνθη διὰ τὸ μὴ ἔχειν ἰκμάδα.

Some fell on the rock, and when it grew up, it withered away, **because it had** no moisture.

Luke 18:5 . . . διά γε τὸ παρέχειν μοι κόπον τὴν χήραν ταύτην ἐκδικήσω αὐτήν, ἵνα μὴ εἰς τέλος ἐρχομένη ὑπωπιάζῃ με.

. . . yet **because this widow troubles me**, I will give her justice, so that she doesn't wear me out by her coming.

John 2:24 αὐτὸς δὲ Ἰησοῦς οὐκ ἐπίστευεν αὐτὸν αὐτοῖς **διὰ τὸ αὐτὸν** γινώσκειν πάντας.

But Jesus did not entrust himself to them, **because he knew** all people.

Ezekiel 34:5 καὶ διεσπάρη τὰ πρόβατά μου **διὰ τὸ μὴ εἶναι** ποιμένας καὶ ἐγενήθη εἰς κατάβρωμα πᾶσι τοῖς θηρίοις τοῦ ἀγροῦ.

And my sheep were scattered **because there were no** shepherds, and they became food for all the animals of the field.

Such infinitival constructions account for the majority of present infinitival usage. As for present infinitives that do not function within these constructions, their unifying characteristics are related to the portrayal of events, actions, or descriptions in a manner that is simply best described as internal in viewpoint.

THE AORIST INFINITIVE

Though once again difficult to appreciate at times, aorist infinitives semantically encode perfective aspect. This aspect is pragmatically expressed in a variety of ways, primarily through infinitival constructions that commonly require it. For many of these constructions, the preference for the aorist infinitive is clearly due to its perfective aspect.

Three of these constructions are related to temporal expression—one expressing antecedent time (μετὰ τό + infinitive) and two expressing subsequent time (πρὸ τοῦ + infinitive, and πρίν + infinitive). The perfective aspect of the aorist infinitive fits these temporal constructions that indicate antecedent and subsequent action. In a manner similar to that of the aorist participle, the undefined and summary viewpoint of the perfective aspect of the aorist infinitive naturally suits the depiction of action occurring on *either side* of the leading verb, temporally speaking.

Μετὰ Τό + Aorist Infinitive

The perfective aspect of the aorist infinitive suits the expression of antecedent time, as seen in the construction μετὰ τό + aorist infinitive, which is translated "after..."

Mark 16:19 Ὁ μὲν οὖν κύριος Ἰησοῦς **μετὰ τὸ λαλῆσαι** αὐτοῖς ἀνελήμφθη εἰς τὸν οὐρανὸν καὶ ἐκάθισεν ἐκ δεξιῶν τοῦ θεοῦ.

So the Lord Jesus, **after speaking** to them, was taken up into heaven and sat down at the right hand of God.

Luke 12:5 ὑποδείξω δὲ ὑμῖν τίνα φοβηθῆτε· φοβήθητε τὸν **μετὰ τὸ ἀποκτεῖναι** ἔχοντα ἐξουσίαν ἐμβαλεῖν εἰς τὴν γέενναν. ναὶ λέγω ὑμῖν, τοῦτον φοβήθητε.

But I will warn you whom you should fear: fear him who, **after he has killed**, has authority to cast into hell. Yes, I tell you, fear him!

Acts 10:41 οὐ παντὶ τῷ λαῷ, ἀλλὰ μάρτυσιν τοῖς προκεχειροτονημένοις ὑπὸ τοῦ θεοῦ, ἡμῖν, οἵτινες συνεφάγομεν καὶ συνεπίομεν αὐτῷ **μετὰ τὸ ἀναστῆναι αὐτὸν** ἐκ νεκρῶν.

... not by all the people, but by us whom God appointed as witnesses, who ate and drank with him **after he rose** from the dead.

Daniel 8:1 Ἔτους τρίτου βασιλεύοντος Βαλτασαρ ὅρασις, ἣν εἶδον ἐγὼ Δανιηλ **μετὰ τὸ ἰδεῖν με** τὴν πρώτην.

During the third year, when Baltasar was king, there was a vision, which I, Daniel, saw **after I saw** the first one.

Πρὸ Τοῦ + Aorist Infinitive

The perfective aspect of the aorist infinitive suits the expression of subsequent time, as seen in the construction πρὸ τοῦ + aorist infinitive, which is translated "before..."

Luke 22:15 καὶ εἶπεν πρὸς αὐτούς, Ἐπιθυμίᾳ ἐπεθύμησα τοῦτο τὸ πάσχα φαγεῖν μεθ' ὑμῶν **πρὸ τοῦ με παθεῖν.**

And he said to them, "I have eagerly desired to eat this Passover with you **before I suffer.**"

John 13:19 ἀπ᾽ ἄρτι λέγω ὑμῖν **πρὸ τοῦ γενέσθαι,** ἵνα πιστεύσητε ὅταν γένηται ὅτι ἐγώ εἰμι.

I am telling you now **before it happens,** so that when it does happen you will believe that I am he.

Galatians 3:23 Πρὸ τοῦ δὲ ἐλθεῖν τὴν πίστιν ὑπὸ νόμον ἐφρουρούμεθα συγκλειόμενοι εἰς τὴν μέλλουσαν πίστιν ἀποκαλυφθῆναι.

Before this faith came, we were confined under the law, imprisoned until the coming faith was revealed.

Isaiah 42:9 τὰ ἀπ᾽ ἀρχῆς ἰδοὺ ἥκασιν, καὶ καινὰ ἃ ἐγὼ ἀναγγελῶ, καὶ **πρὸ τοῦ ἀνατεῖλαι** ἐδηλώθη ὑμῖν.

The past events have indeed happened. Now I declare new events; I announce them to you **before they occur.**

Πρίν + Aorist Infinitive

The perfective aspect of the aorist infinitive suits the expression of subsequent time, as seen in the construction πρίν + aorist infinitive, which is translated "before..."

Matthew 26:34 ἔφη αὐτῷ ὁ Ἰησοῦς, Ἀμὴν λέγω σοι ὅτι ἐν ταύτῃ τῇ νυκτὶ **πρὶν ἀλέκτορα φωνῆσαι** τρὶς ἀπαρνήσῃ με.

"Truly I tell you," Jesus said to him, "tonight, **before the rooster crows,** you will deny me three times."

John 4:49 λέγει πρὸς αὐτὸν ὁ βασιλικός, Κύριε, κατάβηθι **πρὶν ἀποθανεῖν τὸ παιδίον μου.**

The official said to him, "Sir, come down **before my child dies.**"

Acts 7:2 ὁ δὲ ἔφη, Ἄνδρες ἀδελφοὶ καὶ πατέρες, ἀκούσατε. Ὁ θεὸς τῆς δόξης ὤφθη τῷ πατρὶ ἡμῶν Ἀβραὰμ ὄντι ἐν τῇ Μεσοποταμίᾳ **πρὶν ἢ κατοικῆσαι αὐτὸν** ἐν Χαρράν.

"Brothers and fathers," he replied, "listen: The God of glory appeared to our father Abraham when he was in Mesopotamia, **before he settled in Haran.**"

Exodus 1:19 εἶπαν δὲ αἱ μαῖαι τῷ Φαραω Οὐχ ὡς γυναῖκες Αἰγύπτου αἱ Εβραῖαι, τίκτουσιν γὰρ **πρὶν ἢ εἰσελθεῖν πρὸς αὐτὰς τὰς μαίας·** καὶ ἔτικτον.

The midwives said to Pharaoh, "The Hebrew women are not like the Egyptian women, for they are vigorous and give birth **before the midwife can get to them.**"

EXERCISES FOR NON-INDICATIVE TENSE-FORMS

For each non-indicative verb encountered, work out whether it is found within an established construction (such as πρὸ τοῦ + infinitive or ἕως + subjunctive). Then identify the aspect of the non-indicative verb and describe what it is doing in the context.

Example:
Romans 4:8 μακάριος ἀνὴρ οὗ **οὐ μὴ λογίσηται** κύριος ἁμαρτίαν.

How happy is the man whom the Lord **will never charge** with sin!

1. Does the non-indicative verb occur within a construction?
    Yes: οὐ μή + aorist subjunctive (emphatic future negative).
2. What is the aspectual value?
    The aorist subjunctive is perfective in aspect.
3. What is the non-indicative doing in the context?
    In this construction the aorist subjunctive conveys an action that will emphatically not occur in the future.

Matthew 6:8 μὴ οὖν ὁμοιωθῆτε αὐτοῖς· οἶδεν γὰρ ὁ πατὴρ ὑμῶν ὧν χρείαν ἔχετε πρὸ τοῦ ὑμᾶς **αἰτῆσαι** αὐτόν.

Don't be like them, because your Father knows the things you need before you **ask** him.

1. Does the non-indicative verb occur within a construction?

2. What is the aspectual value?

3. What is the non-indicative doing in the context?

1 Corinthians 8:9 **βλέπετε** δὲ μή πως ἡ ἐξουσία ὑμῶν αὕτη πρόσκομμα γένηται τοῖς ἀσθενέσιν.

But **be careful** that this right of yours in no way becomes a stumbling block to the weak.

1. Does the non-indicative verb occur within a construction?

2. What is the aspectual value?

3. What is the non-indicative doing in the context?

Hebrews 10:13 τὸ λοιπὸν ἐκδεχόμενος ἕως **τεθῶσιν** οἱ ἐχθροὶ αὐτοῦ ὑποπόδιον τῶν ποδῶν αὐτοῦ.

He is now waiting until his enemies are **made** his footstool.

1. Does the non-indicative verb occur within a construction?

2. What is the aspectual value?

3. What is the non-indicative doing in the context?

Galatians 5:26 μὴ γινώμεθα κενόδοξοι, ἀλλήλους **προκαλούμενοι,** ἀλλήλοις **φθονοῦντες.**

Let us not become conceited, **provoking** one another, **envying** one another.

1. Does the non-indicative verb occur within a construction?

2. What is the aspectual value?

3. What is the non-indicative doing in the context?

Matthew 12:13 τότε λέγει τῷ ἀνθρώπῳ, Ἔκτεινόν σου τὴν χεῖρα. καὶ ἐξέτεινεν καὶ ἀπεκατεστάθη ὑγιὴς ὡς ἡ ἄλλη.

Then he told the man, "**Stretch out** your hand." So he stretched it out, and it was restored, as good as the other.

1. Does the non-indicative verb occur within a construction?

2.　What is the aspectual value?

3.　What is the non-indicative doing in the context?

Luke 9:7 Ἤκουσεν δὲ Ἡρῴδης ὁ τετραάρχης τὰ γινόμενα πάντα καὶ διηπόρει διὰ τὸ **λέγεσθαι** ὑπό τινων ὅτι Ἰωάννης ἠγέρθη ἐκ νεκρῶν.

Herod the tetrarch heard about everything that was going on. He was perplexed, because some **said** that John had been raised from the dead.

1.　Does the non-indicative verb occur within a construction?

2.　What is the aspectual value?

3.　What is the non-indicative doing in the context?

Romans 6:9 . . . εἰδότες ὅτι Χριστὸς **ἐγερθεὶς** ἐκ νεκρῶν οὐκέτι ἀποθνῄσκει, θάνατος αὐτοῦ οὐκέτι κυριεύει.

. . . **knowing** that Christ, **having been raised** from the dead, will not die again. Death no longer rules over him.

1.　Does the non-indicative verb occur within a construction?

2.　What is the aspectual value?

3.　What is the non-indicative doing in the context?

Deuteronomy 23:23 ἐὰν δὲ μὴ **θέλῃς** εὔξασθαι, οὐκ ἔστιν ἐν σοὶ ἁμαρτία.

But if you do not **wish** to make a vow, it will not be counted against you as sin.

1. Does the non-indicative verb occur within a construction?

2. What is the aspectual value?

3. What is the non-indicative doing in the context?

CHAPTER 11

More Participles

While the basic operations of adverbial participles are discussed in the previous chapter, the topics of periphrastic participles, adjectival and substantival participles, and participles of attendant circumstance are worth discussing separately.

PERIPHRASTIC PARTICIPLES

Periphrastic participles are participles that form a construction with a finite auxiliary verb that provides a net meaning. For most of these constructions, the net meaning of the construction corresponds to the meaning of a particular finite

The Forms of the Periphrastic Participle

Finite Verb (of εἰμί)	+ Participle	= Finite Tense Equivalent
Present	+ Present	= Present
Imperfect	+ Present	= Imperfect
Future	+ Present	= Future
Present	+ Perfect	= Perfect
Imperfect	+ Perfect	= Pluperfect

form. Periphrases in the New Testament involve only the present and perfect participles, which may be combined with present, imperfect, or future finite auxiliaries, normally of εἰμί, as the table below sets forth.[1]

Following are examples of each type of periphrasis.

PRESENT PERIPHRASIS

John 1:41 εὑρίσκει οὗτος πρῶτον τὸν ἀδελφὸν τὸν ἴδιον Σίμωνα καὶ λέγει αὐτῷ, Εὑρήκαμεν τὸν Μεσσίαν, ὅ **ἐστιν μεθερμηνευόμενον** Χριστός.

He first found his own brother Simon and told him, "We have found the Messiah!" (which **is translated** "Anointed One").

IMPERFECT PERIPHRASIS

John 1:28 Ταῦτα ἐν Βηθανίᾳ ἐγένετο πέραν τοῦ Ἰορδάνου, ὅπου **ἦν** ὁ Ἰωάννης **βαπτίζων**.

All this happened in Bethany across the Jordan, where John **was baptizing**.

FUTURE PERIPHRASIS

Luke 1:20 καὶ ἰδοὺ **ἔσῃ σιωπῶν** καὶ μὴ δυνάμενος λαλῆσαι ἄχρι ἧς ἡμέρας γένηται ταῦτα.

Now listen! **You will become silent** and unable to speak until the day these things take place.

PERFECT PERIPHRASIS

John 3:27 ἀπεκρίθη Ἰωάννης καὶ εἶπεν, Οὐ δύναται ἄνθρωπος λαμβάνειν οὐδὲ ἓν ἐὰν μὴ **ᾖ δεδομένον** αὐτῷ ἐκ τοῦ οὐρανοῦ.

John responded, "No one can receive a single thing unless **it is given** to him from heaven."

---

1. The table is from Daniel B. Wallace, *Greek Grammar Beyond the Basics: An Exegetical Syntax of the New Testament* (Grand Rapids: Zondervan, 1996), 648.

PLUPERFECT PERIPHRASIS

Matthew 9:36 Ἰδὼν δὲ τοὺς ὄχλους ἐσπλαγχνίσθη περὶ αὐτῶν, ὅτι ἦσαν ἐσκυλμένοι καὶ ἐρριμμένοι ὡσεὶ πρόβατα μὴ ἔχοντα ποιμένα.

When he saw the crowds, he felt compassion for them, because **they were weary** and **worn out**, like sheep without a shepherd.

In terms of verbal aspect, participial periphrastic constructions convey the same aspectual and spatial semantic values that their finite equivalents convey—with one exception, which will be noted below. This is because the aspect of the periphrasis is determined by the participle, not by the auxiliary. Once an indicative verb begins to function as the auxiliary within a periphrastic construction, it becomes "aspectually vague" and therefore does not contribute aspect to the net outcome.[2]

As such, a review of the table above reveals that all periphrastic constructions are imperfective in aspect, since the present and perfect participles that form these constructions are imperfective in aspect. In four out of five cases, the imperfective aspect of the periphrasis matches the imperfective aspect of the finite equivalent. For example, the imperfect periphrasis consists of the imperfect auxiliary and the present participle, which results in a periphrasis that expresses imperfective aspect. This is the same aspectual value as the imperfect indicative tense-form.

The one exception is the future periphrasis. If the aspectual value of the periphrasis is determined by the participle and not the auxiliary, then the future periphrasis must be imperfective in aspect, since the present participle that helps to form the periphrasis is imperfective. This is not, therefore, the same as the aspectual value of the future indicative tense-form, which is perfective in aspect. While such issues are difficult to resolve with certainty, it is most likely that the future periphrasis does not simply replicate the future indicative; rather, it provides an imperfective option for the future. Consequently, there is aspectual choice for the future—the perfective option is provided by the future indicative, while the imperfective option is provided by the future periphrasis.

Once these factors are appreciated, we may treat periphrastic constructions just as we have learned to deal with their finite counterparts. The same principles of exegesis apply, as do the various relationships between aspect, lexeme, and *Aktionsart*.

---

2. See Constantine R. Campbell, *Verbal Aspect and Non-Indicative Verbs: Further Soundings in the Greek of the New Testament*, Studies in Biblical Greek 15 (New York: Peter Lang, 2008), 33–34.

ADJECTIVAL
PARTICIPLES

Adjectival participles are participles that function like adjectives. They modify a noun, just as a normal adjective would, though they retain a verbal nuance. Nearly all adjectival participles are present or perfect. Why? Because offering description is a natural function of imperfective aspect.

Luke 7:32 ὅμοιοί εἰσιν παιδίοις τοῖς ἐν ἀγορᾷ **καθημένοις** καὶ **προσφωνοῦσιν** ἀλλήλοις.

They are like children **sitting** in the marketplace and **calling** to each other.

John 4:11 λέγει αὐτῷ ἡ γυνή, Κύριε, οὔτε ἄντλημα ἔχεις καὶ τὸ φρέαρ ἐστὶν βαθύ· πόθεν οὖν ἔχεις τὸ ὕδωρ τὸ **ζῶν**;

"Sir," the woman said to him, "You don't even have a bucket, and the well is deep. So where do you get this 'living water'?"

Romans 12:1 Παρακαλῶ οὖν ὑμᾶς, ἀδελφοί, διὰ τῶν οἰκτιρμῶν τοῦ θεοῦ παραστῆσαι τὰ σώματα ὑμῶν θυσίαν **ζῶσαν** ἁγίαν εὐάρεστον τῷ θεῷ, τὴν λογικὴν λατρείαν ὑμῶν.

Therefore, brothers, by the mercies of God, I urge you to present your bodies as a **living** sacrifice, holy and pleasing to God; this is your spiritual worship.

Occasionally, however, an adjectival participle may be aorist. In such cases, the aorist is used in order to describe some kind of antecedence that relates to the noun that the participle modifies. This is a standard function of perfective aspect.

Romans 12:3 Λέγω γὰρ διὰ τῆς χάριτος **τῆς δοθείσης** μοι παντὶ τῷ ὄντι ἐν ὑμῖν μὴ ὑπερφρονεῖν παρ' ὃ δεῖ φρονεῖν ἀλλὰ φρονεῖν εἰς τὸ σωφρονεῖν.

For by the grace **given** to me, I tell everyone among you not to think of himself more highly than he should think.

SUBSTANTIVAL PARTICIPLES

A substantival participle is one that functions as a substantive—that is, as a noun. There are many examples of this usage of the participle.

Luke 1:50 καὶ τὸ ἔλεος αὐτοῦ εἰς γενεὰς καὶ γενεὰς **τοῖς φοβουμένοις** αὐτόν.

His mercy is from generation to generation on **those who** fear him.

John 5:11 ὁ δὲ ἀπεκρίθη αὐτοῖς, Ὁ **ποιήσας** με ὑγιῆ ἐκεῖνός μοι εἶπεν, Ἆρον τὸν κράβαττόν σου καὶ περιπάτει.

He replied to them, "**The man who made** me well told me, 'Pick up your bedroll and walk.'"

John 6:39 τοῦτο δέ ἐστιν τὸ θέλημα **τοῦ πέμψαντός** με.

This is the will of **the one who sent** me.

While several scholars minimize the importance of aspect within this usage of the participle, there is nevertheless good evidence that aspect is relevant, even though the participle functions as a noun.

THE PRESENT SUBSTANTIVAL PARTICIPLE

Imperfective aspect is a semantic feature of the present participle, and this feature continues to play a role in the present participle's use as a substantive. Though functioning as a noun, there is often a verbal nuance to the noun when it is conveyed through a substantival participle. When the present is used, the verbal nuance is normally contemporaneous in time frame, just as the adverbial participle often is. This is a pragmatic outworking of imperfective aspect.

Luke 7:14 καὶ προσελθὼν ἥψατο τῆς σοροῦ, οἱ δὲ **βαστάζοντες** ἔστησαν, καὶ εἶπεν, Νεανίσκε, σοὶ λέγω, ἐγέρθητι.

Then he came up and touched the open coffin, and **those bearing** the coffin stopped. And he said, "Young man, I tell you, get up!"

John 3:36 ὁ **πιστεύων** εἰς τὸν υἱὸν ἔχει ζωὴν αἰώνιον· ὁ δὲ **ἀπειθῶν** τῷ υἱῷ οὐκ ὄψεται ζωήν, ἀλλ' ἡ ὀργὴ τοῦ θεοῦ μένει ἐπ' αὐτόν.

The one who believes in the Son has eternal life, but **the one who refuses to believe** in the Son will not see life; instead, the wrath of God remains on him.

Romans 1:32 οἵτινες τὸ δικαίωμα τοῦ θεοῦ ἐπιγνόντες ὅτι οἱ τὰ τοιαῦτα **πράσσοντες** ἄξιοι θανάτου εἰσίν, οὐ μόνον αὐτὰ ποιοῦσιν ἀλλὰ καὶ συνευδοκοῦσιν **τοῖς πράσσουσιν**.

Although they know full well God's just sentence—that **those who practice** such things deserve to die—they not only do them but even applaud **others who practice them**.

Another pragmatic outworking of imperfective aspect in present substantival participles is the providing of some kind of description or state.

Luke 16:26 καὶ ἐν πᾶσι τούτοις μεταξὺ ἡμῶν καὶ ὑμῶν χάσμα μέγα ἐστήρικται, ὅπως οἱ **θέλοντες** διαβῆναι ἔνθεν πρὸς ὑμᾶς μὴ δύνωνται, μηδὲ ἐκεῖθεν πρὸς ἡμᾶς διαπερῶσιν.

Besides all this, a great chasm has been fixed between us and you, so that **those who want** to pass over from here to you cannot; neither can those from there cross over to us.

Luke 22:36 εἶπεν δὲ αὐτοῖς, Ἀλλὰ νῦν ὁ **ἔχων** βαλλάντιον ἀράτω, ὁμοίως καὶ πήραν, καὶ ὁ **μὴ ἔχων** πωλησάτω τὸ ἱμάτιον αὐτοῦ καὶ ἀγορασάτω μάχαιραν.

Then he said to them, "But now, **whoever has** a money bag should take it, and also a traveling bag. And **whoever doesn't have** a sword should sell his robe and buy one."

A third pragmatic outworking of imperfective aspect is present substantive participles within generic or proverbial statements.

Luke 6:30 παντὶ αἰτοῦντί σε δίδου, καὶ ἀπὸ τοῦ αἴροντος τὰ σὰ μὴ ἀπαίτει.

Give to **everyone who asks** from you, and from **one who takes away** your things, don't ask for them back.

Luke 11:23 ὁ **μὴ ὢν** μετ᾽ ἐμοῦ κατ᾽ ἐμοῦ ἐστιν, καὶ ὁ **μὴ συνάγων** μετ᾽ ἐμοῦ σκορπίζει.

Anyone who is not with me is against me, and **anyone who does not gather** with me scatters.

John 12:45 καὶ ὁ **θεωρῶν** ἐμὲ θεωρεῖ τὸν πέμψαντά με.

And **the one who sees** me sees him who sent me.

THE AORIST SUBSTANTIVAL PARTICIPLE

Perfective aspect is a semantic feature of the aorist participle, and this feature continues to play a role in the aorist participle's use as a substantive. Though functioning as a noun, there is often a verbal nuance to the noun when it is conveyed through a substantivalized participle. When the aorist is used, the verbal nuance is normally antecedent in time frame, just as the adverbial participle often is. This is a pragmatic outworking of perfective aspect.

Luke 7:10 καὶ ὑποστρέψαντες εἰς τὸν οἶκον οἱ **πεμφθέντες** εὗρον τὸν δοῦλον ὑγιαίνοντα.

When **those who had been sent** returned to the house, they found the slave in good health.

John 5:30 Οὐ δύναμαι ἐγὼ ποιεῖν ἀπ᾽ ἐμαυτοῦ οὐδέν· καθὼς ἀκούω κρίνω, καὶ ἡ κρίσις ἡ ἐμὴ δικαία ἐστίν, ὅτι οὐ ζητῶ τὸ θέλημα τὸ ἐμὸν ἀλλὰ τὸ θέλημα **τοῦ πέμψαντός** με.

I am not able to do anything from myself; as I hear, I judge, and my judgment is righteous, because I do not seek my own will but the will **of him who sent** me.

Romans 6:7 ὁ γὰρ **ἀποθανὼν** δεδικαίωται ἀπὸ τῆς ἁμαρτίας.

For **a person who has died** is freed from sin's claims.

THE PERFECT SUBSTANTIVAL PARTICIPLE

Imperfective aspect is a semantic feature of the perfect participle, and this feature continues to play a role in the perfect participle's use as a substantive. Though functioning as a noun, there is often a verbal nuance to the noun when it is conveyed through a substantival participle. When the perfect is used, the verbal nuance is normally contemporaneous in time frame, just as the adverbial participle often is. This is a pragmatic outworking of imperfective aspect, and it mirrors the primary usage of the present substantival participle (e.g., Luke 6:25, below), which is to be expected since the two forms share the same aspect.

Matthew 5:10 μακάριοι οἱ **δεδιωγμένοι** ἕνεκεν δικαιοσύνης, ὅτι αὐτῶν ἐστιν ἡ βασιλεία τῶν οὐρανῶν.

Blessed are **those who are persecuted** for righteousness, because the kingdom of heaven is theirs.

Luke 6:25 οὐαὶ ὑμῖν, οἱ **ἐμπεπλησμένοι** νῦν, ὅτι πεινάσετε. οὐαί, οἱ γελῶντες νῦν, ὅτι πενθήσετε καὶ κλαύσετε.

Woe to you, **those being full** now, because you will be hungry. Woe to you who are laughing now, because you will mourn and weep.

Luke 19:24 καὶ **τοῖς παρεστῶσιν** εἶπεν, Ἄρατε ἀπ᾽ αὐτοῦ τὴν μνᾶν καὶ δότε τῷ τὰς δέκα μνᾶς ἔχοντι.

So he said **to those standing there**, "Take the mina from him and give it to the one who has ten minas."

Sometimes, however, the perfect substantival participles will demonstrate a nuance of past temporal reference. This normally occurs with lexemes of propulsion and introducers of discourse. In other words, the same lexemes that form historical perfects (and historical presents, for that matter) are those that have a sense of antecedent temporal reference with perfect substantival participles.

Matthew 23:37 Ἰερουσαλὴμ Ἰερουσαλήμ, ἡ ἀποκτείνουσα τοὺς προφήτας καὶ λιθοβολοῦσα **τοὺς ἀπεσταλμένους** πρὸς αὐτήν.

Jerusalem, Jerusalem! The city who kills the prophets and stones **those who were sent to her.**

Luke 1:45 καὶ μακαρία ἡ πιστεύσασα ὅτι ἔσται τελείωσις τοῖς **λελαλημένοις** αὐτῇ παρὰ κυρίου.

She who has believed is blessed because **what was spoken** to her by the Lord will be fulfilled!

Luke 14:12 Ἔλεγεν δὲ καὶ **τῷ κεκληκότι** αὐτόν, Ὅταν ποιῇς ἄριστον ἢ δεῖπνον, μὴ φώνει τοὺς φίλους σου μηδὲ τοὺς ἀδελφούς σου μηδὲ τοὺς συγγενεῖς σου μηδὲ γείτονας πλουσίους, μήποτε καὶ αὐτοὶ ἀντικαλέσωσίν σε καὶ γένηται ἀνταπόδομά σοι.

He also said to **the one who had invited** him, "When you give a dinner or a banquet, don't invite your friends, your brothers, your relatives, or your rich neighbors, lest they invite you back, and you be repaid."

PARTICIPLES OF ATTENDANT CIRCUMSTANCE

According to Daniel B. Wallace, a participle of attendant circumstance communicates an action that is coordinate with its finite leading verb and "'piggybacks' on the mood of the main verb."[3] The participle, therefore, takes on the force of a finite verb and ceases, in some sense, to behave like a participle. Again according to Wallace, participles of attendant circumstance are identified by the following features: the tense-form of the participle is usually aorist; the tense-form of the main verb is usually aorist; the mood of the main verb is usually imperative or indicative; the participle will precede the main verb; they occur frequently in narrative. These features are observed in the following examples.

Matthew 2:8 καὶ πέμψας αὐτοὺς εἰς Βηθλέεμ εἶπεν, **Πορευθέντες ἐξετάσατε** ἀκριβῶς περὶ τοῦ παιδίου· ἐπὰν δὲ εὕρητε, ἀπαγγείλατέ μοι, ὅπως κἀγὼ ἐλθὼν προσκυνήσω αὐτῷ.

He sent them to Bethlehem and said, "**Go** and **search** carefully for the child. When you find him, report back to me so that I too may go and worship him."

Matthew 28:7 καὶ ταχὺ **πορευθεῖσαι εἴπατε** τοῖς μαθηταῖς αὐτοῦ ὅτι Ἠγέρθη ἀπὸ τῶν νεκρῶν, καὶ ἰδοὺ προάγει ὑμᾶς εἰς τὴν Γαλιλαίαν, ἐκεῖ αὐτὸν ὄψεσθε· ἰδοὺ εἶπον ὑμῖν.

Then **go** quickly and **tell** his disciples, "He has been raised from the dead. In fact, he is going ahead of you to Galilee; you will see him there." Listen, I have told you.

Luke 1:19 καὶ **ἀποκριθεὶς** ὁ ἄγγελος **εἶπεν** αὐτῷ, Ἐγώ εἰμι Γαβριὴλ ὁ παρεστηκὼς ἐνώπιον τοῦ θεοῦ καὶ ἀπεστάλην λαλῆσαι πρὸς σὲ καὶ εὐαγγελίσασθαί σοι ταῦτα.

The angel **answered** him, "I am Gabriel, who stands in the presence of God, and I was sent to speak to you and tell you this good news."

In terms of aspect, the significance of participles of attendant circumstance is that they are contemporaneous with the leading verb, even though they are aorist participles. In such cases, the perfective aspect of the aorist participle functions to coordinate with the perfective aspect of its aorist leading verb. This

---

3. Wallace, *Grammar*, 640.

is the pragmatic function of perfective aspect here rather than the more usual expression of antecedent temporal reference.

These observations are exegetically significant. As the first two examples above demonstrate, participles of attendant circumstance may take on the meaning of the imperative mood rather than expressing some kind of prior action before a command is to be carried out. A classic example is found in Matthew 28:19.

Matthew 28:19 πορευθέντες οὖν **μαθητεύσατε** πάντα τὰ ἔθνη, βαπτίζοντες αὐτοὺς εἰς τὸ ὄνομα τοῦ πατρὸς καὶ τοῦ υἱοῦ καὶ τοῦ ἁγίου πνεύματος.

Go, therefore, and **make disciples** of all nations, baptizing them in the name of the Father and of the Son and of the Holy Spirit.

It would be a mistake to render this aorist participle "as you go," communicating an action that frames the context in which the command "make disciples" is to take place. Instead, as a participle of attendant circumstance, the aorist takes on the full force of the imperative with which it is coordinate. The command is to go and make disciples.

EXERCISES FOR THE PARTICIPLE

For each participle encountered, work out whether it is periphrastic, adjectival, substantival, or a participle of attendant circumstance. Then identify the aspect of the participle and describe what it is doing in the context.

Example:

John 16:5 νῦν δὲ ὑπάγω πρὸς **τὸν πέμψαντά** με, καὶ οὐδεὶς ἐξ ὑμῶν ἐρωτᾷ με, Ποῦ ὑπάγεις;

But now I am going away to **the one who sent** me, and not one of you asks me, "Where are you going?"

1.   Periphrastic, adjectival, substantival, or attendant circumstance?
     This participle is substantival.

2. What is the aspectual value?

    This aorist participle is perfective in aspect.

3. What is the participle doing in the context?

    This substantival participle conveys a nuance of past temporal reference.

John 5:2 ἔστιν δὲ ἐν τοῖς Ἱεροσολύμοις ἐπὶ τῇ προβατικῇ κολυμβήθρα ἡ **ἐπιλεγομένη** Ἑβραϊστὶ Βηθεσδὰ πέντε στοὰς ἔχουσα.

By the Sheep Gate in Jerusalem there is a pool, **called** Bethesda in Hebrew, which has five colonnades.

1. Periphrastic, adjectival, substantival, or attendant circumstance?

2. What is the aspectual value?

3. What is the participle doing in the context?

Luke 16:6 ὁ δὲ εἶπεν, Ἑκατὸν βάτους ἐλαίου. ὁ δὲ εἶπεν αὐτῷ, Δέξαι σου τὰ γράμματα καὶ **καθίσας** ταχέως γράψον πεντήκοντα.

"A hundred measures of oil," he said. "Take your invoice," he told him, "**sit down** quickly, and write fifty."

1. Periphrastic, adjectival, substantival, or attendant circumstance?

2. What is the aspectual value?

3. What is the participle doing in the context?

John 13:23 ἦν **ἀνακείμενος** εἷς ἐκ τῶν μαθητῶν αὐτοῦ ἐν τῷ κόλπῳ τοῦ Ἰησοῦ, ὃν ἠγάπα ὁ Ἰησοῦς.

One of his disciples, the one Jesus loved, was **reclining** close beside Jesus.

1. Periphrastic, adjectival, substantival, or attendant circumstance?

2. What is the aspectual value?

3. What is the participle doing in the context?

Romans 7:14 Οἴδαμεν γὰρ ὅτι ὁ νόμος πνευματικός ἐστιν, ἐγὼ δὲ σάρκινός εἰμι **πεπραμένος** ὑπὸ τὴν ἁμαρτίαν.

For we know that the law is spiritual; but I am made out of flesh, **sold** into sin's power.

1. Periphrastic, adjectival, substantival, or attendant circumstance?

2. What is the aspectual value?

3. What is the participle doing in the context?

Acts 5:5 ἀκούων δὲ ὁ Ἀνανίας τοὺς λόγους τούτους **πεσὼν** ἐξέψυξεν, καὶ ἐγένετο φόβος μέγας ἐπὶ πάντας τοὺς ἀκούοντας.

When he heard these words, Ananias **dropped** dead, and a great fear came on all who heard.

1. Periphrastic, adjectival, substantival, or attendant circumstance?

2. What is the aspectual value?

3. What is the participle doing in the context?

John 3:24 οὔπω γὰρ ἦν **βεβλημένος** εἰς τὴν φυλακὴν ὁ Ἰωάννης.

For John had not yet **been thrown** into prison.

1. Periphrastic, adjectival, substantival, or attendant circumstance?

2. What is the aspectual value?

3. What is the participle doing in the context?

Mark 14:69 καὶ ἡ παιδίσκη ἰδοῦσα αὐτὸν ἤρξατο πάλιν λέγειν τοῖς **παρεστῶσιν** ὅτι Οὗτος ἐξ αὐτῶν ἐστιν.

When the servant saw him again she began to tell those **standing** nearby, "This man is one of them!"

1. Periphrastic, adjectival, substantival, or attendant circumstance?

2. What is the aspectual value?

3. What is the participle doing in the context?

APPENDIX

The Greek Verb Revisited Revisited[1]

This is an important volume that deserves careful consideration.
It will no doubt occupy a significant position within modern
discussions of the Greek verbal system, and rightly so.

That is my endorsement printed on the back cover of *The Greek Verb Revisited*.[2] And I stand by it. Whatever else I might say about this imposing collection of essays, it remains true that it *is* an important volume, and it does deserve careful consideration. There is much to affirm and celebrate. The editors and contributors are to be congratulated. But careful consideration means that we must also question, probe, and prod. And that's what I intend to do here. I have five main points.

1. FRESH INSIGHTS

Nicholas Ellis offers a helpful overview of a cognitive-linguistic framework for analyzing the Greek verbal system. And the volume as a whole is held together by the contributors' common embrace of a cognitive approach. This is useful and

---

1. This is a paper I delivered to the Biblical Greek Language and Linguistics unit at the Society of Biblical Literature annual meeting in Boston, MA, November 18, 2017.

2. Steven E. Runge and Christopher J. Fresch, eds., *The Greek Verb Revisited: A Fresh Approach for Biblical Research* (Bellingham, WA: Lexham, 2016).

illuminating. Cognitive grammar offers interesting avenues into the Greek verbal system. Some interesting insights into verbal function within narrative texts are offered, such as Stephen Levinsohn's chapter on grounding in narrative and Patrick James's chapter on the indicative verbs in John 11—though, I have to admit, it was personally disappointing that neither interacted with my work on aspectual function within narrative frameworks.

Amalia Moser's chapter on tense and aspect before and after the New Testament is excellent. We know that the ancient Greek perfect and pluperfect synthetic forms dropped out of usage, and in Modern Greek there is only a perfect periphrasis. But I did not know that for a thousand years (ca. from the third to the thirteenth centuries AD) there was no perfect represented at all in the Greek language. Moser is right to point out the significance of this, saying,

> I believe that the morphological loss of one of the three stems, a change of immense magnitude in an otherwise remarkably conservative morphology, cannot be insignificant.[3]

Moreover, I would add that it is significant because—for those who maintain three aspects in Greek—one of those three has dropped out, fundamentally reshaping the entire aspectual network. But that is only a problem if Greek did in fact have three aspects . . . *let the hearer understand.*

Rachel Aubrey on the middle voice is also excellent. She concludes that the "middle voice indicates a marked choice for which the participant is brought into the spotlight for the event . . . while the patient, as the affected entity, is secondary."[4] I agree and find her analysis compelling.

2. THE POSTURE OF THE BOOK

Steve Runge and Chris Fresch say in the introduction:

> We wanted to see what a diverse team of scholars, working within compatible linguistic frameworks, could achieve in solving a problem

---

3. Amalia Moser, "Tense and Aspect after the New Testament," in Runge and Fresch, *Greek Verb Revisited*, 539–62 (543).

4. Rachel Aubrey, "Motivated Categories, Middle Voice, and Passive Morphology," in Runge and Fresch, *Greek Verb Revisited*, 563–625 (618).

that none of us felt had been adequately resolved. Instead of bickering or posturing, the conference and the ensuing discussion resulted in a collegial collaboration that few of us had ever experienced.[5]

Our goal for this volume is not to end the entrenched debate, but rather to break the impasse and to see the discussion move forward.[6]

But by sidestepping those who might critique it, I don't see how the volume breaks the impasse between us. It offers another approach to consider, which may or may not be better than previous approaches. There is nothing wrong with proposing another way. But the editors should recognize what they are doing and not claim for themselves more than that. Rather than breaking the impasse, this volume attempts to tiptoe around it. Later in the volume, after the essays on the Greek perfect, Runge comments:

[Stanley E.] Porter, [Buist M.] Fanning, and Campbell have each captured important pieces of the puzzle, but none fully assemble them into the whole. Our hope is for the essays on the perfect in this volume to provide a more complete though composite picture.[7]

I'm not sure in what sense these essays assemble the pieces of the puzzle into a whole. Indeed, Geoffrey Horrocks says, "It would be misleading to suggest that the problem of the perfect has at last been cracked."[8] The essays on the perfect barely engage with Porter, Fanning, and my own work, and what engagement does exist is superficial and dismissive. In trying to move beyond the impasse, it seems disingenuous to bypass direct interaction with us. Fanning contributed a "history of the debate" paper at the Cambridge conference, since he happened to be there at the time.

Because I was living and studying at Tyndale House at the time of the conference, the conveners kindly encouraged me to make a brief presentation at the outset. They asked me to reflect on what Stan Porter and

---

5. Runge and Fresch, *Greek Verb Revisited*, 3.
6. Runge and Fresch, *Greek Verb Revisited*, 4.
7. Steven E. Runge, "Discourse Function of the Greek Perfect," in Runge and Fresch, *Greek Verb Revisited*, 458–85 (484–85).
8. Geoffrey Horrocks, "Envoi," in Runge and Fresch, *Greek Verb Revisited*, 626–35 (633).

I were trying to address when we took up the topic of New Testament Greek verbal aspect.[9]

I suppose it was nice to ask one of the Perfect Storm guys to say something—since he happened to be in Cambridge at the time. But Fanning was not invited to contribute to the ideas presented in the book. By excluding our three positions, this volume does not mediate and solve the divides in Greek scholarship; instead, it adds a fourth way.

3. THE HEGEMONY OF LINGUISTICS

A troubling trend is detected throughout the volume. I call it the *hegemony of linguistics*. Now, please don't misunderstand me. I welcome, and indeed have championed, the engagement of linguistic methodology for the study of ancient Greek. But while we once lamented that Greek grammarians were not versed at all in linguistic method, the tide has turned. This is great, but it may have gone too far—at least in some of the attitudes expressed in this volume. Chris Thomson's essay on the definition of aspect is a good example. He frequently points to a linguist or two—implying that *all* linguists say the same thing—then shows how New Testament Greek grammarians are at odds with said linguists. He therefore concludes that the Greek grammarian is wrong. No argument is offered to demonstrate which view is superior. The assumption, instead, is that the linguist is always right.

Moreover, this hegemony of linguistics is seen in evaluating Greek scholars' use of linguistic ideas. Unless the use is exactly as intended by the originating linguist, the Greek scholar shows himself not to know what he is doing. For example, Thomson addresses Isačenko's famous parade illustration:

> The version of the analogy familiar to New Testament scholars is Porter's adaptation, and differs strikingly from Isačenko's own version.[10]

---

9. Buist Fanning, "Porter and Fanning on New Testament Greek Verbal Aspect: Retrospect and Prospect," in Runge and Fresch, *Greek Verb Revisited*, 7–12 (7).

10. Christopher J. Thomson, "What Is Aspect?: Contrasting Definitions in General Linguistics and New Testament Studies," in Runge and Fresch, *Greek Verb Revisited*, 13–80 (21).

Are New Testament scholars allowed to adapt analogies and terminology used in general linguistics? If not, why not? After all, Isačenko's illustration was developed for Russian verbs, which are marked differently from Greek verbs. Since Porter adapted it for Greek verbs, a modification of the analogy is appropriate. The attitude expressed here is: this is what linguists say (though the huge diversity among them is rarely acknowledged); New Testament Greek scholars say something else, so the latter are necessarily wrong. But the study of aspect in Greek goes back 150 years. It has its own trajectory. The advances of linguistics are of course important—and we have been eager to say so—but that does not mean that the trajectory of Greek studies over 150 years becomes irrelevant. The point of linguistic study is to assist our study of Greek. Linguistic methodologies come and go, and there is a widespread variety of opinion. Since there is no prevailing hegemony *within* linguistics, why should we accept the hegemony *of* linguistics? Thomson continues,

> This brief summary of their definitions is sufficient to highlight the fact that Porter, Fanning, and Campbell each depart, though to varying degrees, from the consensus in general linguistics that aspect is at its root a temporal concept. This appears to be not so much a deliberate rejection of the consensus as a misunderstanding of it, for each of the three criticizes the temporal definitions of certain linguists without acknowledging that a temporal understanding is the norm.[11]

Apart from suggesting that we do not really understand what aspect is (though all three of us earned our doctorates on the subject), the statement is flawed. Thomson has *not* demonstrated that a temporal understanding of aspect is the norm among linguists. Besides, we are not naively unaware of alternate definitions of aspect, as found in Bernard Comrie and others. Instead, our understanding of aspect as *viewpoint* is consistent with the history of the discussion, both within and outside Greek studies. Comrie in 1975 stepped away from that trajectory by analyzing aspect in temporal terms.

Though Comrie has many followers today, other linguists prefer a spatial, viewpoint understanding of aspect—*even if they acknowledge a relationship between aspect and time*. Thomson, however, conflates aspect and time so that if a linguist acknowledges a relationship between the two, he declares, "Aha!

---

11. Thomson, "What Is Aspect?," 46.

Aspect is temporal!" I acknowledge a relationship between aspect and time too, but that does not mean that I define aspect in temporal terms. Comrie did not consider how well his temporal understanding of aspect did or did not fit the Greek language. But the goal of our Greek studies is to understand Greek, not to conform as closely as possible to the trends of general linguistics. Thomson confuses these goals when he repeatedly implies that being out of step with linguistic terminology means that Greek scholars are mistaken about Greek.

There are other examples of the hegemony of linguistics. Chris Fresch claims that Gricean principles have been misappropriated in New Testament Greek scholarship.[12] He appears to mean that we should not apply linguistic principles in creative ways. But Stephen Levinsohn—a hero of the Runge/Fresch camp—freely admits to eclectic borrowing from different linguistic schools and even applies linguistic principles in reverse from their original intent. Why does Levinsohn have permission to be creative with linguistic principles but Greek scholars do not?

4. DRESSING UP OLD VIEWS IN NEW CLOTHES

I contend that many of the positions put forth in this volume are old grammatical views dressed up in new linguistic clothes. According to Fresch,

> What I am claiming is not all that different from the historical grammarians. Their intimate knowledge of the Greek language often led them to accurate conclusions even if they did not have the linguistic theory to back it up. The only difference may be that while they viewed these nonpast aorist indicatives as exceptions to the rule, I view them as typologically expected.[13]

This simply baptizes old theories with linguistic typology. But it doesn't actually solve anything since it lacks explanatory power. It is more of an apologetic—"Sorry this happens. We don't really know why, but at least we can

---

12. Christopher J. Fresch, "Typology, Polysemy, and Prototypes: Situating Nonpast Aorist Indicatives," in Runge and Fresch, *Greek Verb Revisited*, 379–415 (400). "Gricean principles" refers to certain maxims developed by British linguist Paul Grice, related to the concept of implicature within pragmatics.

13. Fresch, "Situating Nonpast Aorist Indicatives," 404.

say that the problem is widespread." Resorting to solutions that say, "Well, this is what happens in other languages," is less than satisfying. While we should observe patterns between languages, our solutions should primarily be grounded in Greek—in Greek text and through the lens of Greek scholarship. Fresch says,

> In English, there are certain contexts in which it is acceptable to use a past tense form even though past temporal reference is not being made. It would be a mistake to attempt to corral these uses under one semantic definition. There is no question that English has a past tense, but it is an accepted convention of English usage to use past tense verbs to accomplish certain effects pragmatically, such as counterfactual meanings and pragmatic softening.[14]

But the question is, Why is it used this way? Why does the English past tense function for counterfactual meaning or pragmatic softening? It is not explained. It is just convention and that's that. But what if it *can* be explained beyond just observing the convention? In fact, there are scholars who doubt the accuracy of these terms for English verbs. For example, the leading cognitive theorist Ronald Langacker says that "instead of 'present' vs. 'past' we can speak more generally of a **proximal/distal** contrast in the epistemic sphere."[15] He continues,

> Immediate reality corresponds temporally with the time of speaking, so to the extent that the notion of time is specifically invoked, present time is conceived as one facet of immediate reality.[16]
>
> In precisely analogous fashion, the predication of non-immediate reality is equivalent to one of past time.[17]

While Langacker retains the terms present-tense/past-tense for English, he says "their fundamental semantic characterization pertains to epistemic distance."[18] Now that sounds like a solution! And guess what—it is also the solution I have put forward with respect to Greek! But, I have to admit, it sounds eminently more believable coming from a linguist than from a New Testament

---

14. Fresch, "Situating Nonpast Aorist Indicatives," 402.
15. Ronald W. Langacker, *Foundations of Cognitive Grammar, Volume II: Descriptive Application* (Stanford: Stanford University Press, 1991), 245 (emphasis original).
16. Langacker, *Foundations of Cognitive Grammar*, 245–46.
17. Langacker, *Foundations of Cognitive Grammar*, 246.
18. Langacker, *Foundations of Cognitive Grammar*, 249.

scholar. Or it is more believable coming from a classical Greek scholar, such as Rutger Allan. In this volume, Allan makes the same point:

> I proposed . . . to describe the abstract meaning of the secondary indicative . . . as expressing deictic distance from the vantage point of the conceptualizer (speaker/hearer): the event referred to by a secondary indicative is construed as not directly accessible to the experience of the speaker and hearer. In the prototypical case, distance is interpreted in terms of temporal distance. In its counterfactual use, on the other hand, the past tense form signals that the event is located in a virtual world that is epistemically at a distance from the actual reality surrounding the interlocutors.[19]

Allan says it better than I have articulated it, but this is exactly what I have claimed about *remoteness* (what Allan calls distance), of which temporal reference is a subset. Allan does not interact with my work on this point, but it is gratifying to see the idea endorsed—in direct contradiction to Fresch.

In general, finding a real solution is better than explaining away exceptions through linguistic typology. In Rachel Aubrey's essay on the middle voice, she says,

> When -(θ)η- does not live up to expectation, the traditional response is to dismiss such cases as exceptions, suggesting they have somehow skirted the rules and taken on an active role: "passive in form but active in meaning."[20]

In contrast to the traditional "these are just exceptions" approach, she claims,

> Instead of an exclusively passive form with random deviants, -(θ)η- is better understood as a diachronically and synchronically motivated form with multiple functions, all of which fit within the semantic scope of the middle domain.[21]

---

19. Rutger J. Allan, "Tense and Aspect in Classical Greek: Two Historical Developments; Augment and Perfect," in Runge and Fresch, *Greek Verb Revisited*, 81–121 (96–97n37).

20. Aubrey, "Motivated Categories, Middle Voice, and Passive Morphology," 565–66.

21. Aubrey, "Motivated Categories, Middle Voice, and Passive Morphology," 565.

In other words, Aubrey suggests a better understanding of the semantics of the form that can account for its variety of usage. This sounds like our debates about aspect and tense in the indicative mood. Several contributors to this volume say that exceptions to the rule are to be typologically expected. But like Aubrey, let's not dismiss exceptions to the rules; instead, let's look for better rules.

5. SOME POINTS OF DISAGREEMENT

First, consider Thomson:

> I have suggested that the precise sense in which aspect relates to time, and the various ways in which it interacts with procedural character, are clarified when one abandons visual and spatial metaphors and adopts a more literal time-referential definition.[22]

What is a "literal time-referential definition"? Is time *literal*? What does that mean? Time is an *abstract* concept that we can only really grasp through metaphor, and spatial metaphors at that. Time rests on space. We measure time based on the rotation of the earth and the earth's orbit around the sun. Those are literal, spatial realities. Time is a construct we superimpose on those spatial realities. It cannot be measured without spatial entities. Thomson's biggest mistake is to assume that temporal reality is more fundamental than spatial reality, and this reveals his modern, Western, time-oriented mindset. It says nothing about ancient Greek.

Sociology demonstrates that not all cultures (and therefore not all languages) are equally preoccupied with time. Indeed, a basic principle of cognitive linguistics is that spatial concepts evolve into temporal senses over a period of diachronic development (e.g., as seen with Greek prepositions). English speakers need to step outside our own cultural prejudice to appreciate that time is not the only framework by which to understand the world.

Similarly, Randall Buth argues against a spatial understanding of the augment:

---

22. Thomson, "What Is Aspect?," 70.

Renaming the augment as a "remote proximity" marker simply uses a spatial metaphor for something that is not related to locational space. Let me explain this in English: "He was standing" is not farther away geographically than "he is standing." Calling the Greek augment a remoteness marker means that the remoteness metaphor requires a definition and that definition is time related.[23]

This assumes that for ancient speakers time is more concrete than metaphorical space. This is not the case, as I have already explained. I refer again to Langacker on *epistemic distance* as well as the cognitive principle that spatial concepts are basic, while abstract notions (including time) are extensions of spatial reasoning.

Second, several contributors (especially Buth and Nicholas Ellis) argue for the combinative perfect, according to which two aspects are combined into one form. But how plausible is it that *one* form conveys *two* aspects at once? On the viewpoint understanding of aspect, this seems impossible. How can we view an event from the outside as a whole *and* from within the event as it unfolds *at the same time*? On Comrie's internal temporal constituency view it is also impossible. Thus, the two major definitions of aspect are incompatible with combinative aspect.

The claim is only possible if we conceive of aspect in different ways regarding the same event—with respect to the event, plus the *effects* of that event. Ellis defines the combinative aspect as "reflecting the perfective nature of the verbal event and the imperfective nature of its ongoing relevance."[24]

In effect, each perfect form conveys *two* verbal activities, each with their own aspect. But this is neither standard nor a trivial departure from the norm. Moreover, we come to the problem of usage. Some perfects clearly fit at a pragmatic level—they indicate a past action with present consequences. But many do not—they either convey a past action with no present state implied (so called aoristic perfects—though I prefer the term "historical perfects"), or they convey a state with no past action implied. For the semantics to be *both* perfective and imperfective, we should expect to see more of the perfects actually displaying these characteristics at once. But that is not what we see.

---

23. Randall Buth, "Perfect Greek Morphology and Pedagogy," in Runge and Fresch, *Greek Verb Revisited*, 416–29 (424).

24. Nicholas J. Ellis, "Aspect-Prominence, Morpho-Syntax, and a Cognitive-Linguistic Framework for the Greek Verb," in Runge and Fresch, *Greek Verb Revisited*, 122–60 (143).

CONCLUSION

The most enduring contribution of *The Greek Verb Revisited* is its firm introduction of cognitive grammar to the study of the Greek verbal system. While it is not the first time such an approach has been applied to Greek verbs, this volume heralds its arrival. This is a positive and welcome advance. Nevertheless, while the volume represents a major milestone, I feel that it claims too much for itself. The volume more or less claims, "We are going to solve the problems that Porter, Fanning, and Campbell got stuck in the mud trying to resolve." The success of solving these problems is sometimes in the eye of the beholder, and sometimes the appearance of success comes from not properly engaging with those who see things differently. Nevertheless, I shall close as I opened:

> This is an important volume that deserves careful consideration. It will no doubt occupy a significant position within modern discussions of the Greek verbal system, and rightly so.

Verbal Glossary

AKTIONSART

A category of pragmatics that describes actional characteristics, such as iterative, punctiliar, ingressive, etc. *Aktionsart* describes the combination of aspect with lexeme and context. It is therefore cancelable.

ASPECT

The view of an action presented by the author. Internal or external viewpoints are the usual aspects. Not to be confused with *Aktionsart*. Aspect is semantic and therefore uncancelable.

CANCELABILITY

A value is cancelable if it is not expressed with *every* use of a particular form. A value is uncancelable if it is expressed with every use of a particular form. Verbal semantic values are uncancelable, while pragmatic values are cancelable.

CONATIVE *AKTIONSART*

A verb depicts an attempted (but not accomplished) action. This may occur with imperfect tense-forms and any type of lexeme. Context indicates that the action was unsuccessfully attempted.

DEICTIC MARKERS

Factors within language that indicate time, person, location, etc. Temporal deixis is most relevant here and encompasses words such as "now," "later," "before," "yesterday," etc. Narrative will often express temporal deixis without explicit markers since it is usually assumed to be referring to the past.

GNOMIC *AKTIONSART*

A verb depicts a timeless and universal action. This may occur with either aspect and any type of lexeme. Context alone determines whether or not an action is gnomic.

HISTORICAL PERFECT

A perfect tense-form that refers to the past.

HISTORICAL PRESENT

A present tense-form that refers to the past.

IMPERFECTIVE ASPECT

The internal aspect/viewpoint. This depicts an action from the inside *as though* unfolding, without reference to the beginning or end of the action. It does not imply progression or incompleteness, though these *Aktionsarten* are naturally expressed with imperfective aspect in combination with other factors. The present, imperfect, perfect, and pluperfect tense-forms are imperfective in aspect.

IMPLICATURE

A specific function of a verb form when in combination with certain pragmatic features. Every verbal form is capable of expressing a variety of implicatures, depending on the combination of pragmatic features at work in any given text.

INGRESSIVE *AKTIONSART*

A verb depicts the beginning, and subsequent progression, of an action. This may occur with imperfective aspect and any nonpunctiliar/nonstative lexeme when the context indicates a shift or new direction. Alternatively, this may occur with perfective aspect and a stative lexeme.

INTRANSITIVE LEXEME

A lexeme that does not perform an action upon an object. It may actually take an object, but strictly speaking the action is not *done* to the object. The action may be done with reference to someone or something.

ITERATIVE *AKTIONSART*

A verb depicts a repeated action. This may occur when imperfective aspect combines with a punctiliar lexeme. Alternatively, the context may create an iterative action even if the lexeme is not punctiliar.

LEXEME
A particular word, such as *run*, *write*, *see*, *fly*, etc.

MAINLINE
The basic outline, or skeletal structure, of a narrative. The narrative mainline is typically portrayed through the use of perfective aspect.

OFFLINE
Narrative background and supplemental information that describes details, provides reasons and explanations, and elucidates motivations of actions on the narrative mainline. Narrative offline is typically portrayed by imperfective aspect.

PERFECTIVE ASPECT
The external aspect/viewpoint. This depicts an action as undefined, in summary. It does not imply completion or punctiliarity, though these *Aktionsarten* are naturally expressed with perfective aspect in combination with other factors. The aorist and future are perfective in aspect.

PRAGMATICS
The cancelable outcome of all textual/lexical/deictic factors in combination. What a verb ends up "doing" in the context.

PROGRESSIVE *AKTIONSART*
A verb depicts a process or action in progress. This may occur when imperfective aspect combines with any lexeme that is not punctiliar or stative and when the context allows progression.

PROXIMITY
The spatial quality of nearness. Used as a spatial replacement for present tense. Spatial proximity may be expressed pragmatically through present temporal reference or through logical intimacy (such as intensity or prominence).

PUNCTILIAR *AKTIONSART*
A verb depicts a punctiliar action. This may occur with perfective aspect and a punctiliar lexeme.

PUNCTILIAR LEXEME
A type of transitive lexeme that is instantaneous and once occurring. While a punctiliar action may be repeated, it cannot be performed with any duration.

REMOTENESS

The spatial quality of distance. Used as a spatial replacement for past tense. Spatial remoteness may be expressed pragmatically through past temporal reference or through logical obliqueness (such as within negative conditions).

SEMANTICS

The uncancelable core value(s) of a verb form. With respect to Greek verbs (verbal semantics, grammatical semantics), the semantic values are aspect and remoteness or proximity (or tense).

STATIVE *AKTIONSART*

A verb depicts a state. This may occur when imperfective aspect combines with a stative lexeme. Sometimes the context can create a stative *Aktionsart* even if the lexeme is not itself stative.

STATIVE ASPECT

Refers either to the state of the subject (McKay) or of "the situation" (Porter). The latter is roughly equivalent to the "present consequence" of the traditional rendering of the perfect as past action with present implications. It does not, in my view, accommodate transitive verbs very well. Under my analysis, stativity is properly understood as an *Aktionsart* category (as it is in general linguistics) rather than as aspectual.

STATIVE LEXEME

A type of intransitive lexeme that conveys a state of being.

SUMMARY *AKTIONSART*

A verb depicts a process or action in summary. This may occur with perfective aspect and any type of lexeme that is not punctiliar or stative.

SYSTEMIC LINGUISTICS

A school within functional linguistics, foundational especially to Porter's analysis. This conceives language use as a series of choices made in opposition to other possible choices. A language, therefore, is a network of oppositions.

TENSE

Cancelable temporal reference. Tense has been mistakenly assumed by some to be semantic alongside aspect, but it is better regarded as a pragmatic outcome of various factors in context. In fact, on this definition one might say that tense does not exist; there is only temporal reference (except for the future, which is a real tense).

TRANSITIVE LEXEME

A lexeme that performs an action upon an object.

Answers to Exercises

PRESENT AND IMPERFECT INDICATIVE TENSE-FORMS

For each passage, (1) write about the semantic meaning of the indicative verb, (2) state the contribution of the lexeme, and (3) discuss the function of the verb in context. Once you have written your answers, summarize your findings in the boxes below each passage.

Example:

Luke 8:45 (x2) καὶ εἶπεν ὁ Ἰησοῦς, Τίς ὁ ἁψάμενός μου; ἀρνουμένων δὲ πάντων εἶπεν ὁ Πέτρος, Ἐπιστάτα, οἱ ὄχλοι **συνέχουσίν** σε καὶ **ἀποθλίβουσιν.**

"Who touched Me?" Jesus asked. When they all denied it, Peter said, "Master, the crowds **are hemming** you in and **pressing against** you."

1. Semantic meaning of the indicative verb. The present indicative semantically encodes imperfective aspect and the spatial value of proximity.
2. Contribution of the lexeme. The lexemes are transitive (perform an action upon an object). They are not punctiliar or stative.
3. Function in context. The context makes it clear that these actions are taking place continuously at the time of speech. Thus, these indicative verbs are conveying progressive action.

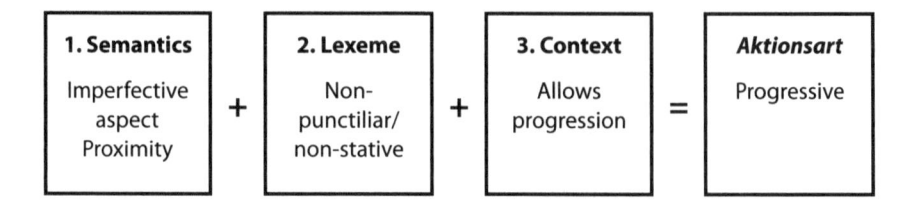

1. Semantics		2. Lexeme		3. Context		Aktionsart
Imperfective aspect Proximity	+	Non-punctiliar/ non-stative	+	Allows progression	=	Progressive

John 7:42 οὐχ ἡ γραφὴ εἶπεν ὅτι ἐκ τοῦ σπέρματος Δαυὶδ καὶ ἀπὸ Βηθλέεμ τῆς κώμης ὅπου ἦν Δαυὶδ **ἔρχεται** ὁ Χριστός;

Doesn't the Scripture say that the Christ **comes** from David's offspring and from the town of Bethlehem, where David once lived?

1. Semantic meaning of the indicative verb. The present indicative semantically encodes imperfective aspect and the spatial value of proximity.
2. Contribution of the lexeme. The lexeme is intransitive (does not take an object) but is not stative. This is also a verb of propulsion.
3. Function in context. The context makes it clear that a general statement about reality is being made. The indicative verb is therefore gnomic. Jesus is asserting the general statement that the Messiah comes from David's offspring.

1. Semantics		2. Lexeme		3. Context		Aktionsart
Imperfective aspect Proximity	+	Intransitive / propulsion	+	Gnomic	=	Gnomic

Other considerations: Since ἔρχεται is a verb of propulsion, it would be appropriate to wonder if it is an historical present (e.g., "the Christ **came** from David's offspring"). But this possibility is ruled out by the forward-looking expectation of Scripture ("Doesn't the Scripture say . . . ?"). The verb cannot be a historical present since it is clearly not past referring in this context.

John 5:16 καὶ διὰ τοῦτο **ἐδίωκον** οἱ Ἰουδαῖοι τὸν Ἰησοῦν, ὅτι ταῦτα ἐποίει ἐν σαββάτῳ.

Therefore, the Jews **began persecuting** Jesus because he was doing these things on the Sabbath.

1. Semantic meaning of the indicative verb. The imperfect indicative semantically encodes imperfective aspect and the spatial value of remoteness.
2. Contribution of the lexeme. The lexeme is transitive (takes an object) but not punctiliar.
3. Function in context. The wider context makes it clear that the action has just begun, and as such the action is ingressive.

1. Semantics	2. Lexeme	3. Context	Aktionsart
Imperfective aspect Remoteness	Transitive	Beginning of action	Ingressive

(with + between boxes 1 and 2, + between boxes 2 and 3, and = between box 3 and Aktionsart)

Other considerations: Admittedly, it is not really possible to know that this action has just begun from the verse alone. From the information provided, it would be possible to understand ἐδίωκον as a progressive *Aktionsart* (e.g., "they were persecuting"). However, if the wider context is taken into account, it becomes clear that John's Gospel presents this event as the beginning of the persecution of Jesus.

Romans 1:18 Ἀποκαλύπτεται γὰρ ὀργὴ θεοῦ ἀπ' οὐρανοῦ ἐπὶ πᾶσαν ἀσέβειαν καὶ ἀδικίαν ἀνθρώπων τῶν τὴν ἀλήθειαν ἐν ἀδικίᾳ κατεχόντων.

For God's wrath **is revealed** from heaven against all godlessness and unrighteousness of people who by their unrighteousness suppress the truth.

1. Semantic meaning of the indicative verb. The present indicative semantically encodes imperfective aspect and the spatial value of proximity.
2. Contribution of the lexeme. The lexeme is transitive. It is not punctiliar or stative. (See "Other considerations" below).
3. Function in context. The context does not make it clear whether the action is progressive or stative. On the one hand, it may refer to God's wrath being revealed continuously (God's wrath is being revealed); on the other, it may refer to a state of affairs (God's wrath has been revealed and is now evident). Wider context is needed to decide which option is best (i.e., theological context). An iterative reading is unlikely, since the lexeme is not punctiliar.

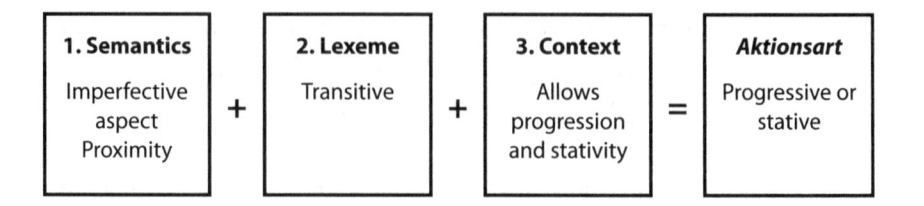

1. Semantics		2. Lexeme		3. Context		Aktionsart
Imperfective aspect Proximity	+	Transitive	+	Allows progression and stativity	=	Progressive or stative

Other considerations: Since ἀποκαλύπτεται is in the passive voice, it may seem that the lexeme is stative, when really that is not the case. The passive voice creates this effect rather than the lexeme itself. It is best to temporarily "unpassify" the lexeme to its active meaning to see that it is, in fact, transitive.

Romans 8:3 τὸ γὰρ ἀδύνατον τοῦ νόμου ἐν ᾧ **ἠσθένει** διὰ τῆς σαρκός, ὁ θεὸς τὸν ἑαυτοῦ υἱὸν πέμψας ἐν ὁμοιώματι σαρκὸς ἁμαρτίας καὶ περὶ ἁμαρτίας κατέκρινεν τὴν ἁμαρτίαν ἐν τῇ σαρκί.

What the law could not do since **it was limited** by the flesh, God did. He condemned sin in the flesh by sending his own Son in flesh like ours under sin's domain, and as a sin offering.

1. Semantic meaning of the indicative verb. The imperfect indicative semantically encodes imperfective aspect and the spatial value of remoteness.
2. Contribution of the lexeme. The lexeme is stative in that it refers to being in a state of weakness.
3. Function in context. The context allows stativity but locates this within a past temporal context. Thus, the verb conveys a (past) state.

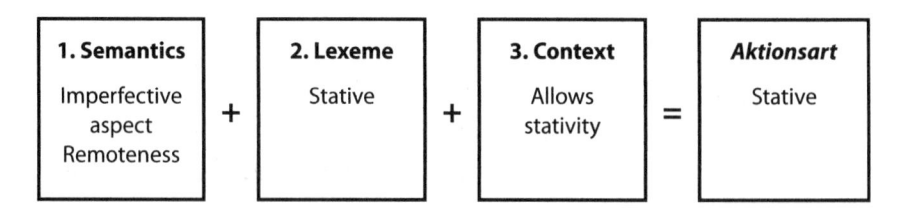

1. Semantics		2. Lexeme		3. Context		Aktionsart
Imperfective aspect Remoteness	+	Stative	+	Allows stativity	=	Stative

John 15:27 (x2) καὶ ὑμεῖς δὲ **μαρτυρεῖτε**, ὅτι ἀπ᾽ ἀρχῆς μετ᾽ ἐμοῦ **ἐστε**.

You also **will testify**, because you **have been** with me from the beginning.

1. Semantic meaning of the indicative verb. The present indicative semantically encodes imperfective aspect and the spatial value of proximity.

2. Contribution of the lexeme. The first lexeme is intransitive (does not take an object) but is not stative; the second is stative.

3. Function in context. The wider context makes it clear that the first verb is progressive in nature and future in temporal reference. It is clear that the second verb refers to a state that began in the past ("from the beginning") and implies that the state exists at the time of speaking.

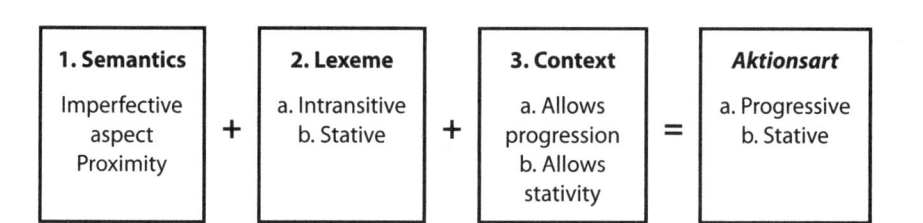

1. Semantics		2. Lexeme		3. Context		Aktionsart
Imperfective aspect Proximity	**+**	a. Intransitive b. Stative	**+**	a. Allows progression b. Allows stativity	**=**	a. Progressive b. Stative

Other considerations: The previous verse (John 15:26) sets the future temporal reference in this instance, since it looks forward to the time when the Counselor comes, who will testify about Jesus. Without this information, it would be possible to read μαρτυρεῖτε in 15:27 as present referring ("you testify").

Romans 6:8 εἰ δὲ ἀπεθάνομεν σὺν Χριστῷ, **πιστεύομεν** ὅτι καὶ συζήσομεν αὐτῷ.

Now if we died with Christ, **we believe** that we will also live with him.

1. Semantic meaning of the indicative verb. The present indicative semantically encodes imperfective aspect and the spatial value of proximity.

2. Contribution of the lexeme. The lexeme is stative.

3. Function in context. The context allows for a stative interpretation.

1. Semantics		2. Lexeme		3. Context		Aktionsart
Imperfective aspect Proximity	**+**	Stative	**+**	Allows stavtivity	**=**	Stative

Other considerations: The occurrence of πιστεύομεν in the apodosis of a conditional sentence might lead to some confusion. Does conditionality affect the "state" of the stative lexeme? The answer is no, because the protasis ("if we died with Christ") is not really conditional in the context. Paul is not genuinely raising the question "if" believers died with Christ, since this is already an established fact (6:3–4). The conditional sentence is used for rhetorical purposes, thus there is no genuine conditionality that might compromise the "reality" of the state of believing.

John 3:22 Μετὰ ταῦτα ἦλθεν ὁ Ἰησοῦς καὶ οἱ μαθηταὶ αὐτοῦ εἰς τὴν Ἰουδαίαν γῆν καὶ ἐκεῖ διέτριβεν μετ᾽ αὐτῶν καὶ **ἐβάπτιζεν**.

After this, Jesus and his disciples went to the Judean countryside, where he spent time with them and **was baptizing**.

1. Semantic meaning of the indicative verb. The imperfect indicative semantically encodes imperfective aspect and the spatial value of remoteness.
2. Contribution of the lexeme. The lexeme is punctiliar in that a baptism (lit. "to dip") is an instantaneous action.
3. Function in context. The context implies that this action was repeated and is therefore iterative.

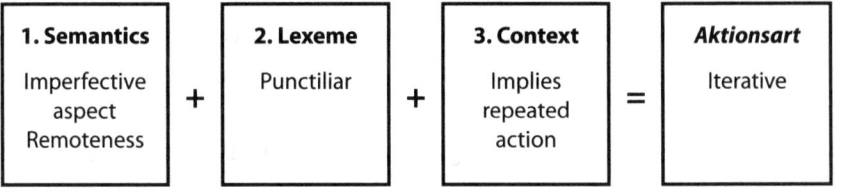

Other considerations: In fact, βαπτίζω is not necessarily a punctiliar lexeme, since it can mean *immerse*, *submerge*, or *sink* in various contexts. However, baptism involves a momentary "dipping" of a person underwater, drawing on the lexeme's ability to refer to an instantaneous event.[1] As such, ἐβάπτιζεν is correctly regarded as iterative in this context.

Romans 8:13 (x3) εἰ γὰρ κατὰ σάρκα **ζῆτε**, **μέλλετε** ἀποθνῄσκειν· εἰ δὲ πνεύματι τὰς πράξεις τοῦ σώματος **θανατοῦτε**, ζήσεσθε.

For if **you live** according to the flesh, **you are going** to die. But if by the Spirit **you put to death** the deeds of the body, you will live.

---

1. Franco Montanari, *The Brill Dictionary of Ancient Greek*, ed. Madeleine Goh and Chad Schroeder (Leiden: Brill, 2015), s.v. βαπτίζω (p. 375).

1. Semantic meaning of the indicative verb. The present indicative semantically encodes imperfective aspect and the spatial value of proximity.
2. Contribution of the lexeme. The first lexeme is stative; the second is an auxiliary to an infinitive (and is kind of stative); the third is transitive (*to put to death, to cause to die, to kill*).[2]
3. Function in context. The context allows the first and second verbs to be stative; the third is most likely progressive.

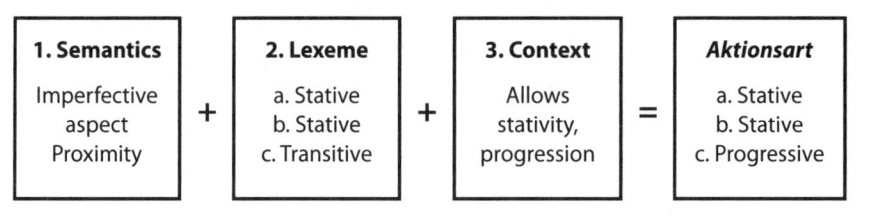

Other considerations: This example, along with others, demonstrates that the same tense-form (in this case, the present active indicative) is capable of multiple *Aktionsart* expressions in a single context. The variable is the lexeme, which illustrates how important it is to consider properly the input of each lexeme.

Psalm 101:9 ὅλην τὴν ἡμέραν ὠνείδιζόν με οἱ ἐχθροί μου, καὶ οἱ ἐπαινοῦντές με κατ᾽ ἐμοῦ ὤμνυον.

All day long my enemies **reproach** me, and those who used to commend me **swear** against me.

1. Semantic meaning of the indicative verb. The imperfect indicative semantically encodes imperfective aspect and the spatial value of remoteness.
2. Contribution of the lexeme. The first lexeme is transitive; the second is normally intransitive, but in this case it takes an object ("against me").
3. Function in context. The temporal phrase "all day long" (ὅλην τὴν ἡμέραν) indicates that the actions are ongoing.

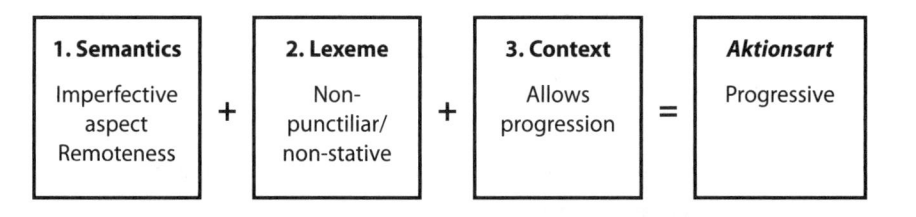

---

2. Montanari, *Brill Dictionary of Ancient Greek*, s.v. θανατόω (p. 925).

Other considerations: Without the temporal phrase, "all day long," this example could be understood as gnomic, expressing the general reality that the psalmist is reviled by his enemies. But the inclusion of the temporal phrase creates the sense of ongoing, progressing actions.

AORIST AND FUTURE INDICATIVE TENSE-FORMS

For each passage, (1) write about the semantic meaning of the indicative verb, (2) state the contribution of the lexeme, and (3) discuss the function of the verb in context. Once you have written your answers, summarize your findings in the boxes below each passage.

Example:
John 19:34 ἀλλ᾽ εἷς τῶν στρατιωτῶν λόγχῃ αὐτοῦ τὴν πλευρὰν **ἔνυξεν**, καὶ ἐξῆλθεν εὐθὺς αἷμα καὶ ὕδωρ.

But one of the soldiers **pierced** his side with a spear, and at once blood and water came out.

1. Semantic meaning of the indicative verb. The aorist indicative semantically encodes perfective aspect and the spatial value of remoteness.
2. Contribution of the lexeme. The lexeme is punctiliar; it is an instantaneous action.
3. Function in context. The context allows for a punctiliar interpretation.

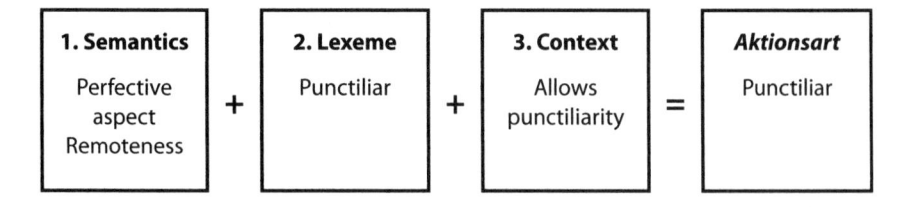

John 7:32 (x2) Ἤκουσαν οἱ Φαρισαῖοι τοῦ ὄχλου γογγύζοντος περὶ αὐτοῦ ταῦτα, καὶ **ἀπέστειλαν** οἱ ἀρχιερεῖς καὶ οἱ Φαρισαῖοι ὑπηρέτας ἵνα πιάσωσιν αὐτόν.

The Pharisees **heard** the crowd muttering these things about him, so the chief priests and the Pharisees **sent** temple police to arrest him.

1. Semantic meaning of the indicative verb. The aorist indicative semantically encodes perfective aspect and the spatial value of remoteness.
2. Contribution of the lexeme. The first lexeme is intransitive, the second is transitive. Neither lexeme is punctiliar or stative.
3. Function in context. The context allows for both to be interpreted as summary aorists.

1. Semantics		2. Lexeme		3. Context		Aktionsart
Perfective aspect Remoteness	**+**	Non-punctiliar/ non-stative	**+**	Allows summary	**=**	Summary

Other considerations: Though ἤκουσαν takes an object (the Pharisees heard *the crowd*), this does not make it transitive according to our definition. Remember that a lexeme is transitive if it *affects* or *impacts* its object somehow. Hearing the noise made by a crowd does not do anything to the crowd, so ἤκουσαν is intransitive (see chapter 6). On the other hand, ἀπέστειλαν is transitive because its object (the temple police) are *sent*. They are affected by the action.

Romans 6:14 ἁμαρτία γὰρ ὑμῶν **οὐ κυριεύσει**· οὐ γὰρ ἐστε ὑπὸ νόμον ἀλλὰ ὑπὸ χάριν.

For sin **will not rule** over you, because you are not under law but under grace.

1. Semantic meaning of the indicative verb. The future indicative semantically encodes perfective aspect and future temporal reference.
2. Contribution of the lexeme. The lexeme is not punctiliar or stative (though it *could be* understood as stative; see "Other considerations" below).
3. Function in context. The context allows for the verb to be interpreted as a summary future.

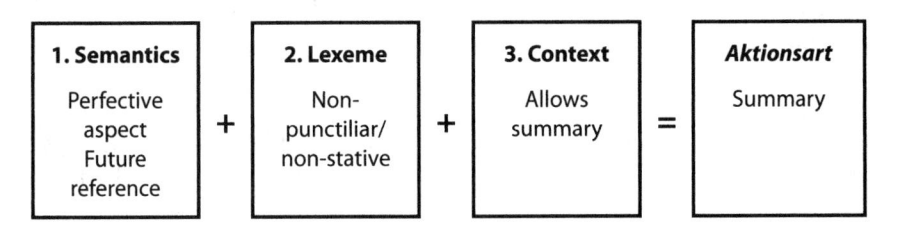

1. Semantics		2. Lexeme		3. Context		Aktionsart
Perfective aspect Future reference	**+**	Non-punctiliar/ non-stative	**+**	Allows summary	**=**	Summary

Other considerations: The lexeme κυριεύω here most likely refers to exercising authority or control over its object (transitive), but it can also refer to the state of being master or lord over something (stative).[3] If the lexeme is taken as stative, the *Aktionsart* outcome would be affected. Perfective aspect in combination with a stative lexeme normally creates an ingressive *Aktionsart*, yielding the sense, "sin will not *begin to* rule over you." Such a reading is unlikely, however, for theological/contextual reasons: Paul clearly believes that people *were* under the rule of sin until they were set free in Christ (see the wider context; e.g., Romans 6:6–7).

Romans 3:23 πάντες γὰρ **ἥμαρτον** καὶ ὑστεροῦνται τῆς δόξης τοῦ θεοῦ.

For all **have sinned** and fall short of the glory of God.

1. Semantic meaning of the indicative verb. The aorist indicative semantically encodes perfective aspect and the spatial value of remoteness.
2. Contribution of the lexeme. The lexeme is not punctiliar or stative.
3. Function in context. The context allows for the verb to be interpreted as a summary aorist. It could perhaps provide a gnomic context ("For all sin . . ."), but this is tentative at best.

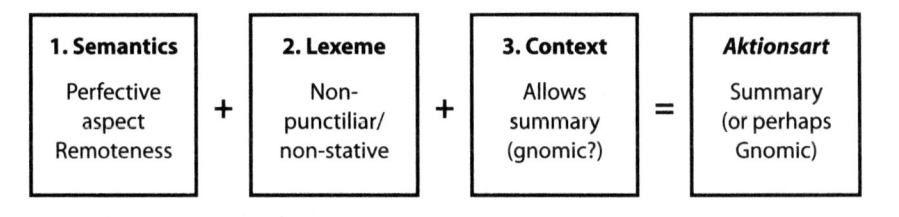

1. Semantics		**2. Lexeme**		**3. Context**		*Aktionsart*
Perfective aspect Remoteness	**+**	Non-punctiliar/ non-stative	**+**	Allows summary (gnomic?)	**=**	Summary (or perhaps Gnomic)

Other considerations: It is possible to understand this context as gnomic so that the phrase is rendered, "All **sin** and fall short of the glory of God." This would then be a general statement about reality (i.e., all people sin) rather than a depiction of something that happened in the past. While the gnomic reading is possible, it is probably best to understand the context as past referring, so that Paul comments on a historical reality: all **have sinned**. This is a fact that requires the solution of justification in Christ (3:24).

---

3. Frederick W. Danker, Walter Bauer, William F. Arndt, and F. Wilbur Gingrich, *Greek-English Lexicon of the New Testament*, 3rd ed. (Chicago: University of Chicago Press, 2000), s.v. κυριεύω 1, 2 (p. 576).

John 1:10 ἐν τῷ κόσμῳ ἦν, καὶ ὁ κόσμος δι᾽ αὐτοῦ ἐγένετο, καὶ ὁ κόσμος αὐτὸν **οὐκ ἔγνω**.

He was in the world, and the world was created through him, yet the world **did not recognize** him.

1. Semantic meaning of the indicative verb. The aorist indicative semantically encodes perfective aspect and the spatial value of remoteness.
2. Contribution of the lexeme. The lexeme γινώσκω is stative.
3. Function in context. The context allows the entrance into a state.

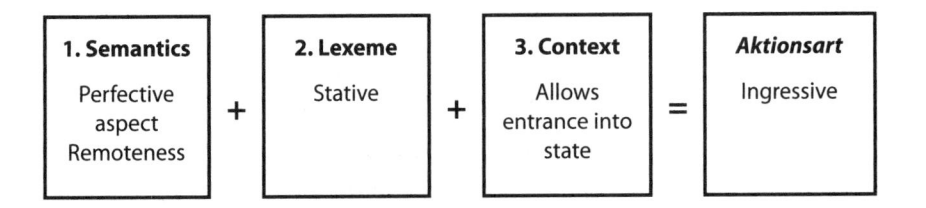

Other considerations: When a stative lexeme is used in combination with perfective aspect, an ingressive *Aktionsart* is implied. This is why the translation is rendered "the world **did not recognize** him," since "recognize" captures the idea of coming to know something. Another possible translation would be "the world **did not come to know** him."

Mark 14:27 καὶ λέγει αὐτοῖς ὁ Ἰησοῦς ὅτι Πάντες σκανδαλισθήσεσθε, ὅτι γέγραπται, Πατάξω τὸν ποιμένα, καὶ τὰ πρόβατα διασκορπισθήσονται.

Then Jesus said to them, "All of you will run away, because it is written: '**I will strike** the shepherd, and the sheep will be scattered.'"

1. Semantic meaning of the indicative verb. The future indicative semantically encodes perfective aspect and future temporal reference.
2. Contribution of the lexeme. The lexeme is punctiliar; it is an instantaneous action.
3. Function in context. The context allows for a punctiliar interpretation.

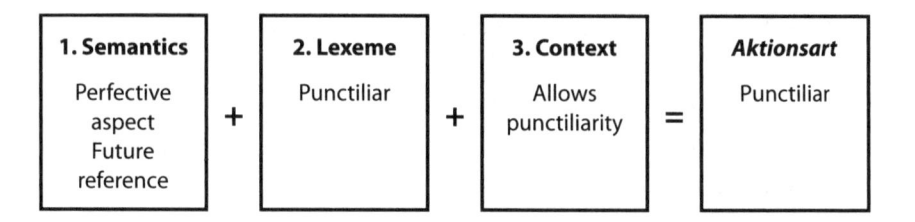

John 7:26 καὶ ἴδε παρρησίᾳ λαλεῖ καὶ οὐδὲν αὐτῷ λέγουσιν. μήποτε ἀληθῶς **ἔγνωσαν** οἱ ἄρχοντες ὅτι οὗτός ἐστιν ὁ Χριστός;

Yet, look! He's speaking publicly and they're saying nothing to him. Can it be true that the authorities **know** he is the Christ?

1. Semantic meaning of the indicative verb. The aorist indicative semantically encodes perfective aspect and the spatial value of remoteness.
2. Contribution of the lexeme. The lexeme γινώσκω is stative.
3. Function in context. The context allows entrance into a state, making an ingressive interpretation possible.

1. Semantics		2. Lexeme		3. Context		Aktionsart
Perfective aspect Remoteness	+	Stative	+	Allows entrance into state	=	Ingressive

Other considerations: As with John 1:10 above, the stative lexeme combines with perfective aspect to create an ingressive *Aktionsart*. Thus, the translation "the authorities **know**" depicts the authorities coming into a state of knowledge that Jesus is the Christ (or at least the question raises this possibility: "Can it be true . . . ?").

Romans 8:11 εἰ δὲ τὸ πνεῦμα τοῦ ἐγείραντος τὸν Ἰησοῦν ἐκ νεκρῶν οἰκεῖ ἐν ὑμῖν, ὁ ἐγείρας Χριστὸν ἐκ νεκρῶν **ζωοποιήσει** καὶ τὰ θνητὰ σώματα ὑμῶν διὰ τοῦ ἐνοικοῦντος αὐτοῦ πνεύματος ἐν ὑμῖν.

And if the Spirit of him who raised Jesus from the dead lives in you, then he who raised Christ from the dead **will also bring** your mortal bodies **to life** through his Spirit who lives in you.

1. **Semantic meaning of the indicative verb.** The future indicative semantically encodes perfective aspect and future temporal reference.
2. **Contribution of the lexeme.** The lexeme is not punctiliar or stative. It does, however, imply ingressive action, since it means "to make alive," which refers to the entrance into a state of being alive.
3. **Function in context.** The context allows for an ingressive interpretation (i.e., entrance into a state).

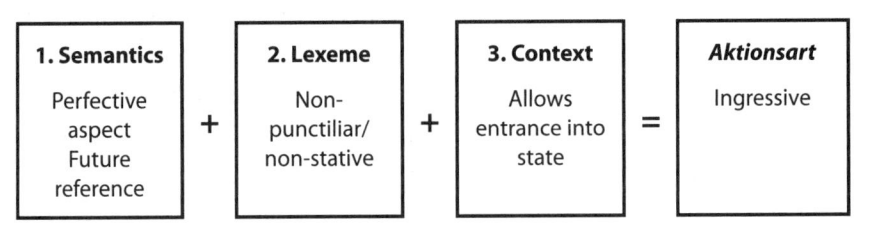

1. Semantics		2. Lexeme		3. Context		Aktionsart
Perfective aspect Future reference	+	Non-punctiliar/ non-stative	+	Allows entrance into state	=	Ingressive

Other considerations: This example demonstrates how an ingressive *Aktionsart* can be created without a stative lexeme, which is the normal way it occurs (in combination with perfective aspect). The lexeme is transitive but leads to the creation of a state, so it already implies ingression.

Romans 8:30 (x6) οὓς δὲ **προώρισεν**, τούτους καὶ **ἐκάλεσεν**· καὶ οὓς **ἐκάλεσεν**, τούτους καὶ **ἐδικαίωσεν**· οὓς δὲ **ἐδικαίωσεν**, τούτους καὶ **ἐδόξασεν**.

And those **he predestines, he** also **calls**; and those **he calls, he** also **justifies**; and those **he justifies, he** also **glorifies**.

1. **Semantic meaning of the indicative verb.** The aorist indicative semantically encodes perfective aspect and the spatial value of remoteness.
2. **Contribution of the lexeme.** The lexemes are not punctiliar or stative.
3. **Function in context.** The context suggests a gnomic reading.

1. Semantics		2. Lexeme		3. Context		Aktionsart
Perfective aspect Remoteness	+	Non-punctiliar/ non-stative	+	Allows gnomic	=	Gnomic

Other considerations: This verse has been notoriously difficult for interpreters who take the aorists as past referring—"Those he predestined, he also called, and those he called, he also justified, and those he justified, he also glorified." Since glorification is normally understood to occur in the future, interpreters tend to claim that the past-referring aorist "glorified" is used because the future is so certain that it can be claimed as being done already. This highly unlikely understanding is not necessary, however, once it is recognized that this string of aorists can be explained as gnomic in function. They do not refer to past events but to a series of activities that God performs—predestining, calling, justifying, and glorifying. As a general statement of reality, the gnomic reading does not require these actions to be locked into any specific timeframe.

Genesis 4:12 ὅτι ἐργᾷ τὴν γῆν, καὶ **οὐ προσθήσει** τὴν ἰσχὺν αὐτῆς δοῦναί σοι· στένων καὶ τρέμων **ἔσῃ** ἐπὶ τῆς γῆς.

For **you will till** the earth, and **it will not continue** to yield its strength to you; **you will be** groaning and trembling on the earth.

1. Semantic meaning of the indicative verb. The future indicative semantically encodes perfective aspect and future temporal reference.
2. Contribution of the lexeme. The first two lexemes are transitive; the third is stative.
3. Function in context. The context allows for all three verbs to be interpreted as summary futures.

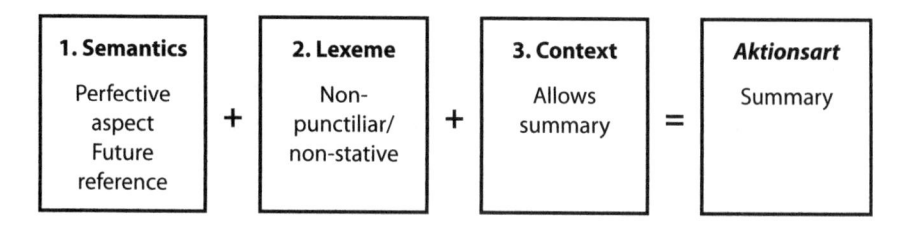

PERFECT AND PLUPERFECT INDICATIVE TENSE-FORMS

For each passage, (1) write about the semantic meaning of the indicative verb, (2) state the contribution of the lexeme, and (3) discuss the function of the verb in context. Once you have written your answers, summarize your findings in the boxes below each passage.

Example:
John 7:27 ἀλλὰ τοῦτον **οἴδαμεν** πόθεν ἐστίν· ὁ δὲ Χριστὸς ὅταν
ἔρχηται οὐδεὶς γινώσκει πόθεν ἐστίν.

But **we know** where this man is from. When the Christ comes, nobody
will know where he is from.

1. Semantic meaning of the indicative verb. The perfect indicative semantically
   encodes imperfective aspect and the spatial value of heightened proximity.
2. Contribution of the lexeme. The lexeme is stative.
3. Function in context. The context allows for a stative interpretation.

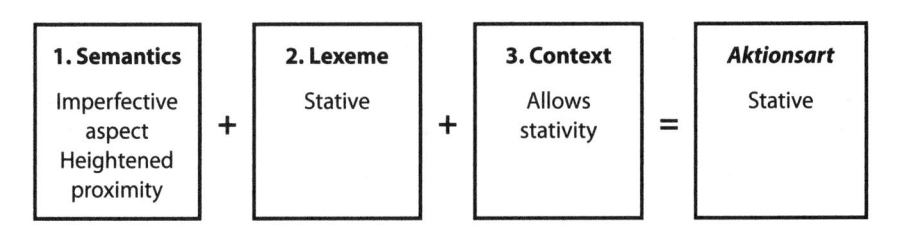

Romans 1:17 δικαιοσύνη γὰρ θεοῦ ἐν αὐτῷ ἀποκαλύπτεται ἐκ πίστεως
εἰς πίστιν, καθὼς **γέγραπται**, Ὁ δὲ δίκαιος ἐκ πίστεως ζήσεται.

For in it God's righteousness is revealed from faith to faith, just as **it is
written**: The righteous will live by faith.

1. Semantic meaning of the indicative verb. The perfect indicative semantically
   encodes imperfective aspect and the spatial value of heightened proximity.
2. Contribution of the lexeme. The lexeme is transitive.
3. Function in context. The context suggests a stative interpretation.

1. Semantics		2. Lexeme		3. Context		*Aktionsart*
Imperfective aspect Heightened proximity	**+**	Transitive	**+**	Implies stativity	**=**	Stative

Other considerations: While the lexeme γράφω is transitive, the passive
voice of γέγραπται implies stativity, which is often the effect of the passive voice

(especially with imperfective aspect). A stative reading suits the context since Habakkuk 2:4 stands written in Scripture.

John 7:30 Ἐζήτουν οὖν αὐτὸν πιάσαι, καὶ οὐδεὶς ἐπέβαλεν ἐπ᾽ αὐτὸν τὴν χεῖρα, ὅτι **οὔπω ἐληλύθει** ἡ ὥρα αὐτοῦ.

Then they tried to seize him. Yet no one laid a hand on him because his hour **had not yet come.**

1. Semantic meaning of the indicative verb. The pluperfect indicative semantically encodes imperfective aspect and the spatial value of heightened remoteness.
2. Contribution of the lexeme. The lexeme is intransitive.
3. Function in context. The context indicates past-past temporal reference.

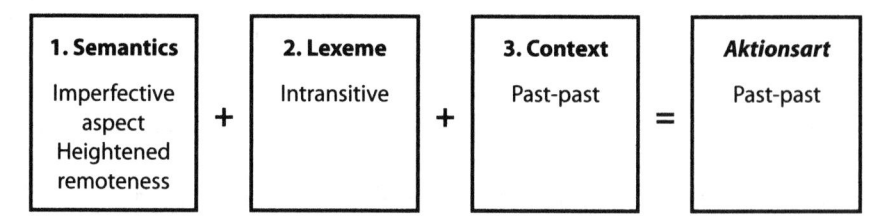

1. Semantics		2. Lexeme		3. Context		Aktionsart
Imperfective aspect Heightened remoteness	**+**	Intransitive	**+**	Past-past	**=**	Past-past

John 16:11 . . . περὶ δὲ κρίσεως, ὅτι ὁ ἄρχων τοῦ κόσμου τούτου **κέκριται.**

. . . and about judgment, because the ruler of this world **is being judged.**

1. Semantic meaning of the indicative verb. The perfect indicative semantically encodes imperfective aspect and the spatial value of heightened proximity.
2. Contribution of the lexeme. The lexeme is transitive and is not punctiliar nor stative.
3. Function in context. The context allows for a progressive interpretation.

1. Semantics		2. Lexeme		3. Context		Aktionsart
Imperfective aspect Heightened proximity	**+**	Non-punctiliar/ non-stative	**+**	Allows progression	**=**	Progressive

Other considerations: Though the lexeme κρίνω is not stative, the passive voice of κέκριται makes a stative reading possible—"The ruler of this world **is judged**." However, the traditional rendering of the perfect—"has been judged"— makes little sense in the context or theologically. Insisting on the "past action with present consequences" interpretation of the perfect evokes misleading and unnecessary complications. The progressive reading of the perfect—though rare (and debated)—works well in the context as Jesus anticipates the process of judgment upon "the ruler of this world."

John 1:15 Ἰωάννης μαρτυρεῖ περὶ αὐτοῦ καὶ **κέκραγεν** λέγων, Οὗτος ἦν ὃν εἶπον, Ὁ ὀπίσω μου ἐρχόμενος ἔμπροσθέν μου γέγονεν, ὅτι πρῶτός μου ἦν.

John testified concerning him and **exclaimed**, "This was the one of whom I said, 'The one coming after me has surpassed me, because he was before me.'"

1. Semantic meaning of the indicative verb. The perfect indicative semantically encodes imperfective aspect and the spatial value of heightened proximity.
2. Contribution of the lexeme. The lexeme introduces discourse.
3. Function in context. The context is past referring, making the historical perfect a suitable interpretation.

1. Semantics		2. Lexeme		3. Context		Aktionsart
Imperfective aspect Heightened proximity	+	Introduces discourse	+	Past referring	=	Historical perfect

Other considerations: This is a good example of the historical perfect functioning in parallel with the historical present (μαρτυρεῖ). In English translations, both verbs are appropriately translated with the simple past tense ("testified," "exclaimed"). Instances of such parallels provide further corroborating evidence that the present and perfect tense-forms share the same imperfective aspect.

Romans 8:38 πέπεισμαι γὰρ ὅτι οὔτε θάνατος οὔτε ζωὴ οὔτε ἄγγελοι
οὔτε ἀρχαὶ οὔτε ἐνεστῶτα οὔτε μέλλοντα οὔτε δυνάμεις . . .

For **I am persuaded** that neither death nor life, nor angels nor rulers,
nor things present, nor things to come, nor powers . . .

1. Semantic meaning of the indicative verb. The perfect indicative semantically
   encodes imperfective aspect and the spatial value of heightened proximity.
2. Contribution of the lexeme. The lexeme is stative.
3. Function in context. The context allows for a stative interpretation.

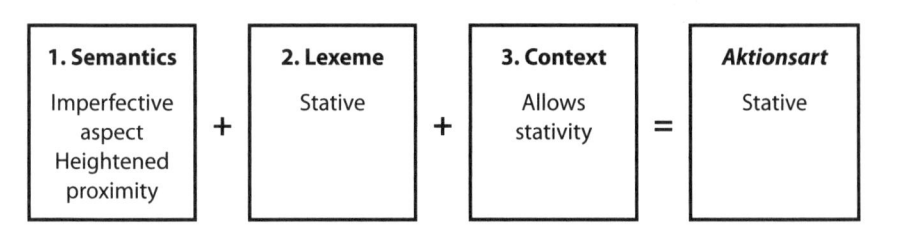

Other considerations: The lexeme πείθω can be transitive or intransitive
in the active voice, but in the middle/passive voices is normally intransitive and
stative.[4] Clearly the lexeme and the context support the notion of stativity as Paul
expresses the unchanging reality of his being persuaded.

Matthew 7:25 καὶ κατέβη ἡ βροχὴ καὶ ἦλθον οἱ ποταμοὶ καὶ
ἔπνευσαν οἱ ἄνεμοι καὶ προσέπεσαν τῇ οἰκίᾳ ἐκείνῃ, καὶ οὐκ ἔπεσεν,
τεθεμελίωτο γὰρ ἐπὶ τὴν πέτραν.

The rain fell, the rivers rose, and the winds blew and pounded that
house. Yet it didn't collapse, because **it was founded** on the rock.

1. Semantic meaning of the indicative verb. The pluperfect indicative semantically encodes imperfective aspect and the spatial value of heightened
   remoteness.
2. Contribution of the lexeme. The lexeme is transitive in the active voice but
   intransitive in the passive voice.

---

4. Montanari, *Brill Dictionary of Ancient Greek*, 1604–5.

3. Function in context. The context implies a stative interpretation.

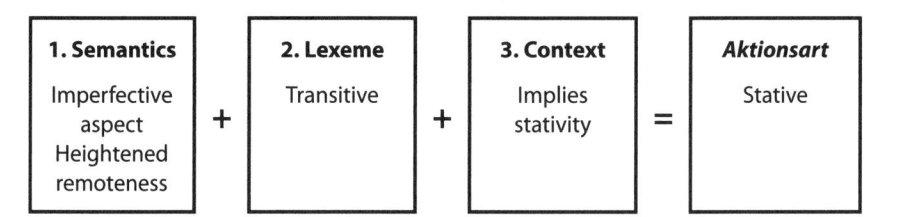

1. Semantics		2. Lexeme		3. Context		Aktionsart
Imperfective aspect Heightened remoteness	+	Transitive	+	Implies stativity	=	Stative

Other considerations: In the active voice, the lexeme θεμελιόω is transitive ("to set on foundations"), but in the passive voice it is intransitive ("to have foundations").[5] The passive voice of τεθεμελίωτο—along with the sense of the house being permanently established on the rock—points to a stative *Aktionsart* reading.

John 19:30 ὅτε οὖν ἔλαβεν τὸ ὄξος ὁ Ἰησοῦς εἶπεν, **Τετέλεσται**, καὶ κλίνας τὴν κεφαλὴν παρέδωκεν τὸ πνεῦμα.

When Jesus had received the sour wine, he said, "**It is finished!**" Then after bowing his head, he gave up his spirit.

1. Semantic meaning of the indicative verb. The perfect indicative semantically encodes imperfective aspect and the spatial value of heightened proximity.
2. Contribution of the lexeme. The lexeme is transitive.
3. Function in context. The context implies a stative interpretation.

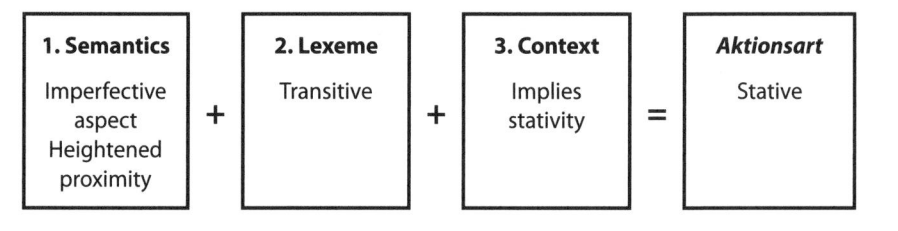

1. Semantics		2. Lexeme		3. Context		Aktionsart
Imperfective aspect Heightened proximity	+	Transitive	+	Implies stativity	=	Stative

Other considerations: While the transitive lexeme with imperfective aspect could render a progressive reading ("it is being finished"), the context strongly supports a stative reading. Just prior to giving up his spirit, Jesus expresses that his work is complete.

---

5. Montanari, *Brill Dictionary of Ancient Greek*, 931.

John 20:11 Μαρία δὲ εἱστήκει πρὸς τῷ μνημείῳ ἔξω κλαίουσα. ὡς οὖν ἔκλαιεν, παρέκυψεν εἰς τὸ μνημεῖον.

But Mary **was standing** outside facing the tomb, crying. As she was crying, she stooped to look into the tomb.

1. Semantic meaning of the indicative verb. The pluperfect indicative semantically encodes imperfective aspect and the spatial value of heightened remoteness.
2. Contribution of the lexeme. The lexeme is stative.
3. Function in context. The context allows for a stative interpretation.

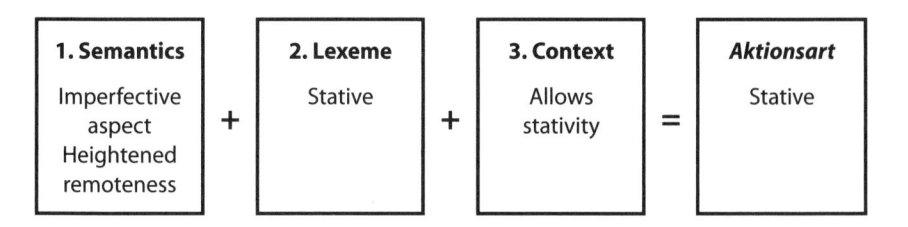

1. Semantics		2. Lexeme		3. Context		Aktionsart
Imperfective aspect Heightened remoteness	**+**	Stative	**+**	Allows stativity	**=**	Stative

2 Samuel 3:22 καὶ ἰδοὺ οἱ παῖδες Δαυιδ καὶ Ιωαβ παρεγίνοντο ἐκ τῆς ἐξοδίας καὶ σκῦλα πολλὰ ἔφερον μετ᾽ αὐτῶν· καὶ Αβεννηρ οὐκ ἦν μετὰ Δαυιδ εἰς Χεβρων, ὅτι **ἀπεστάλκει** αὐτὸν καὶ **ἀπεληλύθει** ἐν εἰρήνῃ.

Just then David's soldiers and Joab returned from a raid and brought a large amount of plundered goods with them. Abner was not with David in Hebron because David **had dismissed** him, and **he had gone** in peace.

1. Semantic meaning of the indicative verb. The pluperfect indicative semantically encodes imperfective aspect and the spatial value of heightened remoteness.
2. Contribution of the lexeme. The first lexeme is transitive; the second is intransitive.
3. Function in context. The context suggests a past-past interpretation.

1. Semantics		2. Lexeme		3. Context		Aktionsart
Imperfective aspect Heightened remoteness	**+**	a. Intransitive b. Transitive	**+**	Past-past	**=**	Past-past

Non-Indicative Tense-Forms

For each non-indicative verb encountered, work out whether it is found within an established construction (such as πρὸ τοῦ + infinitive or ἕως + subjunctive). Then identify the aspect of the non-indicative verb and describe what it is doing in the context.

Example:
Romans 4:8 μακάριος ἀνὴρ οὗ **οὐ μὴ λογίσηται** κύριος ἁμαρτίαν.

How happy is the man whom the Lord **will never charge** with sin!

1. Does the non-indicative verb occur within a construction?
   Yes: οὐ μή + aorist subjunctive (emphatic future negative)
2. What is the aspectual value?
   The aorist subjunctive is perfective in aspect.
3. What is the non-indicative doing in the context?
   In this construction the aorist subjunctive conveys an action that will emphatically not occur in the future.

Matthew 6:8 μὴ οὖν ὁμοιωθῆτε αὐτοῖς· οἶδεν γὰρ ὁ πατὴρ ὑμῶν ὧν χρείαν ἔχετε πρὸ τοῦ ὑμᾶς **αἰτῆσαι** αὐτόν.

Don't be like them, because your Father knows the things you need before you **ask** him.

1. Does the non-indicative verb occur within a construction? Yes: πρὸ τοῦ + infinitive.
2. What is the aspectual value? The aorist infinitive is perfective in aspect.
3. What is the non-indicative doing in the context? In this construction the aorist infinitive expresses subsequent action.

1 Corinthians 8:9 βλέπετε δὲ μή πως ἡ ἐξουσία ὑμῶν αὕτη πρόσκομμα γένηται τοῖς ἀσθενέσιν.

But **be careful** that this right of yours in no way becomes a stumbling block to the weak.

1. Does the non-indicative verb occur within a construction? No.
2. What is the aspectual value? The present imperative is imperfective in aspect.
3. What is the non-indicative doing in the context? The present imperative conveys a general command.

Hebrews 10:13 τὸ λοιπὸν ἐκδεχόμενος ἕως **τεθῶσιν** οἱ ἐχθροὶ αὐτοῦ ὑποπόδιον τῶν ποδῶν αὐτοῦ.

He is now waiting until his enemies are **made** his footstool.

1. Does the non-indicative verb occur within a construction? Yes: ἕως + subjunctive.
2. What is the aspectual value? The aorist subjunctive is perfective in aspect.
3. What is the non-indicative doing in the context? In this construction the aorist subjunctive conveys a point in the future at which a new situation is inaugurated.

Galatians 5:26 μὴ γινώμεθα κενόδοξοι, ἀλλήλους **προκαλούμενοι,** ἀλλήλοις **φθονοῦντες.**

Let us not become conceited, **provoking** one another, **envying** one another.

1. Does the non-indicative verb occur within a construction? No.
2. What is the aspectual value? The present participle is imperfective in aspect.
3. What is the non-indicative doing in the context? Both present participles express action that is contemporaneous with the action expressed by their leading verb.

Matthew 12:13 τότε λέγει τῷ ἀνθρώπῳ, Ἔκτεινόν σου τὴν χεῖρα. καὶ ἐξέτεινεν καὶ ἀπεκατεστάθη ὑγιὴς ὡς ἡ ἄλλη.

Then he told the man, "**Stretch out** your hand." So he stretched it out, and it was restored, as good as the other.

1. Does the non-indicative verb occur within a construction? No.
2. What is the aspectual value? The aorist imperative is perfective in aspect.
3. What is the non-indicative doing in the context? The aorist imperative conveys a specific command.

Luke 9:7 Ἤκουσεν δὲ Ἡρῴδης ὁ τετραάρχης τὰ γινόμενα πάντα καὶ διηπόρει διὰ τὸ **λέγεσθαι** ὑπό τινων ὅτι Ἰωάννης ἠγέρθη ἐκ νεκρῶν.

Herod the tetrarch heard about everything that was going on. He was perplexed, because some **said** that John had been raised from the dead.

1. Does the non-indicative verb occur within a construction? Yes: διὰ τό + infinitive.
2. What is the aspectual value? The present infinitive is imperfective in aspect.
3. What is the non-indicative doing in the context? In this construction the present infinitive conveys a causal action.

Romans 6:9 . . . εἰδότες ὅτι Χριστὸς **ἐγερθεὶς** ἐκ νεκρῶν οὐκέτι ἀποθνῄσκει, θάνατος αὐτοῦ οὐκέτι κυριεύει.

. . . **knowing** that Christ, **having been raised** from the dead, will not die again. Death no longer rules over him.

1. Does the non-indicative verb occur within a construction? No (x2).
2. What is the aspectual value? The perfect participle is imperfective in aspect; the aorist participle is perfective in aspect.
3. What is the non-indicative doing in the context? The perfect participle conveys a contemporaneous state; the aorist participle conveys an antecedent action.

Deuteronomy 23:23 ἐὰν δὲ μὴ **θέλῃς** εὔξασθαι, οὐκ ἔστιν ἐν σοὶ ἁμαρτία.

But if you do not **wish** to make a vow, it will not be counted against you as sin.

1. Does the non-indicative verb occur within a construction? No.
2. What is the aspectual value? The present subjunctive is imperfective in aspect.
3. What is the non-indicative doing in the context? The present subjunctive conveys a stative notion.

MORE PARTICIPLES

For each participle encountered, work out whether it is periphrastic, adjectival, substantival, or a participle of attendant circumstance. Then identify the aspect of the participle and describe what it is doing in the context.

Example:

John 16:5 νῦν δὲ ὑπάγω πρὸς **τὸν πέμψαντά** με, καὶ οὐδεὶς ἐξ ὑμῶν ἐρωτᾷ με, ποῦ ὑπάγεις;

But now I am going away to **the one who sent** me, and not one of you asks me, "Where are you going?"

1. Periphrastic, adjectival, substantival, or attendant circumstance? This participle is substantival.
2. What is the aspectual value? This aorist participle is perfective in aspect.
3. What is the participle doing in the context? This substantival participle conveys a nuance of past temporal reference.

John 5:2 ἔστιν δὲ ἐν τοῖς Ἱεροσολύμοις ἐπὶ τῇ προβατικῇ κολυμβήθρα ἡ **ἐπιλεγομένη** Ἑβραϊστὶ Βηθεσδὰ πέντε στοὰς ἔχουσα.

By the Sheep Gate in Jerusalem there is a pool, **called** Bethesda in Hebrew, which has five colonnades.

1. Periphrastic, adjectival, substantival, or attendant circumstance? This participle is adjectival.
2. What is the aspectual value? This present participle is imperfective in aspect.
3. What is the participle doing in the context? This adjectival participle describes the noun it qualifies.

Luke 16:6 ὁ δὲ εἶπεν, ἑκατὸν βάτους ἐλαίου. ὁ δὲ εἶπεν αὐτῷ, δέξαι σου τὰ γράμματα καὶ **καθίσας** ταχέως γράψον πεντήκοντα.

"A hundred measures of oil," he said. "Take your invoice," he told him, "**sit down** quickly, and write fifty."

1. Periphrastic, adjectival, substantival, or attendant circumstance? This is a participle of attendant circumstance.
2. What is the aspectual value? This aorist participle is perfective in aspect.
3. What is the participle doing in the context? This participle conveys imperatival force.

John 13:23 ἦν **ἀνακείμενος** εἷς ἐκ τῶν μαθητῶν αὐτοῦ ἐν τῷ κόλπῳ τοῦ Ἰησοῦ, ὃν ἠγάπα ὁ Ἰησοῦς.

One of his disciples, the one Jesus loved, was **reclining** close beside Jesus.

1. Periphrastic, adjectival, substantival, or attendant circumstance? This participle forms an imperfect periphrasis.
2. What is the aspectual value? This present participle is imperfective in aspect.
3. What is the participle doing in the context? This participle combines with the imperfect auxiliary to provide the lexical meaning of the imperfect periphrasis.

Romans 7:14 Οἴδαμεν γὰρ ὅτι ὁ νόμος πνευματικός ἐστιν, ἐγὼ δὲ σάρκινός εἰμι **πεπραμένος** ὑπὸ τὴν ἁμαρτίαν.

For we know that the law is spiritual; but I am made out of flesh, **sold** into sin's power.

1. Periphrastic, adjectival, substantival, or attendant circumstance? This participle is adjectival.
2. What is the aspectual value? This perfect participle is imperfective in aspect.
3. What is the participle doing in the context? This adjectival participle conveys a nuance of past temporal reference (with a verb of propulsion).

Acts 5:5 ἀκούων δὲ ὁ Ἀνανίας τοὺς λόγους τούτους **πεσὼν** ἐξέψυξεν, καὶ ἐγένετο φόβος μέγας ἐπὶ πάντας τοὺς ἀκούοντας.

When he heard these words, Ananias **dropped** dead, and a great fear
came on all who heard.

1. Periphrastic, adjectival, substantival, or attendant circumstance? This is a
   participle of attendant circumstance.
2. What is the aspectual value? This aorist participle is perfective in aspect.
3. What is the participle doing in the context? This participle conveys the force
   of an aorist indicative.

John 3:24 οὔπω γὰρ ἦν **βεβλημένος** εἰς τὴν φυλακὴν ὁ Ἰωάννης.

For John had not yet **been thrown** into prison.

1. Periphrastic, adjectival, substantival, or attendant circumstance? This participle forms a pluperfect periphrasis.
2. What is the aspectual value? This perfect participle is imperfective in aspect.
3. What is the participle doing in the context? This perfect participle combines
   with the imperfect auxiliary to form a pluperfect periphrasis.

Mark 14:69 καὶ ἡ παιδίσκη ἰδοῦσα αὐτὸν ἤρξατο πάλιν λέγειν τοῖς
παρεστῶσιν ὅτι Οὗτος ἐξ αὐτῶν ἐστιν.

When the servant saw him again she began to tell those **standing** nearby,
"This man is one of them!"

1. Periphrastic, adjectival, substantival, or attendant circumstance? This is a
   substantive participle.
2. What is the aspectual value? This perfect participle is imperfective in aspect.
3. What is the participle doing in the context? This participle conveys a nuance
   of contemporaneous temporal reference.

Bibliography

Allan, Rutger J. "Tense and Aspect in Classical Greek: Two Historical Developments; Augment and Perfect." Pages 81–121 in *The Greek Verb Revisited: A Fresh Approach for Biblical Exegesis*. Edited by Steven E. Runge and Christopher J. Fresch. Bellingham, WA: Lexham, 2016.

Aubrey, Rachel. "Motivated Categories, Middle Voice, and Passive Morphology." Pages 563–625 in *The Greek Verb Revisited: A Fresh Approach for Biblical Exegesis*. Edited by Steven E. Runge and Christopher J. Fresch. Bellingham, WA: Lexham, 2016.

Bache, Carl. "Aspect and Aktionsart: Towards a Semantic Distinction." *Journal of Linguistics* 18 (1982): 57–72.

Burton, Ernest de Witt. *Syntax of the Moods and Tenses in New Testament Greek*. 3rd edition. Chicago: University of Chicago Press, 1900. Repr., Grand Rapids: Kregel, 1976.

Buth, Randall. "Perfect Greek Morphology and Pedagogy." Pages 416–29 in *The Greek Verb Revisited: A Fresh Approach for Biblical Exegesis*. Edited by Steven E. Runge and Christopher J. Fresch. Bellingham, WA: Lexham, 2016.

Campbell, Constantine R. *Advances in the Study of Greek: New Insights for Reading the New Testament*. Grand Rapids: Zondervan Academic, 2015.

———. "Aspect and Tense in New Testament Greek." Pages 37–53 in *Linguistics and New Testament Greek: Key Issues in the Current Debate*. Edited by David Alan Black and Benjamin L. Merkle. Grand Rapids: Baker Academic, 2020.

———. "Finished the Race? 2 Timothy 4:6–7 and Verbal Aspect." Pages 169–75 in *Donald Robinson: Selected Works, Appreciation*. Edited by Peter G. Bolt and Mark D. Thompson. Sydney: Australian Church Record/Moore College, 2008.

———. *Verbal Aspect, the Indicative Mood, and Narrative: Soundings in the Greek of the New Testament*. Studies in Biblical Greek 13. New York: Peter Lang, 2007.

———. *Verbal Aspect and Non-Indicative Verbs: Further Soundings in the Greek of the New Testament*. Studies in Biblical Greek 15. New York: Peter Lang, 2008.

Campbell, Constantine R., Buist M. Fanning, and Stanley E. Porter. *The Perfect Storm: Critical Discussion of the Semantics of The Greek Perfect Tense under Aspect Theory*. Edited by D. A. Carson. Studies in Biblical Greek 21. New York: Peter Lang, 2021.

Carson, D. A. *Exegetical Fallacies*. 2nd edition. Grand Rapids: Baker, 1996.

———. "An Introduction to the Porter/Fanning Debate." Pages 18–25 in *Biblical Greek Language and Linguistics: Open Questions in Current Research*. Edited by Stanley E. Porter and D. A. Carson. Journal for the Study of the New Testament Supplement Series 80. Sheffield: Sheffield Academic Press, 1993.

Cirafesi, Wally V. *Verbal Aspect in Synoptic Parallels: On the Method and Meaning of Divergent Tense-Form Usage in the Synoptic Passion Narratives*. Linguistic Biblical Studies 7. Leiden: Brill, 2013.

Clark, H. H. "Space, Time, Semantics, and the Child." Pages 27–63 in *Cognitive Development and the Acquisitions of Language*. Edited by T. E. Moore. New York: Academic Press, 1973.

Comrie, Bernard. *Aspect: An Introduction to the Study of Verbal Aspect and Related Problems*. Cambridge Textbooks in Linguistics. Cambridge: Cambridge University Press, 1976.

Crellin, Robert S. D. *The Syntax and Semantics of the Perfect Active in Literary Koine Greek*. Publications of the Philological Society 47. West Sussex: Wiley Blackwell, 2016.

Curtius, Georg. *Die Bildung der Tempora und Modi im Griechischen und Lateinischen sprachvergleichend dargestellt*. Berlin: Wilhelm Besser, 1846.

———. *The Greek Verb: Its Structure and Development*. Translated by Augustus S. Wilkins and Edwin B. England. London: John Murray, 1880.

Decker, Rodney J. *Temporal Deixis of the Greek Verb in the Gospel of Mark with Reference to Verbal Aspect*. Studies in Biblical Greek 10. New York: Peter Lang, 2001.

Ellis, Nicholas J. "Aspect-Prominence, Morpho-Syntax, and a Cognitive-Linguistic Framework for the Greek Verb." Pages 122–60 in *The Greek Verb Revisited: A Fresh Approach for Biblical Research*. Edited by Steven E. Runge and Christopher J. Fresch. Bellingham, WA: Lexham, 2016.

Evans, T. V. "Future Directions for Aspect Studies in Ancient Greek." Pages 199–206 in *Biblical Greek Language and Lexicography: Essays in Honor of Frederick W. Danker*. Edited by Bernard A. Taylor et al. Grand Rapids: Eerdmans, 2004.

———. *Verbal Syntax in the Greek Pentateuch: Natural Greek Usage and Hebrew Interference*. Oxford: Oxford University Press, 2001.

Fanning, Buist M. "Approaches to Verbal Aspect in New Testament Greek: Issues in Definition and Method." Pages 46–62 in *Biblical Greek Language and Linguistics: Open Questions in Current Research*. Edited by Stanley E. Porter and D. A. Carson. Journal for the Study of the New Testament Supplement Series 80. Sheffield: Sheffield Academic Press, 1993.

———. "Porter and Fanning on New Testament Greek Verbal Aspect: Retrospect and Prospect." Pages 7–12 in *The Greek Verb Revisited: A Fresh Approach for Biblical Exegesis*. Edited by Steven E. Runge and Christopher J. Fresch. Bellingham, WA: Lexham, 2016.

———. *Verbal Aspect in New Testament Greek*. Oxford Theological Monographs. Oxford: Clarendon, 1990.

Freney, Samuel J. *Aspectual Substitution: Verbal Change in New Testament Quotations of the Septuagint*. Studies in Biblical Greek 20. New York: Peter Lang, 2020.

Fresch, Christopher J. "Typology, Polysemy, and Prototypes: Situating Nonpast Aorist Indicatives." Pages 379–414 in *The Greek Verb Revisited: A Fresh Approach for Biblical Research*. Edited by Steven E. Runge and Christopher J. Fresch. Bellingham, WA: Lexham, 2016.

Grimm, H. "On the Child's Acquisition of Semantic Structure Underlying the Wordfield of Prepositions." *Language and Speech* 18 (1975): 97–119.

Haspelmath, Martin. *From Space to Time—Temporal Adverbials in the World's Languages*. Munich: LINCOM Europa, 1997.

Holt, Jens. *Études d'aspect*. Acta Jutlandica Aarsskrift for Aarhus Universitet 15.2. Copenhagen: Munksgaard, 1943.

Horrocks, Geoffrey. "Envoi." Pages 626–35 in *The Greek Verb Revisited: A Fresh Approach for Biblical Exegesis*. Edited by Steven E. Runge and Christopher J. Fresch. Bellingham, WA: Lexham, 2016.

Huffman, Douglas S. *Verbal Aspect Theory and the Prohibitions in the Greek New Testament*. Studies in Biblical Greek 16. New York: Peter Lang, 2014.

Isačenko, A. V. *Grammaticheskij stroj russkogo jazyka v sopostavlenii s slovatskim: Morfologija*. Bratislava: The Slovak Academy of Sciences Press, 1960.

Langacker, Ronald W. *Foundations of Cognitive Grammar, Volume II: Descriptive Application*. Stanford: Stanford University Press, 1991.

Maddox, Randy L. "The Use of the Aorist Tense in Holiness Exegesis." *Wesleyan Theological Journal* 16 (1981): 168–79.

Mathewson, David L. *Verbal Aspect in the Book of Revelation: The Function of Greek Verb Tenses in John's Apocalypse.* Linguistic Biblical Studies 4. Leiden: Brill, 2010.

McKay, K. L. *A New Syntax of the Verb in New Testament Greek: An Aspectual Approach.* Studies in Biblical Greek 5. New York: Peter Lang, 1994.

———. "The Use of the Ancient Greek Perfect Down to the Second Century A.D." *Bulletin of the Institute of Classical Studies* 12 (1965): 1–21.

Montanari, Franco. *The Brill Dictionary of Ancient Greek.* Edited by Madeleine Goh and Chad Schroeder. Leiden: Brill, 2015.

Moser, Amalia. "Tense and Aspect after the New Testament." Pages 539–62 in *The Greek Verb Revisited: A Fresh Approach for Biblical Exegesis.* Edited by Steven E. Runge and Christopher J. Fresch. Bellingham, WA: Lexham, 2016.

Olsen, Mari Broman. *A Semantic and Pragmatic Model of Lexical and Grammatical Aspect.* Outstanding Dissertations in Linguistics. New York: Garland, 1997.

Pang, Francis G. H. *Revisiting Aspect and* Aktionsart*: A Corpus Approach to Koine Greek Event Typology.* Linguistic Biblical Studies 14. Leiden: Brill, 2016.

Porter, Stanley E. *Idioms of the Greek New Testament.* 2nd edition. Biblical Languages: Greek 2. Sheffield: Sheffield Academic Press, 1994.

———. *Verbal Aspect in the Greek of the New Testament with Reference to Tense and Mood.* Studies in Biblical Greek 1. New York: Peter Lang, 1989.

Porter, Stanley E., and D. A. Carson, eds. *Biblical Greek Language and Linguistics: Open Questions in Current Research.* Journal for the Study of the New Testament Supplement Series 80. Sheffield: Sheffield Academic Press, 1993.

Rijksbaron, Albert. *The Syntax and Semantics of the Verb in Classical Greek: An Introduction.* Amsterdam: Gieben, 1984.

Ruipérez, Martín S. *Estructura del Sistema de Aspectos y Tiempos del Verbo Griego Antiguo: Análisis Funcional Sincrónico.* Theses et Studia Philologica Salmanticensia 7. Salamanca: Colegio Trilingüe de la Universidad, 1954.

Runge, Steven E. "Discourse Function of the Greek Perfect." Pages 458–85 in *The Greek Verb Revisited: A Fresh Approach for Biblical Exegesis.* Edited by Steven E. Runge and Christopher J. Fresch. Bellingham, WA: Lexham, 2016.

Runge, Steven E., and Christopher J. Fresch, eds. *The Greek Verb Revisited: A Fresh Approach for Biblical Research.* Bellingham, WA: Lexham, 2016.

Swain, Tony. *A Place for Strangers: Towards a History of Australian Aboriginal Being.* Cambridge: Cambridge University Press, 1993.

Thomson, Christopher J. "What Is Aspect?: Contrasting Definitions in General Linguistics and New Testament Studies." Pages 13–80 in *The Greek Verb Revisited: A Fresh Approach for Biblical Exegesis*. Edited by Steven E. Runge and Christopher J. Fresch. Bellingham, WA: Lexham, 2016.

Wackernagel, Jakob. "Studien zum griechischen Perfektum." Pages 3–24 in *Studien zum griechischen Perfektum: Programm zur akademischen Preisverteilung 1904* (Göttingen: Dieterich, 1904). Repr., pages 1000–1021 in idem, *Kleine Schriften*. Vol. 1. Akademie der Wissenschaften. Göttingen: Vandenhoeck & Ruprecht, 1953.

Wallace, Daniel B. *Greek Grammar Beyond the Basics: An Exegetical Syntax of the New Testament*. Grand Rapids: Zondervan, 1996.

Scripture Index

Subject Index

Reading Biblical Greek Pack

Richard J. Gibson and Constantine R. Campbell

The *Reading Biblical Greek Pack* contains everything you need to grasp of the fundamentals of the Greek language so you can read and translate the Greek of the New Testament. The learning approach revolves around three core elements: grammar, vocabulary, reading, and translation.

The *Reading Biblical Greek Pack* includes:

- *Reading Biblical Greek*, a Greek textbook introducing first-year Greek students to the essential information—no more and no less—optimizing their grasp of the fundamentals of the Greek language
- *Reading Biblical Greek Workbook*, a companion resource to the main grammar that breaks up the Greek text of Mark 1–4 into manageable portions and provides the vocabulary and grammatical assistance required for beginning students
- *Reading Biblical Greek Video Lectures*, consisting of 82 micro-lessons of up to 10 minutes each, presenting the information in small, digestible chunks

The *Reading Biblical Greek Pack* provides all the essential information needed to learn the basics of the Greek language and helps individuals on their own or in a classroom setting begin reading and translating the New Testament.

ISBN 978-0-310-53434-1

ZONDERVAN ACADEMIC

Advances in the Study of Greek: New Insights for Reading the New Testament

Constantine R. Campbell

Advances in the Study of Greek offers an introduction to issues of interest in the current world of Greek scholarship. Those within Greek scholarship will welcome this book as a tool that puts students, pastors, professors, and commentators firmly in touch with what is going on in Greek studies. Those outside Greek scholarship will warmly receive *Advances in the Study of Greek* as a resource to get themselves up to speed in Greek studies. Free of technical linguistic jargon, the scholarship contained within is highly accessible to outsiders.

Advances in the Study of Greek provides an accessible introduction for students, pastors, professors, and commentators to understand the current issues of interest in this period of paradigm shift.

ISBN 978-0-310-51595-1

ZONDERVAN
ACADEMIC

Paul and Union with Christ: An Exegetical and Theological Study

Constantine R. Campbell

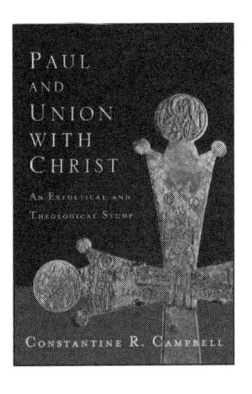

Paul and Union with Christ fills the gap for biblical scholars, theologians, and pastors pondering and debating the meaning of union with Christ.

Following a selective survey of the scholarly work on union with Christ through the twentieth century to the present day, Greek scholar Constantine Campbell carefully examines every occurrence of the phrases "in Christ," "with Christ," "through Christ," "into Christ," and other related expressions, exegeting each passage in context and taking into account the unique lexical contribution of each Greek preposition. Campbell then builds a holistic portrayal of Paul's thinking and engages contemporary theological discussions about union with Christ by employing his evidence-based understanding of the theme.

This volume combines high-level scholarship and a concern for practical application of a topic currently debated in the academy and the church. More than a monograph, this book is a helpful reference tool for students, scholars, and pastors to consult its treatment of any particular instance of any phrase or metaphor that relates to union with Christ in the Pauline corpus.

ISBN 978-0-310-32905-3

**ZONDERVAN
ACADEMIC**